Information Governance Technologies

Information Governance Technologies

A Guide

William Saffady

ROWMAN & LITTLEFIELD
Lanham • Boulder • New York • London

Published by Rowman & Littlefield
An imprint of The Rowman & Littlefield Publishing Group, Inc.
4501 Forbes Boulevard, Suite 200, Lanham, Maryland 20706
www.rowman.com

86-90 Paul Street, London EC2A 4NE

Copyright © 2025 by The Rowman & Littlefield Publishing Group, Inc.

All rights reserved. No part of this book may be reproduced in any form or by any electronic or mechanical means, including information storage and retrieval systems, without written permission from the publisher, except by a reviewer who may quote passages in a review.

British Library Cataloguing in Publication Information Available

Library of Congress Cataloging-in-Publication Data Available

ISBN 978-1-5381-8774-6 (cloth)
ISBN 978-1-5381-8775-3 (pbk.)
ISBN 978-1-5381-8776-0 (electronic)

Contents

Introduction		1
1	Enterprise Content Management	13
2	Records Management Application Software	59
3	Digital Preservation Applications	93
4	Email Archiving	127
5	Digital Asset Management	159
6	Web and Social Media Archiving Applications	189
7	E-Discovery Software	217
8	GRC Software	247
9	Database Archiving Software	275
Finding More Information		299
Index		305
About the Author		321

Introduction

"Governance" is a well-established concept and a widely used term. The *Oxford English Dictionary*, citing usage that dates from the fourteenth century, defines it as "the action or manner or governing, in the sense of directing and controlling with the authority of a superior."[1] *Encyclopedia Brittanica*, noting the term's long history in the English language, defines "governance" as "patterns of rule or practices of governing."[2] Other dictionaries and encyclopedias, as well as numerous academic publications, provide comparable definitions that emphasize direction and control as essential aspects of governance.

As a noun, "governance" is often preceded by an adjective that indicates the entity or activity being governed. Examples include "organizational governance," also termed "corporate governance," which refers to the systems and principles by which a company, nonprofit entity, or other organization is directed and controlled; "public governance," which encompasses the policies and processes that direct and control the work of public officials and governmental institutions; "project governance," which defines roles, responsibilities, and performance criteria for project management; "process governance," which focuses and coordinates policies and responsibilities for specific business processes; "innovation governance," which develops strategies, policies, and incentives that promote innovation and align it with organizational objectives; and "healthcare governance," which relates to the systems and processes for accountability and quality in healthcare organizations.

Broadly defined, information governance is a focused aspect of organizational governance. It encompasses strategies, policies, responsibilities, and processes to direct and control the data, documents, and other recorded information that an organization creates, receives, maintains, and disseminates. Standards and professional associations have played an important role in defining information governance and articulating its purpose, scope, and essential characteristics. For example:

- ISO 24143:2022, *Information and documentation—Information Governance—Concept and principles*, the first international standard to deal specifically with information governance, defines it as "a strategic framework for governing information assets across an entire organization in order to enhance coordinated support for the achievement of business outcomes and obtain assurance that the risks to its information and thereby the operation capabilities and integrity of the organization, are effectively identified and managed."[3] The definition notes that information governance includes "policies, processes, procedures, roles and controls" that address an organization's regulatory, legal, risk, and operational requirements.
- ARMA International's *Glossary of Records and Information Governance Terms*, a technical report registered with the American National Standards Institute, defines information governance as a "strategic, cross-disciplinary framework composed of standards, processes, roles, and metrics that hold organizations and individuals accountable for the proper handling of information assets."[4] ARMA International has also developed an Information Governance Implementation Model, which identifies eight key components for a successful information governance program; an Information Governance Maturity Model, which is based on ARMA's Generally Accepted Recordkeeping Principles; and the Information Governance Body of Knowledge, which provides strategic advice, policy guidance, and process recommendations for information governance implementations and stakeholder collaboration.
- The Gartner Information Technology Glossary, a widely cited, web-based reference resource, defines information governance as "the specification of decision rights and an accountability framework to ensure appropriate behavior in the valuation, creation, storage, use, archiving, and deletion of information."[5] Like ISO 24143:2022, the Gartner definition notes that information governance includes "processes, roles and policies, standards and metrics" that enable an organization to achieve its goals.
- According to the Sedona Conference, a nonprofit research and educational institute dedicated to the study of law and policy, information governance is "a coordinated, inter-disciplinary approach to satisfying information compliance requirements and managing

information risks while optimizing information value."[6] This definition establishes compliance, risk, and value as key concepts in information governance initiatives.
- A glossary issued by the Association of Corporate Counsel defines information governance as "the accountability for the management of an organization's information assets (especially its records), in order to achieve its business purposes and compliance with any relevant legislation or regulations."[7]
- Several international standards reflect the healthcare industry's involvement with information governance. ISO/TS 14441:2013, *Health informatics—Security and privacy requirements of EHR systems for use in conformity assessment* defines information governance as "processes by which an organization obtains assurance that the risks to its information, and thereby the operational capabilities and integrity of the organization, are effectively identified and managed."[8] The same definition is used in ISO 22287:2024, *Health informatics—Workforce roles and capabilities for terminology and terminology services in healthcare (term workforce)* and ISO 13972:2022, *Health informatics—Clinical information models—Characteristics, structures, and requirements.*
- ISO 5477:2023, *Health informatics—Interoperability of public health emergency preparedness and response information systems* defines information governance as an "overall strategy that outlines the responsibility for ensuring appropriate behavior when valuing, creating, storing, using, archiving, and deleting information for an enterprise." The definition further notes that information governance is "a fundamental component of enterprise governance." [9]
- A glossary of records management terms issued by the National Institutes of Health defines information governance as a "set of multi-disciplinary structures, policies, procedures, processes and controls implemented to manage information at an enterprise level, supporting an organization's immediate and future regulatory, legal, risk, environmental and operational requirements."[10] The inclusion of "environmental" requirements recognizes the importance of sustainable information-related practices.
- According to the American Health Information Management Association (AHIMA), information governance is "an organization-wide framework for managing information throughout its lifecycle and supporting the organization's strategy, operations, regulatory, legal, risk, and environmental requirements."[11] The healthcare profession's interest in information is strongly motivated by concerns about the security and confidentiality of patient data, but AHIMA defines information governance's scope broadly to include all information maintained by a healthcare enterprise, not just health information.

In many organizations, information governance coexists and interacts with other governance initiatives that deal with specific information-related matters. Widely cited examples include data governance, which deals with databases and other collections of structured content; information technology governance, which is concerned with stewardship and cost-effective management of an organization's information technology infrastructure; and information security governance, which mitigates risks related to confidentiality, integrity, and accessibility of information. Like information governance, these initiatives are aspects of organizational governance. Compared to information governance, however, they have a narrower purpose and scope. Their objectives, policies, and best practices are defined by international standards and by guidance developed by professional associations and industry groups.

CONSTITUENT DISCIPLINES

The definitions cited above collectively delineate the key characteristics of information governance: an enterprise-wide scope, a multidisciplinary perspective, strategic alignment with an organization's goals and objectives, and an emphasis on accountability, compliance, risk control, and management of the information lifecycle—all of which are grounded in a recognition that information is a valuable asset that an organization is obligated to protect. Information governance's multidisciplinary approach depends on collaboration and cooperation among an organization's information-related business units and functions, most of which predate the introduction of an information governance program. These business units and functions include, but are not necessarily limited to, the following:

- Information Technology, which develops, maintains, operates, and optimizes the computing and networking infrastructure that creates, stores, retrieves, distributes, and creates backup copies of digital content, the most important category of information assets in most organizations. Information Technology play a critical role in information governance initiatives. It supplies the technical resources, expertise, and support required to implement the technologies discussed in this book.
- Information Security, which is responsible for preventing and responding to data breaches, failures of control, and other incidents that involve unauthorized disclosure, use, alteration, or destruction of an organization's nonpublic information assets. Information Security develops and oversees policies and practices related to sensitive

personal data, trade secrets, business plans, and other confidential information.
- Records Management, which develops and implements policies, guidelines, and business processes for retention and disposition of an organization's information assets in full compliance with applicable legal and operational requirements. While it's role in an information governance program focuses on lifecycle management of record information, Records Management is broadly involved with creation, collection, organization, storage, use, and distribution of information in all parts of an organization.
- Compliance, which is responsible for developing and overseeing policies and practices that conform to legal and regulatory requirements, contractual obligations, industry standards and norms, internal codes of conduct, and societal expectations. Compliance must work closely with other constituent disciplines to ensure that an organization's information-related initiatives and operations are aligned with internal and external mandates.
- Risk Management, which is responsible for identifying internal and external threats, assessing vulnerabilities, and mitigating adverse consequences related to an organization information assets. Risk Management is closely aligned with Compliance—noncompliance with regulatory recordkeeping requirements poses significant risks—and with Information Security, which protects information from threats that Risk Management identifies.
- Legal Affairs, which is responsible for aligning information-related policies and practices with an organization's legal obligations and requirements, including protection and production of information deemed relevant for litigation, government investigations, or other legal proceedings. These responsibilities have a direct or indirect impact on all information governance activities and constituent disciplines.
- Archival Administration, which is responsible for identifying and preserving information of continuing value for historical, cultural, scholarly, or research reasons. Archival administration is well-established in government, where it is mandated by law, and in nonprofit organizations. Archival programs are less commonly encountered in for-profit entities.
- Data Science, which collects, processes, and analyzes an organization's digital information using machine learning, pattern recognition, statistics, predictive modeling, and other tools. Data Science depends on Information Technology's ability to store and process large quantities of digital data, which may be subject to internal risks, compliance requirements, and security concerns.

Independent or competitive operations among these disciplines are incompatible with effective governance, which depends on communal pursuit of organizational interests through interaction, cooperation, and consensus-building. In a fully realized information governance implementation, each constituent discipline consults with and informs other disciplines about specific activities and business processes for which it is responsible and accountable.

Some constituent disciplines interact regularly and frequently with the other disciplines about matters of common interest. Information Technology, for example, must consult with and inform other disciplines about decisions and initiatives related to storage, processing, accessibility, dissemination, and reliability of digital information. Similarly, Records Management must consult with and inform Compliance, Risk Management, and Legal Affairs and other disciplines about record retention rules and disposition processes. The relationship between Compliance and Risk Management was noted above. Some constituent disciplines, like Data Science and Archival Administration, have specialized responsibilities that are more likely to be affected by than impact the work of other disciplines.

Information governance is sometimes characterized as an umbrella concept for its constituent disciplines rather than a discipline in its own right, but that view misunderstands the difference between governance and management. Governance is concerned with vision and purpose; management is responsible for operations and performance. Information governance is concerned with alignment of information-related strategies, policies, and initiatives with organizational priorities and objectives. By contrast, the constituent disciplines are responsible for the storage, retention, availability, retrieval, reliability, protection, and disposition of information that come within their scope of authority. The collaboration promoted by information governance creates an environment in which the constituent disciplines can operate more efficiently and efficiently.

Business Need

Information governance is a widely publicized concept and a frequent topic of discussion at professional meetings, but interest in it developed slowly. It was seldom mentioned before the mid-2000s. In the 1990s, a few articles and conference papers described information governance as an emerging, though vaguely defined, field with records management, legal, and information technology as key stakeholders and collaborators. These early publications did not use the phrase in the sense that it is understood today. In particular, they did not clearly differentiate information governance from information management or articulate its strategic significance and relationship to organizational governance. Some publications treated information governance as a broad concept that subsumed other information-related initiatives, while others limited its scope; in England, for example, healthcare organizations initially equated information governance with policies and procedures to protect the security, accuracy, and confidentiality of patient data.

Using Google Scholar as a bibliometric gauge of academic and professional interest, citations to articles and conference papers that pre-date 2010 account for just one-half of one percent of the more than thirty thousand publications that contain the phrase "information governance." According to Google Trends, which tracks the popularity of web queries, there were few Google searches for information governance as a phrase or a topic before 2010, but search activity increased steadily and significantly in subsequent years as concerns about the retention and disposition of growing accumulations of digital information, security and privacy of personal data, compliance with new regulatory requirements, preservation and discovery of information for legal proceedings, and other factors stimulated awareness and interest by information professionals, business managers, researchers, and the general public. A Google Trends analysis indicates that web searches for "information governance" as a phrase or topic have been at consistently high levels since 2020.

In large part, interest in information governance is based on the view that effective governance mechanisms add value through close monitoring and prudent stewardship of organizational assets, which are ultimately the responsibility of the organization's board of directors or equivalent governing body. In companies, government agencies, and nonprofit entities, the business case for organizational governance is based on this value proposition. In this context, information governance's value contribution goes beyond regulatory requirements or operational needs. It derives from diligent oversight of an organization's information assets, which are essential for business operations, planning, and decision making. In particular, information governance aligns policies and practices for maintenance, use, and disposition of information assets with organizational objectives and priorities. This strategic alignment ensures compliance with internal and external mandates, reduces risk, and strengthens an organization's internal controls.

The Role of Technology

Definitions developed by standardization bodies, professional associations, and other groups emphasize strategy, policy, and process as key components of information governance. They rarely mention technology, but the Sedona Conference and other authorities recommend that organizations incorporate technology into their information governance programs. The reason is clear: Most information is created, stored, and distributed by technological resources, and the constituent disciplines discussed in the preceding section depend on technology to organize and analyze information, manage the information lifecycle, retrieve information needed for a given purpose, and address risk management, compliance, and security requirements related to information.

While some constituent disciplines, such as Records Management and Archival Administration, must deal with information in all formats, information governance is principally concerned with digital information. The information governance technologies discussed in this book consist of software, which may be installed and operated on an organization's own computers or acquired as a service from cloud-based providers. The chapters that follow discuss nine technologies that support the business case for information governance:

- Electronic Content Management (ECM) systems, which automate the organization, storage, retrieval, and distribution of digital documents and other unstructured digital content.
- Records Management Application (RMA) software, which manage the retention and disposition of digital documents and other unstructured digital content.
- Digital Preservation applications, which store digital content in stable, accessible condition for the foreseeable future.
- Email Archiving systems, which manage the retention and disposition of email messages and attachments.
- Digital Asset Management (DAM) systems, which are specifically designed for organization, storage, retrieval, and distribution of digital photographs, video recordings, and other visual and audio content.
- Web and Social Media Archiving applications, which collect and preserve websites and information posted on social media platforms.
- E-Discovery software, which supports the identification, collection, preparation, review, and production of digital content in response to legal discovery requests.
- GRC software, which addresses an organization's governance, risk, and compliance requirements and initiatives.
- Database Archiving software, which manages the retention and disposition of computer databases and other structured digital content.

Some of these technologies are well known and widely implemented. ECM, for example, is the technology of choice for digital content with demanding retrieval requirements. It important for all information governance disciplines and many business operations. Other technologies, such as E-discovery software, RMA software, and Digital Preservation applications, support specialized business operations. Still others deal with specific types of information, such as email, audio-visual recordings, and web and social media content. Some organizations may need a few of the technologies discussed in this book. Others may utilize all of them.

ORGANIZATION OF THIS BOOK

This book is intended for information governance specialists, information technology managers, records managers, and others who are responsible for evaluating, acquiring, and implementing technology that enhances the efficient and effectiveness of an organization's information governance program and the work of its constituent disciplines. The book will also prove useful for information security specialists, data privacy managers, compliance officers, risk managers, attorneys, data scientists, archivists, and other stakeholders whose roles and responsibilities are affected by information governance technology.

Each of the chapters that follow explains and discusses one of the nine technologies listed in the preceding section. The chapters are divided into sections that present pertinent information in the following order:

- An introduction provides an overview of the technology, explains its role in information governance, identifies the types of information it can process and the circumstances in which it likely to prove useful, and defines essential terms and concepts.
- A historical section summarizes the technology's development and progress toward commercial availability. Some of the technologies discussed in this book date from the late 1990s and early 2000s. Others became commercially available in the 2010s or later. All of the technologies have been enhanced significantly since their introduction.
- A section on the business need explains the information-related problems, issues, and concerns that the technology is designed to address.
- Applicable standards and guidelines are identified. International standards and guidance documents developed by professional associations and industry groups are important resources for evaluation and implementation of specific technologies. In some cases, they have influenced product design and development. This book cites the latest versions of standards and guidelines, which are subject to future revision or replacement.

- The longest section of each chapter describes and explains the features and capabilities of available products. The discussion covers basic functions that are supported by all products as well as advanced features and special capabilities, which are extra-cost options that may distinguish one product from another.
- Implementation issues are identified and discussed. For many prospective customers. the most important implementation issue relates to the choice between on-premises installation and a cloud-based service. Each has advantages and limitations, but many organizations have adopted cloud-first implementation policies. Most vendors have added cloud versions to their product lines, and some newer products are exclusively available in cloud configurations.

The treatment in all chapters is practical rather than academic. The discussion is designed to be accessible to readers with limited technical knowledge. All terms and concepts are fully defined and explained in nontechnical language.

Obsolescence is a concern to anyone who writes about technology. This book describes the features and functions of information governance technologies at a particular point in time, but change is inevitable. Vendors must add refinements and innovations to satisfy their existing customers and attract new ones. While innovations are certain to continue, this book emphasizes characteristics and capabilities that are critical for information governance initiatives and that are unlikely to change in ways that will affect the book's usefulness for future readers. The names of specific vendors and products are consequently omitted. A given vendor can be acquired, merge with another company, or go out of business. While the nine technologies discussed in this book are likely to remain viable for the foreseeable future, individual products can be rebranded or withdrawn from the market.

NOTES

1. *Oxford English Dictionary*, s.v. "governance (*n.*)," December 2023, accessed August 27, 2024, https://doi.org/10.1093/OED/9912904824. The *Oxford English Dictionary* notes that governance is one of the five thousand most-common words in modern written English. A subscription or library card is required to access to the online *OED*.

2. M. Bevir, "governance," *Encyclopedia Britannica*, April 11, 2024, accessed August 27, 2024, https://www.britannica.com/topic/governance.

3. *Information and documentation—Information Governance—Concept and principles*, ISO 24143:2022 (International Organization for Standardization, May 2022), https://www.iso.org/standard/77915.html.

4. *Glossary of Records and Information Governance Terms, Fifth Edition*, ARMA TR 22-2016 (Overland Park, KS: ARMA International, April 2016), https://webstore.ansi.org/preview-pages/ARMA/preview_ARMA+TR+22-2016.pdf.

5. *Information Technology Glossary*, "information governance," accessed August 27, 2024, https://www.gartner.com/en/information-technology/glossary/information-governance#:~:text=It%20includes%20the%20processes%2C%20roles,organization%20to%20achieve%20its%20goals.

6. "The Sedona Conference Commentary on Information Governance, Second Edition," *Sedona Conference Journal* 20, 94–178 (2019), accessed August 27, 2024, https://thesedonaconference.org/publication/Commentary_on_Information_Governance.

7. Association of Corporate Counsel, *Information Governance—Glossary of Terms*, accessed August 27, 2024, https://www.acc.com/sites/default/files/resources/upload/Contoural%20Glossary%20of%20IG%20Terms%20%28revised%29.pdf.

8. *Health informatics—Security and privacy requirements of EHR systems for use in conformity assessment*, ISO/TS 14441:2013 (International Organization for Standardization, December 2013), https://www.iso.org/standard/61347.html.

9. *Health informatics—Interoperability of public health emergency preparedness and response information systems*, ISO 5477:2023 (International Organization for Standardization, December 2023), https://www.iso.org/standard/81303.html.

10. National Institutes of Health, Glossary of Records Management Terms, accessed August 27, 2024, https://execsec.od.nih.gov/sites/default/files/2023-03/Glossary-of-Records-Management-Terms.pdf.

11. N. Sayles and L. Gordon, eds., *Health Information Management Technology: An Applied Approach, Sixth Edition* (Chicago: AHIMA Press, 2020), https://my.ahima.org/store#/productdetail/53320f8b-434e-ee11-be6e-6045bd095340.

1

Enterprise Content Management

According to ISO 12651-1:2012, *Electronic document management—Vocabulary—Part 1: Electronic document imaging*, enterprise content management encompasses the strategies, methods, and tools needed to capture, manage, store, preserve, and deliver an organization's unstructured information. ISO/TR 22957:2018, *Document management—Analysis, selection and implementation of enterprise content management (ECM) systems* defines unstructured information as having no prescribed or consistent structure or format, as opposed to a database or table that conforms to a strictly defined structure. Similarly, ISO/IEC 20546:2019, *Information Technology—Big Data—Overview and Vocabulary* differentiates structured data, which is organized according to predefined rules, from unstructured data, which is not composed of predefined data elements. Accepting this distinction, most discussions of enterprise content management define unstructured content by default as any information other than a database, table, or other data file that organizes content according to a structured model or schema.

Widely cited examples of unstructured digital content included word-processing documents and other text files, presentation files with textual and multimedia elements, email and text messages, document images, digital photographs, video recordings, audio recordings, web pages, blog posts, and social media posts. Structured data and unstructured content are useful but not mutually exclusive categories. Some unstructured content has structured attributes. Email messages, for example, have predefined data elements for the recipient and subject. Web pages combine unstructured textual content with HTML tags that identify headings, paragraphs, links, and other page elements. Spreadsheet files, which are routinely comingled with unstructured documents on shared drives and in ECM implementations, organize information in a tabular format of rows and columns, but cell content does not conform to a rigid schema.

Of the information governance technologies discussed in this book, electronic content management (ECM) is the best known, most widely implemented, and most commercially successful. It is also the most broadly applicable. ECM's global customer base includes government agencies, manufacturing companies, financial service companies, transportation companies, retail companies, healthcare providers, universities, cultural and philanthropic institutions, and other organizations that need to store digital content efficiently and retrieve it quickly when needed. These customers range from small organizations with a few users in a single office to large government agencies and multinational entities with thousands of users in geographically dispersed locations and complicated business operations that require extensive customization.

ECM technology is principally intended for digital content that is in the active phase of the information lifecycle, the period when digital content must be conveniently available and readily retrievable for analysis, transaction processing, project management, decision making, regulatory compliance, audits, collaboration, knowledge sharing, or other purposes. In this respect, electronic content management differs from records management application software, which is designed to manage the retention of information in the inactive phase of its lifecycle. As discussed in the next chapter, a properly configured ECM application can manage inactive records, but that is not its best use.

The active phase of the information lifecycle begins when a document or other digital content item is created or collected. It ends when the content is no longer needed to support ongoing operations or activities. The active phase for a given content item may be measured in days, weeks, months, or years, depending on its purpose and the specific operations and activities it supports. The active phase for an invoice, for example, begins when it is received by an organization's accounting department and ends when payment is accepted by the payee. Similarly, video surveillance recordings of public areas of a building may be overwritten a few days or weeks after they are created, provided they do not depict incidents that require further investigation. By contrast, a law firm's file for a complex case or a medical clinic's file for a patient with a chronic illness requiring continuing treatment may be open and active for years. Active content must be readily accessible when needed, but the active phase is not invariably associated with frequent use. Deeds and mortgage filings maintained by a county clerk must be available for convenient reference by property owners and prospective buyers, title insurance companies, attorneys, real estate appraisers, and other interested parties, but documents related to a given property may not be needed for decades.

As discussed in the following sections, enterprise content management offers a functionally superior alternative to shared drives and paper filing systems for managed storage and retrieval of active digital content. An ECM application can create and maintain a managed repository that combines a coherent organization of topical folders with in-depth indexing, flexible search mechanisms, effective security mechanisms, and workflow processing of digital content. Oher technologies discussed in this book offer similar capabilities, but they have different business purposes, and some of them are limited to a narrower range of content types.

HISTORY

Enterprise content management technology has been commercially available, in various forms, for more than forty years. Electronic document imaging, ECM's earliest manifestation, was introduced in the early 1980s as high-performance alternatives to paper filing systems and microfilming. It was one of several technologies intended as automated replacements for pre-computer office methods and equipment, the most successful being word processing, which rendered typewriters obsolete. Given their technical complexity and high cost, however, the earliest document imaging systems had a limited market. They were intended for high-volume recordkeeping operations in large government agencies and paperwork-intensive industries, such as banking and insurance. They featured highly customized combinations of computing equipment, document scanners, storage devices, and software that were assembled, installed, configured, and maintained at great expense by computer companies and contractors that specialized in integration of these components. Document images produced by scanning paper records were saved in proprietary file formats on optical disks housed in jukebox-style autochangers, which offered a high-capacity alternative to the hard drives available at that time. These customized implementations were widely publicized and attracted a lot of attention in the computing and records management communities, but few organizations could afford them.

Preconfigured document imaging systems, introduced in the late 1980s and early 1990s, required less customization. They became progressively more capable and less expensive through the end of the decade, as the processing power of personal computers increased, the cost of scanners declined, and the increased capacity of hard drives made optical storage unnecessary. Just as special-purpose word processors were supplanted by affordable word-processing software for personal computers, document-imaging systems that previously required exotic hardware components became available as software for installation and operation on customers' existing computing equipment. This increased the technology's acceptance by government agencies and businesses that did not have the money for or interest in a complicated customized imaging implementation.

By the late 1990s, electronic document-imaging applications were offered by dozens of software developers. Compared to paper filing and microfilming, these products supported a broader, more effective range of document storage and retrieval capabilities, but their market was inherently self-limiting. The commercial viability of document imaging technology depends on the continued proliferation of paper records. Microfilming, which never enjoyed wide market acceptance, similarly depended on the creation of paper documents. In the 1980s, paper was the dominant recordkeeping medium; word processing was simply a more efficient way of producing typed documents for distribution and filing, and computer applications relied on printouts to communicate the results of processing. By the early 2000s, however, many business records were being created in digital form, and organizations increasingly wanted to store them that way, rather than printing them for filing or scanning. In response, electronic document-imaging systems evolved into electronic document-management systems that could store and retrieve word-processing files, spreadsheets, and other digital documents in their native formats.

Over the next several years, document management applications expanded their storage and retrieval capabilities to encompass digital photographs, video recordings, audio recordings, web pages, and other information-bearing objects that are not normally considered documents. Some document management applications also added collaboration, digital asset management, records management, and other components that support features and functions discussed elsewhere in this book. Reflecting these changes, document management vendors reconceptualized and rebranded their products as content management systems, with "enterprise" subsequently added to signify that the enhanced technology could address all of an organization's requirements for storage and retrieval of unstructured information of all types in all formats. By the late 1990s, ECM had become an emerging topic of discussion in business periodicals and conference presentations. A Google Trends analysis indicates that web searches for the phrase "enterprise content management" peaked in the mid-2000s, by which time the concept had become well established. Searches for "document management" and "document imaging" peaked during the same period but have declined steadily and significantly in recent years.

While document imaging continues to be supported by ECM products, its importance has diminished. It is now considered an ECM component rather than a separate information-governance technology. Industry analysts similarly treat document management as a capability of ECM applications rather than a distinct product group, but document management is not an obsolete concept. Some of the international standards discussed in the next section continue to use the phrases "document management" and "content management" interchangeably, and so do existing and prospective customers. Many ECM installations are limited to office documents as opposed to video recordings, audio recordings, web pages, and social media content, for which the technologies discussed in later chapters may be preferable. The abbreviation EDMS, for electronic document management system, continues to be applied to these document-centric ECM implementations. Adding to the confusion, some sources confuse ECM and document management products with the records management applications discussed in chapter 3.

BUSINESS NEED

From its inception, ECM technology provided a computerized solution for a common problem—storage and retrieval of business and other unstructured digital content. In its initial document-imaging incarnation, its potential market encompassed any organization with a filing cabinet. With the transition to document management and, ultimately, content management, the ECM market has expanded to include any organization that saves digital information on shared drives, which may reside on-premises or be maintained by cloud storage providers. While these widely encountered storage repositories may be conveniently accessible, they have significant limitations:

- Shared drives are usually ungoverned or lightly governed storage repositories that are implemented with little planning or user training. While related content may be grouped in folders, few organizations have enterprise-wide rules for organizing and naming files or well-defined procedures for the types of content to be saved in specific folders. Individual employees decide how digital content will be organized and where it will be saved, often without regard to its future retrievability by others. Many shared drives contain vaguely titled folders and files, including some that were created and saved by former employees. In some organizations, shared drives contain folders that are merely identified by a former employee's name without any indication of their contents. Some documents or other digital content may not be saved in folders at all, a practice that is rarely encountered in paper recordkeeping systems.

- Shared drives are decentralized storage repositories. Digital content pertaining to a given matter may be scattered in multiple locations. This dispersal impedes interdepartmental information sharing and promotes duplicate storage. This decentralized approach contrasts sharply with database management practices, which emphasize the creation of enterprise-wide information resources that are shared by multiple parts of an organization.
- Shared drives provide limited indexing and retrieval functionality. Digital content is often saved on a shared drive without metadata other than a file name. To retrieve desired content, an employee must browse through folders and files, which may not be well organized or adequately labeled. Searching a shared drive is particularly difficult when an employee is looking for content that was saved by others. Complicated directory structures with subfolders nested to multiple levels can be confusing and time-consuming to navigate. Some operating systems provide an indexing feature that can find documents on a shared drive that contain specific words, but searches can be slow and do not support Boolean operators, relational expressions, or other advanced retrieval functionality.
- Shared drives provide limited safeguards against unauthorized access to digital content. Access privileges are often defined by the person who saved a file rather than by a central authority as the outcome of a coherent planning process. Even where access to files and folders is restricted to authorized persons, documents can be accidentally or intentionally deleted or modified by anyone who has full access to a given folder.
- Shared drives do not provide effective mechanisms for tracking access to and use of digital content, and there is no accountability for unauthorized viewing, printing, downloading, deletion, or modification of information. Shared drives do not maintain an audit trail that identifies employees who have accessed specific folders or files, and they do not track failed access attempts by unauthorized persons. These security lapses are particularly significant for documents or other digital content that contains trade secrets, proprietary business plans and financial information, personally identifiable information, protected health information, payment card information, or any information that was given to an organization in confidence or with a reasonable expectation of nondisclosure.
- Storage on shared drives is not compatible with workflow processes in which digital content is automatically routed among authorized participants in a prescribed sequence for review, comment, signed approval, or other action. With employees working in multiple loca-

tions, automated routing combined with electronic signing is essential to expedite transaction processing and other business operations.
- These limitations pose problems where digital content must be accessed by or shared with employees who are working remotely or in geographically dispersed office locations, although some of them can be mitigated in an office context. An office worker can ask support staff or colleagues for assistance in locating content that is saved on shared drives. Similarly, an office worker can physically trace the routing path of a document that is delayed or misplaced in the review and approval cycle. Comparable help is not available to employees who are working from home or other out-of-office locations. Remote working is a self-service environment.

A well-planned ECM implementation can address these issues. ECM applications are produced and marketed by dozens of companies, ranging from large computer manufacturers and software developers with diverse product lines and global operations to relatively small, specialized suppliers that focus on ECM applications in selected geographic locations. ECM developers sell their products directly to customers or through dealers, agents, or other authorized representatives, who provide the implementation support and customization services that most organizations need to get an ECM installation up and running.

Industry analysts and technology consultants regularly track the growth of ECM installations in specific regions, survey the characteristics of ECM customers, evaluate features and capabilities supported by new ECM products, and assess the competitive positions of ECM vendors. Studies by industry analysts estimate the size of the market and project its growth. Individual case studies discuss its use in specific work environments, but there have been no comprehensive surveys of the business purpose and scope of ECM installations, the types of content involved, the technology's acceptance by employees and other users, and the efficiency improvements, cost savings, and other advantages expected and obtained. While the technology has been commercially available for many years, the continued pervasiveness of shared drives as storage repositories for an organization's most valuable content suggests that ECM has barely scratched the surface of its potential market and that it may be underutilized in some organizations where it is currently installed.

STANDARDS AND GUIDELINES

International standards view ECM as an all-encompassing technology that supports business process management, workflow automation, enterprise reports management, and other capabilities as well as features and functions customarily associated with document management and document imaging. Unlike the RMA standards discussed in chapter 2, which provide detailed specifications for features and functions that records management applications must support, international ECM standards are written at a higher level of abstraction and have had little impact on the development and acceptance of ECM products. They are seldom, if ever, referenced in requests for proposals, bid invitations, or other procurement solicitations. Most of the standards were issued after ECM's capabilities and market were well established. Vendors of ECM products and service rarely advertise compliance with specific international standards, and there is no mechanism for certifying compliance. Nonetheless, the international standards discussed in the following sections deal with important concepts, issues, and expectations that decision-makers must consider when planning ECM implementations and evaluating ECM products.

General ECM Standards

The following standards address technical and organizational aspects of enterprise content management at varying levels of specificity:

- ECM terms and concepts are defined in ISO 12651-1:2012, *Electronic document management—Vocabulary—Part 1: Electronic document imaging*, which was cited at the beginning of this chapter, and ISO 12652-1:2014, *Electronic document management—Vocabulary—Part 2*. While it has a broader scope, ISO 5127:2017, *Information and documentation—Foundation and vocabulary* defines many terms that are relevant for ECM implementations.
- ISO 19475:2021, *Document management—Minimum requirements for the storage of documents* specifies essential capabilities that maintain the authenticity, integrity, and usability of an electronic document management system's work processes for receipt, storage, and delivery of documents.
- ISO/TR 22957:2018, *Document management—Analysis, selection, and implementation of enterprise content management (ECM) systems* provides vendor-neutral guidelines and best practices for evaluation and implementation of ECM applications.
- ISO 16175-1:2020, *Information and documentation—Processes and functional requirements for software for managing records—Part 1: Functional requirements and associated guidance for any applications that manage digital records* presents high-level requirements and usage guidelines that are applicable to ECM as well as other technologies discussed in

this book. ISO 16175-2:2020, *Information and documentation—Processes and functional requirements for software for managing records—Part 2: Guidance for selecting, designing, implementing and maintaining software for managing records* contains general guidelines for planning and implementing ECM applications and other digital recordkeeping technologies. Criteria for specification of ECM requirements in the context of competitive procurements is also presented in ANSI/AIIM TR27-1996, *Electronic imaging request for proposals (RFP) guidelines*.
- ISO 22938:2017, *Document management—Electronic Content/Document Management (CDM) data interchange format* specifies an XML-based markup format for reliable exchange of documents, metadata, and other content between compliant ECM systems.
- ISO/TR 14105:2011, *Document management—Change management for successful electronic document management system (EDMS) implementation* discusses ergonomic and organizational issues related to planning and implementing an electronic document management system. The standard applies to electronic content management, which it considers synonymous with document management. Nontechnical factors related to ECM installations are also discussed in ANSI/AIIM TR35-1995, *Human and organization issues for successful EIM system implementation*, which predates the transition from document imaging to content management.
- ISO 14641:2018, *Electronic document management—Design and operation of an information system for the preservation of electronic documents—Specifications* provides a reference framework to ensure that digital content will be captured, stored, retrieved, and accessed in a way that ensures its authenticity. The standard is relevant for ECM systems that manage active information and for digital preservation.
- ISO/TR 15801:2017, *Document management—Electronically stored information—Recommendations for trustworthiness and reliability* discusses best practices for implementation and operation of ECM systems to manage digital content in a manner that ensures its authenticity, integrity, and availability.
- ISO 18829:2017, *Document management—Assessing ECM/EDRM implementations—Trustworthiness* provides a methodology for evaluating whether an ECM environment complies with best practices for authenticity and integrity of digital content.
- ISO 13008:2022, *Information and documentation—Digital records conversion and migration process* provides guidance for the conversion of digital content from one format to another and the migration of digital content from one hardware or software platform to another. Much ECM content will require such conversion at some point in its lifecycle.

Document Imaging Standards

Standards have played an important role in acceptance of electronic document imaging technology as a replacement for paper records and for microfilm, itself an imaging technology with a long history of standardization. These standards remain relevant for ECM implementations that include a document scanning component:

- ISO/TR 13028:2010, *Information and documentation—Implementation guidelines for digitization of records* specifies best practices for reliable conversion of paper documents and other nondigital content to digital form. It provides guidance that will permit the destruction of paper records and other nondigital source materials following digitization and accessibility of digital images throughout their retention periods. Digitization of paper documents and microfilm images is also discussed in ANSI/AIIM TR15-1997, *Planning considerations, addressing preparation of documents for image capture.*
- ISO/TR 12033:2009, *Document management—Electronic imaging—Guidance for the selection of document image compression methods* discusses factors that users and system integrators must consider when deciding on an appropriate compression method for digital images of business documents. An earlier treatment of the same topic is presented in ANSI/AIIM TR33-1998, *Selecting an appropriate image compression method to match user requirements.*
- Test targets for document scanning are covered by ISO 12653-1:2000, *Electronic imaging—Test target for the black and white scanning of office documents—Part 1: Characteristics;* ISO 12653-1:2000, *Electronic imaging—Test target for the black and white scanning of office documents—Part 2: Method of use;* and ISO 12653-3:2014, *Electronic imaging—Test target for scanning of office documents—Part 3: Test target for use in lower resolution applications.*
- ISO 19264-1:2021, *Photography—Archiving systems—Imaging systems quality analysis—Part 1: Reflective originals* and ISO 19263-1:2017, *Photography—Archiving systems—Part 1: Best practices for digital image capture of cultural heritage material* discuss quality assurance criteria and methodologies for electronic imaging, with particular emphasis on digitization of archival documents and library materials. Relevant terms are defined in ISO 19264-1:2021, *Photography—Archiving Systems—Vocabulary.* Quality assurance methods for document imaging are also discussed in ANSI/AIIM TR34-1996, *Sampling procedures for inspection by attributes of images in Electronic Image Management (EIM) and micrographic systems.*

- ISO/TR 12654:1997, *Electronic imaging—Recommendations for the management of electronic recording systems for the recording of documents that may be required as evidence, on WORM optical disk* discusses the use of nonrewritable optical storage for retention of digital images. Optical storage technology is covered by other international standards that were widely discussed in the 1990s and early 2000s, but optical storage devices and media have been supplanted by magnetic disks in most ECM implementations, including those that require nonerasable recording to satisfy regulatory mandates.

Metadata Standards

As discussed later in this chapter, ECM implementations use metadata to identify, access, control, and otherwise manage digital content. International metadata standards are relevant for many of the information governance technologies discussed in this book. Most of the following standards provide generic guidance that is applicable to digital and nondigital content:

- ISO/IEC TR 19583-1:2019, *Information technology—Concepts and usage of metadata—Part 1: Metadata concepts* defines and discusses the essential attributes of metadata.
- ISO 23081: 2017, *Information and documentation—Metadata for records—Part 1: Principles* discusses metadata requirements within the framework established in ISO 15489-1:2016, *Information and documentation—Records management—Part 1: Concepts and principles.*
- ISO 23081-2:2021, *Information and documentation—Metadata for managing records—Part 2: Conceptual and implementation issues* and ISO 23081-2:2011, *Information and documentation—Metadata for managing records—Part 3: Self-assessment method* provide a practical approach to implementing and evaluating metadata elements for records in any format. Selection of metadata for document imaging implementations is discussed in ANSI/AIIM TR40-1995, *Suggested index fields for documents in Electronic Image Management (EIM) environments.*
- ISO 15836-1:2017, *Information and documentation—the Dublin Core metadata set—Part 1: Core elements* and ISO 15836-2:2019, *Information and documentation—the Dublin Core metadata set—Part 2: DCMI properties and classes* specify a general-purpose set of fifteen core elements that can describe a wide variety of information resources, including digital documents, digital images, video and audio content, and web pages. All metadata elements are optional and repeatable, which makes the Dublin Core relevant for a wide range of ECM implemen-

tations. The core set can be expanded and refined to describe content with special requirements.
- IEC 82045-1:2001, *Document management—Part 1: Principles and methods* specifies principles and methods to define metadata for the management of documents throughout the information lifecycle. IEC 82045-2:2004, *Document management—Part 2: Metadata elements and information reference model* provides a set of metadata elements for document management. While they can be applied to paper records, these standards are primarily intended for electronic document management implementations. Although it has been reviewed and confirmed as current by ISO, these standards predate the widespread adoption of enterprise content management as a replacement for electronic document management.
- ISO 5963:1985, *Documentation—Methods for examining documents, determining their subjects, and selecting indexing terms* recommends document analysis and concept identification procedures for manual indexing of documents by subject. The procedures are equally applicable to digital content and paper documents. The standard has been reviewed and confirmed multiple time since it was initially issued.
- Where subject terms will be selected from a controlled indexing vocabulary, ISO 5963 can be used with ISO 25964-1:2011, *Information and documentation—Thesauri and interoperability with other vocabularies—Part 1: Thesauri for information retrieval* and ISO 25964-2:2013, *Information and documentation—Thesauri and interoperability with other vocabularies—Part 2: Interoperability with other vocabularies*, which cover the maintenance and development of lists of approved terms for subject indexing.
- For searching textual metadata, ISO 877:1993, *Information and documentation—Commands for interactive text searching* specifies a basic set of retrieval commands that are relevant for ECM applications and other information governance technologies.

The above listing is limited to cross-disciplinary metadata standards that are relevant for ECM implementations in government agencies, companies, and nonprofit organizations. It omits metadata standards developed for specialized knowledge domains, such as physical science or medicine; metadata standards intended for specific content types, such as geospatial data or bibliographic data; and metadata standards intended for a specific purpose, such as preservation of digital content.

FEATURES AND CAPABILITIES

Most ECM applications support more capabilities than any given content collection requires. Some of the features and functions discussed in the following sections are more often discussed than utilized, but customers are not obligated to use all of an ECM application's capabilities in every situation. The person responsible for planning and configuring an ECM application for a given content collection will select the specific functionality required to satisfy users' requirements. A small organization with a few business operations and straightforward requirements may utilize a subset of an ECM application's capabilities. A large organizations with a varied range of content types and complex business processes will usually benefit from a full-featured product that can address its present and future needs.

Content Capture

ECM applications do not create digital content; they collect, store, and manage content that is created by other applications that an organization is currently using or may have used in the recent past. As noted in the introduction to this chapter, enterprise content management is principally concerned with digital content that is in the active phase of the information lifecycle. Older digital content created in obsolete formats by aging or discontinued software can pose usability problems, but that issue is typically associated with records management and digital preservation applications, which are discussed in chapters 2 and 3.

Most ECM applications can accommodate a wide range of unstructured digital content created in a variety of proprietary and nonproprietary file formats including, but not necessarily limited to, word-processing documents and text files, spreadsheets and CSV files, presentations, email messages, PDF files of all types, TIF images with or without compression, digital photographs and other JPG images, HTML and XML files, engineering drawings and other design documents saved as CAD files, video recordings in MP4 and other formats, audio recordings in MP3 and other formats, web pages, and web forms. Content capture is the process of collecting this digital content and importing it from its current storage location into a repository managed by an ECM application. Authorized users can capture digital content in several ways, including:

- Manual transfer of individual files or groups of files by dragging and dropping them from shared drives or other storage locations into specific folders or subfolder within an ECM-managed repository.
- Batch import of digital content from designated directories or subdirectories on network servers, personal computers, or cloud-based repositories.
- Saving digital content to specific folders or subfolders within an ECM-managed repository from within office productivity software,

an email system, or another originating application at the time the content is created.
- Direct input of office documents, engineering drawings, maps, charts, and other hardcopy records that are digitized by document scanners through an ECM application's integral imaging module, which may a standard or optional component. Most ECM imaging modules are compatible with variety of scanners and multifunction scanner/copiers. The imaging module typically includes image clean-up tools that can correct page skewing, remove background blemishes, and otherwise improve the quality of digitized images.
- Customized integration for automatic transfer of digital content from a customer relationship management system, enterprise resource planning system, or another external application that creates or collects content.
- Direct transfer of digital photographs, video recordings, audio recording, or other content generated by smartphones and tablets via automatic uploading or manual activation of a mobile input capability.

These import options may not be available with every ECM product, but most of them are supported or soon will be. When one ECM vendor offers a desirable capability, others must add it to remain competitive. The ability to save documents to an ECM repository from with office productivity applications or to import digital content from smartphones and tablets via a mobile app were once innovative features supported by a few ECM vendors, but they are now commonplace.

Regardless of the import method selected, the capture process must be monitored. Quality checks must be performed to confirm that the desired content was successfully and completely captured. Some ECM applications perform technical validation using checksum verification or other mathematical algorithms to identify content that may have been corrupted during the transfer process. Other quality inspections must be performed manually. Most ECM applications maintain a log or audit trail of import actions that can be used to confirm that all desired content was captured. A sample of the captured content can be examined and, if necessary, compared to the original source material to verify that it can be accessed reliably. Any problems will be routed to a designated employee for further review and corrective action. Damaged content may also be detected by users when captured content is retrieved, but this should occur infrequently. Repeated problems warrant a reexamination of the capture process.

An ECM application should support multiple repositories or allow authorized users to subdivide a given repository to store digital content created by different departments, to isolate content with special security requirements, to separate content with different retention requirements, or for other purposes. Each repository or subrepository must be able to operate independently and be subject to its own rules for input, storage, retrieval, indexing, viewing, printing, and security of digital content.

File Plans and Metadata

ECM applications use file plans to organize and categorize digital content for access by authorized users. ECM applications support customer-defined file plans consisting of a structured framework of folders and subfolders nested to multiple levels. A file plan must be tailored to the requirements of a specific collection of digital content, and it must be scalable to accommodate new categories and subcategories as needed. An ECM application may be able to replicate an existing directory structure of folders and subfolders when uploading content from a shared drive or other storage repository. This directory structure can be modified to reorganize folders, add or delete categories and subcategories, and relabel folders where necessary. As a potentially helpful resource, some ECM applications offer prebuilt file plans or preconfigured templates for specific content types, industries, or organizations. These prebuilt file plans can be customized to address local requirements.

Some ECM applications support both file plans and metadata. Others support metadata only. Like other information governance technologies, ECM applications use metadata to identify, describe, and index digital content, allowing it to be retrieved, controlled, and otherwise managed. Specific metadata elements will vary for one ECM implementation to another, depending on the types of digital content involved and an organization's retrieval and control requirements. With most content, metadata will include a combination of descriptive and administrative information. Some types of content may also benefit from technical and structural metadata.

Examples of descriptive metadata include the content's title or another unique identifier, the content's creator or originator, the content's date, the content's type, and words or phrases that indicate the person, project, activity, event, transaction, or other subject to which the content pertains. Administrative metadata may include the content's status as a draft or final version, access permissions, security and privacy settings, and retention requirements. Administrative metadata may also provide contextual information about the content's purpose, intellectual property rights, version history, and other attributes that may not be contained or immediately apparent in the content itself. Examples of technical metadata include the content's file type and size, encoding or compression method, and, where applicable, image resolution and bit depth. Publications, reports, and other structured content may require additional metadata that indicates how the content is organized, including the total number of pages, section headings, and a table that identifies the document's special features, such as charts, graphs, illustrations, and sidebars.

ECM applications support customer-defined metadata at the folder, subfolder, or content item level. Some ECM applications maintain a composite catalog of metadata fields that have been defined for any purpose. To simplify the data entry process and promote uniform metadata fields across multiple document collections, an organization can define some generally useful fields based on the previously discussed Dublin Core or another resource. Authorized users can select the types of metadata to be assigned to a particular content collection and add fields to satisfy their unique requirements.

Metadata values can be entered manually or derived automatically from information contained in the content itself:

- Metadata can be key-entered by authorized users when folders, subfolders, or documents are imported into an ECM repository. This is the most widely encountered, broadly applicable, and time-consuming approach to metadata entry. ECM applications typically support customizable data entry screens with labeled metadata fields, global editing capabilities, the ability to select metadata values from pick lists, default data values for designated fields, carry-over of designated field values from previous data entry screens, and other techniques to simplify data entry. To minimize keystroking, some ECM applications support a type-ahead feature that anticipates the metadata value to be entered in a given field and automatically completes the entry.
- Some digital content includes embedded metadata. A word-processing file, for example, includes the file type and size, the date and time when the file was created or modified, the name of the author, and any subject terms or other descriptors that the author may have added. A digital photograph contains information about the creator, date and time of creation, the location where the photograph was taken, the image format, the image size, the image resolution, and certain camera characteristics, such as the brand and model, the lens used, the focal length, and the shutter speed.
- Customized scripts can be created to automatically extract specific metadata values from within word-processing documents, spreadsheets, presentations, and other textual content. Optical character recognition (OCR) can extract metadata values from document images that contain textual information or numeric values. Automatic

extraction works best with structured documents, such as business forms, where the metadata values to be extracted are always located in a readily identifiable part of a page.
- Using a combination of automatic extraction and manual intervention, some ECM applications allow data entry personnel to point and click on a name, identifying number, or other information from within a displayed document. The application will insert the highlighted information into a designated metadata field, eliminating the need to type it. If the document is an image, OCR will convert the selected metadata value to character-coded form.
- Automatic extraction can also be used for full-text indexing of textual documents in which every word becomes an index value. In most cases, adverbs, certain adjectives, prepositions, conjunctions, and other words that play no role in retrieval operations are excluded from indexing.
- An ECM application can be integrated with a customer relationship management system, financial management system, human resources information system, email system, or another external resource where the desired metadata values are stored and from which they can be extracted.
- ECM applications can use artificial intelligence to extract metadata values from digital content. A machine-learning algorithm can be trained, for example, to recognize dates, invoice numbers, vendors' names, payment amounts, billing codes, and other metadata values regardless of their location within a document. Similarly, a machine-learning algorithm can be trained to identify particular types of documents, such as contracts or purchase orders, and locate specific metadata values, such as the names of the parties involved, the starting and termination dates, and the amount of the contract or procurement. Results vary with the types of documents involved, the machine learning model employed, and the quality and quantity of data used to train the model.
- Automatic categorization uses machine-learning algorithms to assign digital documents to predefined categories based on the information they contain and other characteristics. The categories may correspond to people, organizations, events, projects, or other matters. If the categories are represented by topical folders in an EMC repository, documents will be assigned to specific folders without human intervention, although human involvement is required to create the framework of topical folders. Automatic categorization has been investigated in research projects for decades. Recent developments in artificial intelligence have extended categorization functionality to a broad range of content, including digital photographs

and other nontextual documents. These developments have made impressive progress in the accuracy of categorization and continued advances are likely. Some ECM applications can be configured with an automatic categorization engine as an optional component. These categorization engines must be trained on a sample of documents that are manually categorized by subject experts or other knowledgeable persons. The sample must be large enough to accurately represent the collection of documents to be categorized. Performance can be improved by adding documents to the sample or by manually recategorizing documents when errors are detected.

Search and Retrieval

As discussed in preceding sections, ECM technology—like its predecessors, electronic document imaging and electronic document management—is designed to manage digital content that is in the active phase of the information lifecycle. For many organizations, the ability to retrieve recorded content quickly and conveniently to support information-dependent operations and activities is the principal motivation and business justification for an ECM implementation. If an ECM application is appropriately selected and configured, properly instructed users should be able to find and retrieve the digital content they need for transaction processing, decision making, customer service, or other purposes.

Authorized users can search for digital content by manually browsing through the folders and subfolders maintained in an ECM repository, but the same level of retrieval performance can be obtained with a well organized shared drive or, for that matter, a well-organized filing cabinet, assuming that remote access is not required. The advantages of computerized retrieval operations are obtained by searching the metadata values associated with folders, subfolders, or individual content items or by searching for specific words or phrases contained in textual documents, assuming that full-text indexing is applied:

- Search and retrieval capabilities supported by ECM applications have expanded and improved steadily and significantly since the technology's introduction. Search functionality that was once limited to leading-edge or experimental information retrieval systems is now commonplace. Even entry-level products enable users to conduct complex metadata searches based on numeric values or on exact or partial matches of specified words or phrases, although variations in the way a given search function is implemented by a given ECM application can affect ease of use and, consequently, the results obtained.

- All ECM applications support Boolean operators (AND, OR, NOT), which allow users to narrow or broaden searches by combining search terms and including or excluding specific metadata values. Boolean AND operations may be explicit or implicit, as is customary with web search engines when two metadata values are included in the same search specification. The Boolean OR and NOT operators, which may not be as familiar or easy to use as the AND operator, must be explicitly entered in a search specification. Some ECM applications allow different Boolean operators to be combined in the same search, but that capability should be limited to expert users. It requires the use of parentheses to control the order in which Boolean operations are performed. Multiple searches can usually obtain the same results with less confusion.
- A metadata search may be based on an exact match of a specified numeric value or search term, which may be a single word or a multiword phrase. Alternatively, relational expressions can be used to search for metadata values that are greater than or less than a specified number or date. Term truncation, also known as root word search, will match any word or phrase that begins with a specified string of characters. Wildcard symbols can be used to match one or more characters within a search term.
- Among less common retrieval capabilities, some ECM applications support inexact matches, including phonetic searches, which is useful for names or words that are subject to spelling variations; synonym searches, which uses an integral thesaurus to match metadata values that have the same meaning as a specified search term; and fuzzy searches, which match metadata values that are similar to a specified search term in spelling, length, or other characteristics. Some ECM applications allow users to initiate searches from within an external application by simply clicking on a word in a displayed document. The ECM application will launch a search for other documents that contain the word.
- With some ECM applications, frequently repeated searches can be saved for future execution.
- As a complement or alternative to metadata searches, full-text retrieval allows authorized users to search for words or phrases in all or part of a word-processing file, email message, or other textual content. Full-text retrieval is possible with document images if optical character recognition is used to create text versions for indexing. Once reserved for library databases, this feature is now widely supported by ECM applications, which create and maintain a searchable index of the words that documents contain, excluding prepositions, conjunctions, interjections, adverbs, and certain adjectives that rarely

convey subject content. With most ECM applications, full-text indexing capability should be able to be turned on or off, as appropriate, for specific content. Full text indexing and retrieval can be applied to metadata as well as to digital content.
- Full-text search specifications may include Boolean operators, truncated search terms, or wildcard symbols. Less common full-text retrieval capabilities include case-sensitive searching; conflated searching, which can match different verb tenses or related forms of nouns; proximity searching for two words in the same sentence, paragraph, or page; and quorum searching, which will retrieve documents that contain a specified number of listed terms, such as any three search terms from a list of seven.
- ECM applications typically respond to searches by displaying a list of retrieved documents or other content, from which the searcher can select one or more items for viewing. As the default action, most ECM applications will open the selected content in its native format if its originating application or a compatible equivalent is accessible on the retrieval workstation.
- Most ECM applications provide a multiviewer that can display retrieved content if the originating application is no longer in service or otherwise not available, but that is most likely to occur with inactive content that is managed by the records management or digital preservation applications discussed in other chapters. Those information governance technologies must be able to manage aging content created by discontinued applications. ECM applications are principally intended for active content, for which the originating applications are still in use or only recently taken out of service.
- Authorized users can scroll through or print displayed content. Depending on the ECM application, they may also be able to annotate retrieved content, stamp it with a date and time, add a watermark to identify its status, redact it, print it, email it, download it, move it, copy it, delete it, or edit it. Most ECM applications allow retrieved content to be printed once its relevance is confirmed without the necessity of viewing it in its entirety. Most ECM applications allow authorized users to download retrieved content in the format in which it is stored.
- If an ECM application maintains multiple content repositories, authorized users may be able to search them simultaneously. Some ECM applications support federated searching, which can expand a retrieval operation to encompass repositories maintained by another ECM application, a records management application, a digital asset management system, email archiving system, or other external sources. To support this capability, an ECM application may main-

tain a unified index to multiple content sources. Alternatively, the ECM application may transmit a search statement in an appropriate format to external content sources, which have their own indexes. Search results may be displayed individually for each content source or consolidated to interleave results from multiple sources and remove duplicates. Search results are limited to information that a user is authorized to access. While federated searching can facilitate retrieval of scattered content, its effectiveness may be limited by variations in the search functionality, metadata schemes, security controls, and other characteristics of individual content repositories.

Access and Security

ECM applications support a full range of safeguards to ensure the security, integrity, reliability, confidentiality, and controlled availability of digital content and its associated metadata:

- Most organizations designate a system administrator who is authorized to set up user accounts, modify menus and screens, define user privileges, and otherwise configure an ECM application. The system administrator may designate one or more super users at the department, division, or office level. A super user will have access to all system functions except those reserved for the system administrator.
- The system administrator or authorized super users can determine the content that individual employees or other users are authorized to access and the actions they are allowed to perform. User groups or individual users can have full or partial access privileges for creating, importing, retrieving, moving, duplicating, editing, viewing, printing, downloading, sharing, and deleting content and its associated metadata. A system administrator can broaden, narrow, revoke, or otherwise redefine access privileges.
- Access control lists define user privileges at the repository, subrepository, folder, subfolder, or content item levels. Access privileges typically flow down from folders to subfolders to individual content items unless an exception is specified. Organizations can broaden, narrow, revoke, or otherwise redefine access privileges as circumstances warrant. Confidentiality requirements for particular content may increase of decrease over time, for example. An ECM application may prevent copying, printing, or downloading of content related to an active contract, but those restrictions may be lessened or removed when the contract terminates.
- ECM applications provide reliable mechanisms to authenticate users who are allowed to access content and verify their specific privileges.

The customary combination of username and password is typically used to verify a given user's identity, but some ECM applications support biometric or multifactor authentication. In some implementations, role-based access privileges may be associated with specific job functions or duties. Access privileges can be integrated with an organization's existing user authentication mechanisms.

- In addition to user authentication and verification, an ECM application may support IP address restrictions, content encryption, session timeouts, automatic termination of idle sessions, and other security measures to prevent unauthorized access to digital content.
- Most ECM applications maintain an audit log of input, editing, retrieval, viewing, printing, downloading, and deletion activities for users, documents, and metadata. The audit log provides a comprehensive record of user interactions with specific content items. It identifies the date, the user, and the type of interaction (input, view, add, move, delete, edit, annotate, etc.) in sufficient detail to determine the circumstances in which the interaction occurred and to identify unauthorized access attempts, possible security breaches, or suspected mishandling of content or its associated metadata. The audit log can be used to troubleshoot access issues, to highlight matters that may require further investigation, and to respond to security incidents, trace their source, and assess their impact. Users' awareness that an audit log is being maintained may serve as a deterrent to unauthorized actions.
- Unlike the records management applications discussed in chapter 2, ECM products allow authorized users to modify digital content. Most ECM applications require authorized users to check out digital content that is downloaded for editing by an external application. When editing is completed, the revised version is checked in. Depending on the ECM application and the way it is configured, the new version may replace the original content, but many ECM applications provide version control functionality that saves all revisions as specific representations of a given content item at particular points in time. The resulting revision history documents all changes made by specific users and allows revised content to be compared to prior versions. Some ECM applications allows authorized users to restore a previous version of edited content.
- When content is checked out for editing by a given user, most ECM applications lock it to prevent its retrieval or modification by others. Locked content is typically marked to indicate that is being edited. The locked content will remain inaccessible until the changes are completed and it is checked in, which releases it for retrieval. Content is typically revised because it is out of date, incomplete, or incor-

rect. Content locking is necessary to prevent the use of information that is in the process of being corrected or enhanced, although some ECM applications support read-only viewing of previous versions of content while it is undergoing revision. Content locking also prevents inconsistent or conflicting editing by multiple users, but some ECM applications allow locking to be disabled on a case-by-case basis to permit simultaneous collaborative editing of content.

Other Capabilities

A given ECM application may support the following capabilities as a standard feature or optional component:

- Workflow process automation has been closely associated with content management products since the 1990s. A workflow process will automatically route documents or other digital content from user to user in a prescribed sequence for review, approval, transaction processing, or other purposes. To accomplish this, an ECM application supports the creation of a workflow script, a custom-written program that defines the order in which specific tasks will be performed, ensures that the responsible parties will receive the content required to complete those tasks, monitors the progress of the work, and notifies relevant parties when delays or other problems require supervisory intervention. A workflow script may be written by a trained employee, by the ECM vendor, or by a contractor or consultant who specializes in workflow implementations. Novice users can learn an ECM application's scripting language at a level of proficiency that is sufficient to automate simple workflows, but scripting of complex workflow processes with multiple decision points and integration with external information resources requires a knowledge of programming concepts and significant experience with workflow scripting. Like all computer programs, workflow scripts must be tested to detect and correct logical and syntactical errors before an automated process becomes operational.
- Early document imaging and document management applications required the installation of special client software at each user's workstation, which increased the cost of implementation and the level of technical support required. ECM applications now allow digital content and metadata to be accessed through widely installed web browsers, which greatly simplifies and reduces the cost of ECM implementations, especially those with many workstations. Web clients allows authorized users to interact with an ECM application via familiar software that is readily available. When they were initially

introduced, web clients were limited to a subset of ECM operations and they performed poorly in installations with unreliable internet connections and inadequate bandwidth. They have since been enhanced for improved responsiveness and compatibility with a broad range of ECM capabilities, although special client software may be necessary or preferable for some functions, such as document scanning, or where reliable internet connections are unavailable. Web clients are a precondition for cloud-based ECM implementations. Some ECM applications also support access from popular email clients.
- Web clients provide convenient ECM access from desktop or laptop computers. Mobile apps allow authorized users to search for and retrieve digital content and its associated metadata from smartphones and tablets. They are particularly useful for employees who are traveling or working in field locations or other situations where personal computers and web browser are unavailable or unusable. A mobile app's interface is optimized for small screens and touch-activated commands, but a mobile app may not support all ECM functions and a mobile device's limited display size may be poorly suited to digital content that requires careful study, lengthy examination, or extensive editing. Some mobile apps support biometric authentication, voice input, uploading of digital photos and video recordings, and other capabilities of smartphones and tablets. Cellular data service allows a mobile app to be used where internet connectivity is unavailable, but the app's performance will be affected by the quality of cellular connections.
- Many ECM applications support electronic signing of digital documents that are retrieved from an ECM repository. Electronic signing functionality is not incorporated into the ECM application. The retrieved document is transmitted to an external electronic signature platform, which will interact with the signing party and return the signed document to the ECM application for storage. The electronic signature provider handles signatory identification and verification. The ECM application maintains an audit trail of the signing party's actions. E-sign integration is essential for an automated review and approval process based on a predefined workflow. Most contracts and other documents that require signatures originate in digital form. Without electronic signing, such documents must be printed to obtain handwritten signatures then scanned to return them to the ECM application in electronic form.
- Some ECM application will convert digital content from its native format to a PDF file for storage, retention, distribution, or portability. Digital documents and other content may be converted individually or in bulk. PDF conversion may be done by the ECM application

itself or by a separate application that is integrated with the ECM application. Some ECM applications can display PDF content without launching an external viewer. They can also generate thumbnail representations of PDF pages to simplify navigation through large files.
- Machine-learning algorithms that support metadata extraction and automatic categorization of digital content were discussed in a preceding section. ECM applications can be expected to incorporate additional features and functions based on developments in artificial intelligence. Examples include natural language searching, automatic creation of summaries that extract the most important information from lengthy documents, automatic retrieval of documents with similar content, and personalized content recommendations based on a user's job title, previous search activity, or other factors.

Enterprise content management is a self-contained technology, but it is not necessarily implemented in isolation. An organization may want to integrate its ECM application with a human resources information system so that authorized persons will have the option of viewing documents from an employee's personnel file when the employee's database record is retrieved. Similarly, an organization may want to integrate its ECM application with a financial information system so that authorized persons can view invoices along with the corresponding records from an accounts payable database. ECM vendors provide a variety of methods and tools, including application programming interfaces and data synchronization mechanisms, to support such integration, but they can require time and effort to implement. Often, integration with external applications requires customization services from the ECM vendor or another qualified provider.

Some ECM applications can be optionally configured with add-on modules that support records management, digital asset management, and other aspects of information governance that are closely related to, but not identical with, content management. As discussed in later chapters, these optional modules position ECM as an alternative to special-purpose information governance technologies, but they may not offer the full range of features and functions that some organizations require.

IMPLEMENTATION ISSUES

An ECM implementation begins with the selection of a product that can satisfy an organization's technological requirements. Assuming those requirements are clearly defined, product evaluation is the easiest aspect of an ECM implementation. Excellent ECM applications are widely available from many qualified suppliers, but technology is just one component of an ECM implementation. An appropriate governance mechanism must provide the leadership, planning, and coordination necessary for a successful implementation, and a file plan and metadata scheme must be developed to support the organization and retrieval of digital content. The cost of an ECM implementation and the advantages and limitation of on-premises installation versus a cloud-based application must be considered. Finally, planners and decision-makers must assess the risks that may be encountered in an ECM implementation and develop an effective mitigation strategy.

Product Evaluation

Selection of an ECM application begins with the evaluation of proposals submitted by qualified vendors in response to a solicitation that specifies an organization's objectives and the requirements that a proposed ECM product must satisfy. Depending on an organization's purchasing policies and practices, the solicitation may consist of a formal request for proposals or bid invitation that is widely publicized, the goal being to obtain competitive responses from multiple vendors through a fair and open procurement process. Alternatively, an organization may simplify identify several qualified ECM suppliers and ask them to submit proposals. Less commonly, an organization may request a proposal from a single vendor that it is already in its supply chain. Such sole source procurements can be difficult justify, although government agencies may be able to buy certain ECM products without competitive bidding through prenegotiated contracts.

Regardless of procurement procedures, an ECM application and its vendor must satisfy the following general requirements:

- Most ECM implementations are designed to address an immediate need. To merit serious consideration, an ECM application must be commercially available in a fully operational general-release version at the time of procurement. Experimental, developmental, or near-release products are unacceptable for digital content that warrants managed storage and retrieval. The commercial availability requirement applies to all standard and optional ECM components that a customer has ordered, including add-on modules developed by an ECM vendor's business partners or other external parties. If operation of the ECM application depends upon additional software components, such as a database management system that the customer does not already own, those components must be included and implemented with the ECM application. The vendor must be able to

deliver and install the ECM application within a reasonable period of time after an order is placed.
- In addition to commercial availability, an ECM application must be actively marketed and fully supported by its vendor. A given vendor may offer multiple ECM applications, some of which were acquired from other companies. In such cases, the ECM vendor may not have decided whether and to what extent it will continue to develop and support an acquired product.
- An organization considering a given ECM application must have reasonable assurance that it will remain commercially viable for the foreseeable future as evidenced by recent sales of the application to new customers and a recent history of product upgrades. This is important because a full rollout of enterprise-wide ECM implementation will likely require multiple years to complete. A customer must not be required to replace the ECM application before the rollout is completed and fully integrated into its information governance practices.
- An ECM application intended for on-premises installation must be fully compatible with a prospective customer's existing computing and networking infrastructure, including but not necessarily limited to computers, peripheral devices, operating systems, database management software, and network connections. An organization may need to acquire additional storage capacity or document scanners, but its information technology unit is presumably capable of supporting its existing computing and networking environment and may be reluctant to or unwilling to introduce unfamiliar components that will require additional training or staff. Hardware and software compatibility issues are less significant for cloud-based ECM applications. Whether cloud-based or installed on premises, an ECM application must comply with the customer's information security and backup protection protocols and practices.
- Many organizations want an ECM application with out-of-the-box functionality that can be implemented in a reasonable period of time without extensive and costly customization, but ECM applications are not plug-and-play products. Even the simplest implementation must be configured to address specific customer requirements, possibly including conversion of content from a previously installed document management or document imaging system. At a minimum, an on-premises ECM implementation will require technical assistance for software installation, database configuration, testing, minor customizations, and other implementation tasks. Even a cloud-based ECM implementation will require some technical assis-

tance, which must be provided by the ECM application's developer or by an authorized reseller or other qualified supplier.
- An ECM application intended for enterprise-wide implementation will serve a progressively larger user population and store an increasing quantity and variety of digital content. Even an ECM implementation intended for a single department or a defined collection of digital content is likely to be adopted for other purposes elsewhere within an organization. An ECM application must be able to accommodate this expanded deployment. It must permit the future addition of user licenses, and it must not impose impractical limits on the number, size, or other characteristics of digital content it can accommodate. An ECM application should have a track record of reliable operation in installations that involve large and varied quantities of digital content.
- An ECM application must be easily learned and convenient to use on a day-to-day basis by properly instructed nontechnical employees. Users must be able to perform basic tasks with a minimum of instruction the first time they are encountered. The ECM application must be efficient—that is, users must be able to initiate basic operations with a minimum of commands and the operations must be executed quickly. Users must be able to re-establish proficiency quickly after a period of nonuse. The software must give users an easy method of recovering from input errors or other mistakes. Knowledge of programming concepts or other information system expertise, apart from broad familiarity with computer operations in an office context, must not be required. The ECM vendor must provide appropriate training for frequent and occasional users.
- An ECM application must have a proven history of reliable operation and effective maintenance support in multiple installations, including organizations with requirements that are similar to those of the prospective customer.
- ECM applications often support mission-critical business operations. Prolonged downtime, failure to resolve problems in a timely manner, or a vendor's inability to respond immediately and effectively to urgent requests for technical support cannot be tolerated. For malfunctions that result in system failure, the vendor must be able to restore system operability within one business day from the time the problem is reported unless the customer agrees that the problem's complexity warrants a longer time for correction. For problems that do not result in system inoperability, the vendor must respond to the customer's technical support request within one business day with an accurate assessment of the problem and a realistic timetable for correcting it.

- An ECM vendor must provide clear evidence that it has appropriate knowledge, experience, and resources to support a prospective customer's requirements. To evaluate a vendor's qualifications, an organization will need information about the company's history, including information about the vendor's involvement with document and records management activities and technologies, the vendor's financial stability and likely continued viability as evidenced by the company's latest financial statement or other appropriate documentation, and the number of ECM installations the vendor has successfully completed and types of customers. As evidence of satisfactory performance, the vendor must provide contact information for reference accounts, but a prospective customer should reserve the right to contact other installations.
- An ECM vendor must present a realistic implementation timetable and project management plan, including specific tasks and milestones associated with product delivery, installation, configuration, testing, training, and acceptance. The vendor must specify the qualifications of employees who will be assigned to a prospective customer's implementation as well as employees who will service the customer postinstallation. The ECM vendor must identify subcontractors, business partners, or other third parties who will be involved in the ECM implementation and their specific responsibilities. A prospective customer must review technical support arrangements, including hours of service. An ECM vendor's ability to respond quickly and accurately to questions raised during the product evaluation and selection process may be indicative of the quality of technical support.
- Many ECM developers sell their products through business partners, dealers, or other authorized agents or representatives who are responsible for software installation and testing, database configuration, required customizations, customer training, and postinstallation support. The above considerations apply to such representatives as well to ECM developers. For most organizations, a capable, experienced business partner is critical to the success of an ECM implementation. An organization will often have a closer working relationship with a business partner than with the ECM software developer. All other things being equal, many prospective customers prefer an ECM vendor with a well-established local business partner.

Most of these requirements are also applicable to evaluation and selection of other technology products discussed in this book.

ECM Governance

An enterprise-wide ECM initiative requires enterprise-wide management. An effective governance model that defines authority, roles, and responsibilities for an organization's ECM initiatives is essential for successful deployment and full utilization of ECM technology. An organization must appoint an ECM project manager, who will have principal responsibility for the ECM implementation, and establish an ECM governance team, which will provide strategic direction and oversight for the organization's ECM initiatives:

- The ECM project manager should understand the organization's content management requirements, the ECM's implementation's business objectives and relationship to the organization's information governance initiatives, and the ECM application's capabilities and limitations. The ECM project manager does not have to be an information technology specialist, but he or she needs sufficient technical knowledge to be able to communicate with the ECM vendor and with information technology staff who will be assigned to the ECM implementation. Ideally the ECM project manager will have prior experience directing software implementation projects and the interpersonal skills necessary to manage the needs and expectations of business units that will use the ECM application.
- The ECM governance team will work with the project manager to develop an implementation strategy, oversee the ECM installation, monitor its progress, ensure its alignment with organizational objectives, and address issues and concerns that may arise during the implementation and afterwards. Subject to variations in the scope and complexity of an ECM implementation, team members may include representatives from information governance, records management, information technology, and information security as well as the key business units that will be involved in or affected by the ECM implementation. The governance team will also benefit from the participation of a change management specialist, a training specialist, and legal and regulatory compliance specialists when matters arise that require their expert advice or assistance.
- The ECM governance team will work with the project manager and ECM vendor to establish a realistic plan and timetable for implementation of the ECM application. The timetable will depend on the ECM implementation's scope and business objectives. It will also be affected by stakeholder buy-in, user acceptance of the technology's impact on work processes, and the organization's approach to change management.

- As previously noted, some ECM applications are initially intended for a single business unit or a defined collection of digital content. The initial installation will give the ECM vendor an opportunity to learn about and accommodate an organization's requirements and expectations, and it will give the organization's project manager and ECM governance team and technical staff an opportunity to become familiar with the ECM application's capabilities and limitations. Depending on its scope and complexity, the initial installation may begin with a pilot phase that will test the ECM application with a select group of users and a subset of digital content. The pilot phase, which may span several months or longer, will draw on users' experience and feedback to identify issues that must be addressed and changes that must be made before a full-scale deployment is undertaken.
- When an initial ECM application is fully deployed and reliable operational, the implementation can be expanded to include additional business units or digital content, but this process must not be rushed. A managed rollout at a measured pace will minimize complications and increase the likelihood of a successful deployment. As the expanded implementation proceeds, technical modifications and procedural improvements may be needed to satisfy requirements that were not encountered in the initial installation. Each additional implementation will likely have its own challenges. Widespread rollout in a large organization may require multiple years to complete, but enterprise-wide adoption of ECM technology in all business units is probably an unattainable objective. Unlike typewriters, which were completely supplanted by word processing, shared drives and even paper files are likely to remain in use, albeit at a diminished level, in some business units. The rollout should emphasize high-value digital content that will benefit from the accessibility, retrievability, control, and security, capabilities that ECM technology offers.
- The ECM governance team will work with the ECM vendor and the organization's information technology unit to ensure that the ECM application is properly configured, fully tested, and operating reliably. ECM developers and their authorized business partners provide implementation support services, which are typically included in cost quotes submitted to prospective customers. An organization's information technology unit will coordinate, monitor, and provide technical assistance for on-premises installation and testing of ECM software. Postinstallation, the information technology unit will be responsible for operating and maintaining the ECM application, controlling user access, monitoring the application's performance, and installing software updates.

- A cloud-based ECM implementation will require less involvement by local information technology staff. The ECM project manager, with advice and assistance from the information technology unit, will be responsible for interaction with the cloud service provider, including communicating the organization's requirements and expectations and monitoring the cloud service's performance and availability. The ECM project manager will work with the information technology unit to ensure that users' workstations are properly configured and operating reliably, to oversee migration of digital content to the cloud service, and to integrate the cloud-based ECM with other applications.
- For the initial implementation and subsequent rollout, the ECM project manager, supported by the governance team, will work with business units to identify the specific digital content to be included in the ECM implementation and to determine file plan and metadata requirements, input procedures, user access privileges, storage requirements, security requirements, and workflow procedures for documents associated with specific operations. The ECM project manager will work with information technology staff, the ECM vendor, and individual business units to identify opportunities for and assess the feasibility, benefits, and cost of integrating the ECM application with the organization's existing computer applications and databases.
- The ECM project manager, in consultation with the governance team, will develop, communicate, and monitor the implementation of policies, procedures, standards, and rules for transfer of electronic content and its associated metadata from shared drives to the ECM repository. The ECM project manager will work with individual business units to identify, assess, and resolve problems, issues, and concerns associated with document scanning, metadata entry, storage, retrieval procedures, access privileges, security, user interfaces, and other matters related to operation of the ECM application.
- The ECM project manager, in consultation with the governance team and business unit stakeholders, will determine training requirements and develop and deliver training programs and materials to enable employees and other authorized persons to effectively utilize the ECM application.

As an ECM implementation expands, the original configuration's capabilities may need to be upgraded to deal with different types of digital content and satisfy the needs of a broader user base. The ECM project manager will identify and evaluate requirements, benefits, and costs for additional user licenses, optional software modules, customizations, and other features and functions to be added to the ECM installation. The project manager will also evaluate requirements, develop specifications, determine required resources, identify qualified suppliers, and provide project management for backfile scanning, image format conversions, metadata conversions, data migration, and other services associated with the ECM implementation.

ECM File Plans

An ECM application's technical superiority and a vendor's qualifications are important factors for product evaluation, but they will mean nothing to users if the application fails to retrieve digital content when needed. An ECM repository must be a managed resource with a defined scope that specifies the types of digital content to be included, a coherent file plan that provides a logical framework for organizing the content, and an appropriate metadata scheme that describes the content and indexes it for searching. These elements are crucial for a successful ECM implementation.

A hierarchical file plan is the best practice for organizing content in most ECM repositories. Its tree-like structure provides a top-level folder for each category with one or more levels of subfolders, nested to multiple levels as needed, to represent subcategories. The number of top-level categories and depth of subdivision will depend on the complexity of the topics, business operations, or digital content involved. As an example, a government agency's contract management office may have a relatively flat file plan with a top-level folder for each contract awarded by the agency and second-level folders for specific types of contract-related content.

For example:

Top-level folder: Contract No. 23-0167
   Second-level folder: Executed contract
   Second-level folder: Amendments and addenda
   Second-level folder: Change orders
   Second-level folder: Contractor's insurance and bonding
   Second-level folder: Correspondence and communications
   Second-level folder: Contract performance reports
   Second-level folder: Dispute resolution documentation
   Second-level folder: Contract closeout documentation

File plans developed for other business units or operations may require additional subdivisions. The file plan for a recruitment office may contain a top-level folder for each open position, identified by reference number or job title. Each top-level folder will contain second-level folders for the job posting and applications received. Each of these second-level folders may be further subdivided as follows:

   Top-level folder: 23-024 Data analyst
      Second-level folder: Job posting
         Third-level folder: Internal posting
         Third-level folder: External advertisements
      Second-level folder: Applications received
         Third-level folder: Rejected applicants
         Third-level folder: Applicants interviewed but not hired
         Third-level folder: Applicant(s) hired

The third-level folder for applicants interviewed but not hired might contain a fourth-level folder for each applicant. The fourth-level folder might include the applicant's resume, interview notes, background check reports, reference letters, and other documentation. The third-level folder for applicant(s) hired will contain a fourth-level folder for each successful applicant. That folder will include many of the same records that are maintained for applicants who were not hired plus an offer letter, the applicant's response, an employment agreement, and onboarding documentation.

An ECM file plan must be tailored to the requirements of a specific business operation or content collection and it must be scalable to accommodate new categories and subcategories as needed. A file plan must be developed in consultation with business unit employees who capture and search for documents or other content in the course of their assigned duties. This can be done from the ground up, which will likely require many person-hours of effort, but it will be easier and faster to adapt an existing file taxonomy where available.

ECM applications are rarely implemented in a vacuum; they typically replace a shared drive or paper recordkeeping system. The folder structure in a shared drive directory or filing cabinet can be a useful starting point for development of an ECM file plan, although modifications will typically be required to reorganize folders, add categories or subcategories, and ensure that folders are clearly and consistently labelled. Adapting an existing folder structure will simplify a business unit's transition from a shared drive or paper recordkeeping system to an ECM implementation. As a helpful resource, some ECM vendors and other suppliers offer pre-built taxonomies for commonly encountered business operations, such as human resources and fleet management, and specific industries, including healthcare, pharmaceuticals, engineering and construction, banking, and education. These preconfigured file plans may require customization to align them with an organization's business processes or digital content.

ECM Metadata

A file plan creates a structured framework for digital content. A metadata scheme provides additional information about specific content items or groups of items. As discussed in a preceding section, metadata includes descriptive information that supports retrieval of digital content:

- Metadata and ECM file plans are complementary retrieval mechanisms. They have the same relationship as a library's subject catalog, which is used to search for books about a particular topic, and the library's classification system, which determines the order of books on shelves. While digital content can be retrieved by manually browsing through folders and subfolders in an ECM repository's file plan, it is often faster and more effective to search for metadata values associated with folders, subfolders, or individual content items.
- Careful planning and analysis are necessary to determine how users search for specific content items and to identify the categories of descriptive metadata that will enable them to retrieve the desired items. The Dublin Core and other standards discussed in a preceding section provide an excellent starting point for selecting metadata elements for a particular content collection. The Dublin Core metadata set is sufficiently adaptable to work in a broad range of recordkeeping environments involving a variety of content types, but special requirements must be taken into consideration. A healthcare organization may need metadata elements for patient identifiers or treatment codes, for example. Similarly, a construction company may need metadata elements for part numbers and the location in a building where a particular component is installed. A scientific research laboratory may need metadata elements for funding sources and equipment used in experiments.
- As with file plans, a metadata scheme for a given content collection can be developed by an organization's own staff or by a consultant hired for that purpose. In either case, the development effort will involve investigative, prototype, and test phases.
- In the investigative phase, the developer will work with knowledgeable employees to determine how digital content will be retrieved and used. The developer may also study similar metadata schemes developed by government agencies and other organizations.
- In the prototype phase, the developer will prepare a draft metadata scheme, accompanied by instructions and appropriate supporting

procedures. The draft metadata scheme will be circulated among key stakeholders for review. One or more meetings may be needed to clarify the reviewers' comments and criticisms, which will be incorporated into a revised draft to be recirculated for further review and comment. Several additional drafts may be required to produce an acceptable prototype metadata scheme.
- In the test phase, the prototype will be tested in a pilot installation using the selected ECM application. The developer will monitor the pilot installation, discuss the prototype with knowledgeable persons, and make further revisions as necessary in order to ultimately produce an operational version.

To reflect changing requirements, a metadata scheme must be expandable to accommodate new metadata elements. Most ECM applications impose no significant limitations on the number of metadata elements or the characteristic of metadata values. New metadata elements can be added as needed.

Cost

While the actual cost of an ECM application can only be determined by obtaining a firm quotation for a specific product based on a detailed statement of requirements, most organizations will incur a combination of infrastructure, software, and services costs that vary with the scope and complexity of a given ECM implementation:

- An on-premises ECM implementation may require new or upgraded infrastructure components, including servers on which ECM software will be installed, storage devices for digital content and its associated metadata, and networking components to ensure reliable and secure data communication. Cloud-based ECM applications require a reliable internet connection with effective security protection, which may not be available in all locations. If an on-premises implementation does not need to increase its data storage capacity when an ECM application is installed, it will likely need to do so eventually to accommodate an increasing amount of digital content and metadata. An organization may also need to acquire a specific operating system and database management system, although some organizations avoid this requirement by selecting an ECM application that is compatible with its existing system software and database environment.
- ECM vendors specify workstation requirements for retrieval, scanning, workflow processing, and other operations. Except for aging

equipment, existing workstations seldom require replacement or upgrading for an ECM implementation. Most ECM applications are compatible with widely installed personal computer, mobile devices, and operating systems. Most scanners, printers, and other peripherals are supported as well.
- Older ECM products required special client software installed on all user workstations. That approach optimized responsiveness by performing some operations on the workstation rather than on a remote server, but the burden of installing and updating client software on all user workstations made ECM applications difficult to deploy. ECM applications now support popular web browsers for most operations, although browser plugins or special client software may be needed or preferred for certain functions. ECM mobile apps allow authorized users to capture, retrieve, display, and process content on smartphones and tablets.
- An on-premises ECM implementation requires a server license and one or more user licenses. A server license authorizes an organization to install and operate ECM software on its own servers. With a perpetual server license, the most common scenario, the organization pays a one-time fee that permits unlimited operation of ECM software for an indefinite period of time. With a subscription license, the organization pays a monthly or annual fee to install and operate ECM software on its servers. The license remains in effect for as long as the recurring subscription fee is paid. Some server licenses are priced by the type of server or the number of users in a given ECM implementation. Optional modules that support specific ECM capabilities, such as workflow functionality or document imaging, typically require separate server and user licenses.
- Some server licenses include a specified number of user licenses, which allow individual employees or other authorized users to access and interact with an ECM application. In most cases, user licenses must be purchased separately. Named user licenses are assigned to specific individuals for their exclusive use. Depending on the ECM vendor's terms and conditions, a license may be reassigned if a named user leaves the organization or no longer requires access to an ECM application. A concurrent user license allow a maximum number of users to access an ECM application simultaneously. When the maximum number is active, others must wait until one of them logs off. Most licensing arrangements are scalable within limits that are seldom constraining. An organization can add named user licenses or increase the number of concurrent users to accommodate a growing workforce or an expanded ECM implementation. Some

ECM vendors offer enterprise licenses that allow an unlimited number of simultaneous users within an organization.
- User licenses are required in both on-premises and cloud-based ECM implementations. A full user license allows designated individuals to create, retrieve, view, modify, and delete content and metadata. A super-user license gives a system administrator, selected information technology, and designated others access to administrative privileges, including management of access and permissions for specific users and content, content migration into and from the ECM application, and integration with external applications. Super users may also have access to advanced reporting and analytical tools to monitor system operations and troubleshoot performance issues. Some licenses limit the ECM features and functions that a user can access. With a read-only license, the most common example, a user can search for, view, print, or download content or metadata but cannot create, modify, or delete it.
- ECM applications are not plug-and-play products. They must be properly installed and configured by a knowledgeable provider, who may be the ECM application's developer or a reseller, agent, or other authorized representative. Basic vendor-provided services include consultation to determine implementation requirements and expectations, installation and configuration of ECM software, database setup, minor customizations, fine-tuning of the ECM application's user interface, and training for system administrators and users. Some ECM implementations require advanced vendor services, such as extensive customizations, workflow programming, automated capture of metadata, integration with external applications, and assistance with content migration. Implementation services are a major cost component in ECM installations. Even the cost of basic services can equal or exceed the cost of ECM software. Additional implementation services may be needed if an initial installation is expanded to include optional components.
- An on-premises ECM implementation will incur annual charges for software maintenance and technical support contracts. A software maintenance contract provides bug fixes and patches to remedy defects or address security vulnerabilities that may be detected in an ECM application. It also provides access to new releases of an ECM application, which may offer improved performance or support new features and functions. ECM vendors regularly update their products, but there is no guarantee that a new release will be issued during a given contract period. Software maintenance is typically bundled with technical support that provides knowledgeable advice and instruction about issues or problem encountered by ECM

customers. Technical support may be provided by phone, email, or a website. The hours of service and vendor response time vary. Where an ECM application supports mission-critical operation, an organization's performance expectations for technical support must be discussed with prospective vendors and clearly specified in the ECM contract.

On-Premises vs. Cloud ECM

Most ECM applications are available for on-premises installation on an organization's own servers or in a cloud-based version operated by the ECM software developer or an authorized reseller or agent. Subject to minor variations, the on-premises and cloud-based versions of a given ECM application provide equivalent functionality, but each approach has advantages and limitations:

- An on-premises ECM implementation installed on an organization's own servers and operated by its own staff provides close control over an ECM application and the digital content it manages. The organization determines the location where the servers will operate, the devices that will store digital content, the method and frequency of data backup, and the storage medium, location, and retention period for backup copies. The organization can modify its computing environment and network infrastructure, as necessary, to address uptime and performance issues, accommodate additional users, and add storage capacity, although such improvements may be costly.
- In an on-premises implementation, an organization can prioritize the installation of software upgrades and other maintenance tasks, as well as the customization of ECM components and integration of ECM with external applications. On the other hand, an on-premises installation requires the purchase of ECM software, which may involve a significant capital expenditure, and the organization will incur additional annual charges for software maintenance and technical support.
- Compared to an on-premises installation, a cloud-based ECM application offers the advantages of faster implementation because the ECM software is preinstalled and pretested on the cloud provider's servers, and lower start-up costs because the purchase of ECM software is eliminated and in-house servers are not necessary. The cloud service provider is responsible for the computing environment in which an ECM application operates, for improving performance and increasing storage capacity as needed, for ensuring that the ECM

software is updated to the latest release, and for performing data backup and recovering digital content in the event of a disaster.
- An on-premises ECM implementation will also require a significant commitment of staff resources by an organization's information technology staff, which must receive appropriate training from the ECM vendor. This will not necessarily eliminate the need for implementation services and operating assistance from the ECM vendor. A cloud-based implementation eliminates the need to allocate information technology staff to work with the ECM vendor while the application is being installed and to operate and troubleshoot the application postimplementation. In a cloud implementation, however, the information technology unit may still be responsible for monitoring and evaluating the cloud service's availability and performance. The information technology unit may also work with the cloud provider to address users' problems and concerns, to migrate content and metadata from an on-premises ECM installation or another cloud-based ECM service, to integrate the provider's ECM service with external applications, and to ensure that the cloud provider complies with the organization's security standards.
- Cloud-based ECM providers typically charge an initial fee for configuration services plus annual subscription charges that will vary with the number of licensed users and the amount of storage required for digital content. Annual recurring charges that minimize or eliminate start-up costs are particularly appealing to government agencies, businesses, nonprofit organizations, and other prospective ECM customers that have limited access to capital funds but sufficient annual budgets to manage ongoing expenditures. Cloud-based pricing may also attract well-funded organizations where a lengthy approval process for capital investment will delay an ECM implementation. Over a multiyear period, however, the accumulated annual charges for cloud-based services can exceed the cost of on-premises installation of a given EDMS product.
- Some organizations prefer an on-premises implementation for digital content that contains personal data, trade secrets, and other confidential information with special security requirements, although many cloud providers have implemented stringent security measures to prevent data breaches and corruption. Customers' digital content is encrypted for storage and transmission. ECM cloud services comply with data privacy laws and international security standards. They operate in well-protected data centers with restricted access, surveillance technology, and other physical security measures to prevent intrusion. Firewalls and network security protocols combined with

frequent vulnerability assessments limit the potential for unauthorized network access.
- As a potentially significant limitation, a cloud service offer limitation customization options and it may be unable to integrate will an organization's existing applications. These limitations may be specified in service agreements. An on-premises ECM implementation may be preferable for organizations with complex customization or integration requirements.

Advantages and limitations aside, the decision to use the on-premises or the cloud-based approach will be based on an organization's policies and preferences related to cloud services. Some organizations have adopted a cloud-first strategy that prioritizes software-as-a-service offerings over on-premises implementations to reduce costs, for rapid deployment of applications, to make information resources available to remote workers and geographically dispersed offices, and to simplify management of their information technology infrastructure.

Risk Analysis

Broadly defined, risk is a combination of threats, vulnerabilities, and consequences that pose a danger to an organization's assets or that impair its ability to achieve objectives. A risk management process must identify and describe threats and consequences, identify and evaluate vulnerabilities, and assess options for risk mitigation. Because unrecognized risks cannot be managed, an effective risk management process begins with identification of potential threats, which are sometimes described risk sources. The following risk sources may be encountered in an ECM implementation:

- Infrastructure shortfall. An infrastructure shortfall will occur if an organization's computer and networking infrastructure are inadequate for an ECM implementation. To mitigate this risk, the ECM implementation team must evaluate the existing infrastructure at the server and workstation level and recommend any required modifications and enhancements to ensure that appropriate technology components are in place and fully operational at the inception of the implementation. Procurement of required technology components should be initiated when an ECM vendor is selected and a timetable for the ECM implementation is established. Special computer and networking components are rarely required in ECM implementations. Any required devices should be routinely available from multiple suppliers on short notice, although an organization's purchasing procedures and difficulty obtaining required approvals may cause procurement delays. Progress of the procurement should be monitored until all technology components are delivered, installed, and confirmed to be reliably operational. Infrastructure shortfall is not a significant risk in cloud-based ECM implementations, although some users' workstations may need to be upgraded or replaced.

- Functionality shortfall. A functionality shortfall will occur when an ECM product fails to operate as planned. Given proper procurement and product evaluation procedures, this risk has a low likelihood of occurrence. An organization must incorporate functional specifications into requests for proposals, bid invitations, or other procurement solicitations. ECM products that do not satisfy all requirements must be eliminated. ECM vendors under serious consideration will be required to confirm compliance by demonstrating their products' functionality. Unproven ECM products must be avoided; any product that has not been commercially available for at least ninety days and successfully installed at a minimum of one customer site should be eliminated from further consideration. References for previously installed sites should be requested from ECM vendors and contacted. If the provided references are inconclusive or otherwise inadequate, additional installations should be identified and contacted. The qualifications and experience of resellers, subcontractors, or others participating in software installation, customization, and testing should also be verified during the vendor selection process.
- Cost overrun. There is a risk that an organization will pay more than it had intended for ECM technology. Many ECM implementation projects are funded by a one-time capital allocation, which is presumably based on an informed estimate of the anticipated cost of ECM software and services as well as any required infrastructure upgrades. A cost overrun will occur when the actual cost of an ECM implementation exceeds the allocated amount. Reliable cost information for infrastructure components is readily available but, as previously noted, the actual cost of ECM software and services can only be determined by obtaining firm quotations submitted by qualified suppliers. A competitive procurement based on a request for proposals or bid invitation that clearly specifies an organization's requirements and expectations will increase the likelihood of affordable pricing from multiple ECM vendors. To further reduce uncertainty and establish a likely range of costs for budget purposes, some organizations issue a request for information (RFI) prior to a procurement solicitation. When a vendor is selected, a fixed-price contract will provide a definitive cost for ECM software and related services. The progress of an ECM implementation should be closely

monitored to avoid increased costs resulting from unwarranted additions to functional specifications.
- <u>Schedule overrun</u>. Schedule overrun occurs when an ECM implementation takes longer than anticipated. Delays at one or more stages of implementation are commonplace and probably unavoidable in information technology projects, given the many unanticipated events and other factors that can put a project behind schedule. Supervision is the basis for an effective risk-mitigation strategy for schedule overrun. A realistic implementation timetable must be established and discussed with ECM vendors during the product evaluation process. An organization's ECM project manager must closely monitor the progress of an implementation. The ECM vendor should be expected to submit regular status reports. The project manager must identify potential problems and resolve them as quickly as possible with input from all stakeholders. Action items must be tracked for progress. The implementation timetable must be adjusted, as necessary, to account for delays.
- <u>User pushback.</u> An ECM implementation will transform an organization's existing content management practices, in some cases drastically. While some departments will welcome the changes as necessary to achieve desired improvements and replace inefficient business processes, others may resist the ECM implementation out of concern that established work routines will be disrupted, productivity will be degraded, or information security and data privacy will be compromised. Some employees may have had an unfavorable experience with a poorly conceived ECM implementation in their previous employment, which they report to their colleagues. To minimize the risk of user pushback, an organization must develop an effective change-management strategy and communication plan to bring skeptical employees on board. The ECM implementation should meet with departmental stakeholders to discuss their concerns and explain the technology's benefits. Employees who are uncertain about their ability to adjust to the ECM implementation must be assured that they will receive the necessary training and support. Initial installations in key departments will provide a convincing proof-of-concept to confirm reliable operation of the ECM application and demonstrate its value. Departmental participation should be phased in at a measured pace to allow ample time to address stakeholders' issues and concerns.
- <u>Danger to digital content</u>. There is a risk that a hardware failure, software malfunction, operator error, natural or human-induced disaster, or other adverse event will result in loss or damage to digital

content stored in an ECM repository. This risk can be mitigated by regular backup operations that provide appropriate recoverability.
- <u>Sponsorship shortfall.</u> Senior management support is critical to a successful ECM implementation, but there is a risk that departmental managers will lose enthusiasm and withdraw support if unexplained delays, unforeseen costs, strong user resistance, or other problems are encountered. As a mitigation strategy, close supervision at all stages of an ECM implementation will avoid problems that may lead to withdrawal of management support. Senior management must be kept informed of the implementation's progress on a regular basis. Senior management must also be informed about problems and corrective actions in appropriate detail at an early stage. As discussed in a preceding section, some organizations have established an ECM governance committee to increase senior management's commitment and sense of ownership.

These risks and mitigation strategies are not limited to ECM implementations. They also apply to other information governance technologies discussed in this book and to technology projects generally.

SUMMARY OF MAJOR POINTS

- Enterprise content management (ECM) encompasses strategies, methods, and tools to capture, manage, store, preserve, and deliver an organization's unstructured information, which is broadly defined as any information that does not have a prescribed or consistent structure or format.
- Widely cited examples of unstructured digital content included word-processing documents and other text files, presentation files with textual and multimedia elements, email and text messages, document images, digital photographs, video recordings, audio recordings, web pages, blog posts, and social media posts.
- Enterprise content management evolved from document imaging and document management systems that were introduced in the 1980s and 1990s. Once widely discussed as technological innovations, document imaging and document management are now considered ECM components rather than separate information governance technologies.
- ECM technology offers a functionally superior alternative to shared drives and other ungoverned repositories for digital content that is in the active phase of the information lifecycle, the period when information must be conveniently available and readily retrievable.

- ECM applications are produced and marketed by dozens of companies, ranging from large computer manufacturers and software developers with diverse product lines and global operations to relatively small, specialized suppliers.
- International ECM standards deal with important concepts, issues, and expectations that decision-makers must consider when planning ECM implementations and evaluating ECM products.
- ECM applications can accommodate and a wide range of unstructured digital content created in a variety of proprietary and nonproprietary file formats. ECM applications can capture this content in a variety of ways.
- Like other information governance technologies, ECM applications use metadata to identify, describe, and index digital content, allowing it to be retrieved, controlled, and otherwise managed. Specific metadata elements will vary for one ECM implementation to another, depending on the types of digital content involved and an organization's retrieval and control requirements.
- For many organizations, the ability to retrieve recorded information quickly and conveniently is one of the principal motivations and justifications for an ECM implementation.
- ECM applications support a full range of safeguards to ensure the security, integrity, reliability, confidentiality, and controlled availability of digital content and its associated metadata.
- An appropriate governance mechanism must provide the leadership, planning, and coordination necessary for a successful ECM implementation, and a file plan and metadata scheme must be developed to support the organization and retrieval of digital content.
- Organizations will incur a combination of infrastructure, software, and services costs that vary with the scope and complexity of a given ECM implementation.
- Most ECM applications are available for on-premises installation on an organization's own servers or in a cloud-based version operated by the ECM software developer or an authorized reseller or agent.
- Planners and decision-makers must identify and mitigate the risks that may be encountered in an ECM implementation.

2

✛

Records Management Application Software

As an information governance discipline, records management is responsible for determining how long recorded information must be kept to comply with applicable laws and regulations, to satisfy an organization's operational requirements, and to preserve content of continuing value. Retention determinations are based on the information lifecycle concept, which recognizes that the business value of recorded information varies inversely with the age of the information. That is the fundamental principle that makes retention decisions possible. Most records maintained by companies, government agencies, and nonprofit organizations are referenced frequently while the business operations, transactions, activities, or events to which they pertain are under active consideration. As time passes and those matters are resolved or cease to be of active interest, reference activity diminishes. This may occur gradually or abruptly.

Retention decisions are informed estimates of the lifecycles of specific records. Many records, like email messages and lists of tasks to be completed, deal with routine administrative matters; they have short lifecycles and need not be retained beyond their moment of immediate usefulness. Purchase orders, invoices, and other transaction-oriented documents may be referenced frequently for several weeks or months following their creation or receipt; after the transactions to which they pertain are concluded, they may be consulted occasionally when questions arise about the goods or services purchased, the amount paid, or some other aspect of a past transaction. A department manager may need information about a previously purchased product when a replacement is needed, for example. A risk management specialist may need to review paid insurance claims to determine whether additional or different coverage is required. The records of former employees will prove useful when confirmation of prior employment is requested or a former employee is considered for rehiring. Certain business records, such as technical specifications for products with long service lives and legal documentation for precedent-setting cases, retain their business value for longer periods, perhaps a decade or more. A small percentage of an organization's records may have long-term operational or historical value that warrants permanent preservation.

The information lifecycle is divided, by frequency of reference, into active and inactive (less active) phases. Each phase has well established requirements. The active phase is concerned with timely availability and convenient retrieval of information to support an organization's business objectives and operations. The inactive phase is principally concerned with cost-effective, reliable retention of information. Many if not most records spend a longer portion of their lifecycles in the inactive phase than in the active phase. An invoice, for example, will be in active phase until is paid—ninety days or less in many cases—but most organizations retain inactive invoices for the period of time specified by the statute of limitations on payment-related litigation, which may range from three to ten years, depending on the jurisdiction. Similarly, job applications received for an advertised position may be under active considerations for a few weeks or months until the open position is filled or withdrawn, but government regulations in some countries specify a minimum retention period for hiring records and many organizations choose to retain them until the statutes of limitations for litigation to employment discrimination have elapsed, which may be several years after the records are no longer active.

As its distinctive role in information governance initiatives, records management application (RMA) software manages records that are in the inactive phase of the information lifecycle—that is, records that deal with completed transactions, business operations, activities, or events. As such, RMA software occupies a position on the information governance technology spectrum between enterprise content management, which supports the active phase of the information lifecycle and stores electronic records that must be conveniently available to support an organization's mission, and digital preservation applications, which create and maintain an archival repository for digital content of enduring value. RMA software provides retention functionality that is generally absent from ECM applications and other technologies that manage active records. It tracks the retention of specific records, identifies those with elapsed retention periods, and initiates their appropriate disposition, which may involve destruction of the records, transfer of the records to a designated repository, or—if there is a continued need for the records to support litigation, audits, or unfinished business operations—extension of the retention period. Unlike digital preservation products, RMA software is principally intended for nonpermanent content—so-called temporary records—that will be discarded when a predetermined retention period elapses, but a records management application might also serve as a front-end retention component that transfers permanent content to a digital preservation application after a predetermined amount of time.

HISTORY

While RMA software can track inactive information in any form, including paper files, it is principally designed to manage the retention of word-processing documents, spreadsheets, email messages, digital images, audio recordings, video recordings, web pages, social media posts, and other electronic records. As discussed in the preceding chapter, these digital documents are collectively described as unstructured records to differentiate them from database records, which conform to a predefined field structure. RMA software is not suitable for retention of a structured database records, which is typically handled by the application that maintains a given database, assuming that it has retention functionality, or by the database archiving applications discussed in chapter 9.

RMA software is not a new technology. The first commercially available RMA products were introduced in late 1980s and early 1990s by software developers based in Canada and Australia. As with other records management innovations, the early adopters were government agencies concerned about retention and disposition of their growing accumulations of electronic records, but the prospect of an effective approach to electronic recordkeeping attracted a lot of attention in the broader records management community. Most of the initial RMA products were ultimately acquired by major computer companies and software developers who rebranded them, enhanced their capabilities, and marketed them to their large government and corporate customers. New RMA products were introduced in the late 1990s and early 2000s, and the market broadened to include medium-size organizations in government and the private sector.

Today, RMA software is developed and marketed by several dozen companies, who sell their products directly to customers or through authorized representatives. The earliest RMA products were self-contained applications intended for standalone implementation. That remains the case in many installations, although vendors increasingly emphasize the integration of RMA software's lifecycle management functionality with other software. This capability appeals to prospective customers who want RMA software to interact with office productivity, email, enterprise content management, and other applications that create and store electronic records. As noted in chapter 1 and discussed later in this chapter, some vendors of ECM software have added RMA functionality to their product lines as a standard or optional component for customers who want a unified approach to management of active and inactive digital content.

BUSINESS NEED

RMA products are used by government agencies, companies, and nonprofit organizations, but technology to manage the retention of electronic records attracts less attention and fewer customers than other technologies discussed in this book. In marked contrast with ECM applications, which have been extensively surveyed and evaluated by technology analysts, there is little published information about the number of RMA installations or the estimated size of the global market for RMA products, and there are few case studies that discuss specific customers' experience with RMA implementations. Widely publicized market surveys and comparative evaluations of information governance technologies have largely ignored RMA software as a distinct product group. Where RMA technology is mentioned all, it is typically conflated with enterprise content management, with which it is often associated, or treated as a component of enterprise information archiving, a vaguely defined category of products and services that manage the storage and retention of databases, mobile communications, video and audio recordings, social media and web content, scientific research data, medical imagery, and other voluminous collections of digital information.

Yet RMA software effectively addresses a commonplace and significant information governance problem that is encountered in organizations of all types and sizes. Through the late 1990s, most organizations retained records in physical form on paper or, less commonly, microfilm, but that is no longer the case. Government agencies, companies, and nonprofit entities increasingly rely on word-processing files, spreadsheets, email messages, digitized images, digital photographs, and other electronic records to satisfy regulatory recordkeeping requirements or support their business operations. With the vast majority of information originating in digital form, the once prevalent practice of printing electronic records for retention in office files has been sharply curtailed or discontinued as too costly, or simply impractical. To promote this trend, some organizations have reduced the number of printers installed in offices and put them in inconvenient locations to discourage their use. Many employees who entered the workforce after 2010 are unfamiliar with paper recordkeeping and have little tolerance for its functional limitations and labor-intensive maintenance requirements.

While paper records have not disappeared, file rooms managed by trained clerical employees have been steadily supplanted by shared drives, email servers, cloud-based storage services, and other high-capacity repositories. As discussed in chapter 1, these repositories are easily accessible but largely ungoverned. They pose significant challenges for managed retention of recorded information. Within a shared drive, important records may be comingled with work in progress, drafts, superseded documents, duplicate records, personal files, material downloaded from websites, and other unrelated or transitory content that does not warrant continued retention. Very little housekeeping is typically done to identify and remove these obsolete and redundant files and folders. While much insignificant information is needlessly retained, limited safeguards prevent unauthorized destruction of records that need to be kept for legal, operational, or historical reasons. Access and purging privileges are defined by individual employees rather than by a central authority as the outcome of a coherent planning process. Even where access to files and folders is limited, individual documents can be accidentally or intentionally deleted or modified by anyone who has full access to a given folder.

Poorly managed shared drives are not as visible as cluttered file rooms. Given the increased capacity and declining cost of computer storage, business managers may feel little pressure to delete obsolete content to save space and reduce recordkeeping costs. But lifecycle management remains an important and urgent aspect of information governance, although its focus has shifted from destruction of obsolete records to continued retention of records need for regulatory compliance, operational continuity, and historical preservation. Compared to paper documents, digital content can be retained longer at lower cost, but indefinite retention of large quantities of inactive electronic records is not a sustainable practice. It can compromise the performance of computer systems and software, complicate the organization and retrieval of active records, and create burdensome data migration requirements when applications are replaced.

RMA technology addresses these issues. As discussed in the following sections, RMA software provides effective functionality for retention of electronic records that need to be kept for specified periods of time as well as timely disposition of electronic records when their prescribed retention periods elapse.

STANDARDS AND GUIDELINES

ISO 15489-1:2016, *Information and documentation—Records management—Part 1: Concept and principles* provides high-level guidance for creation, capture, and control of recorded information in all formats; it does not deal exclusively with electronic recordkeeping and does not discuss processes or technologies. Similarly, ISO 30301:2019, *Information and documentation—Management systems for records—Requirements* defines organizational roles, responsibilities, and performance measures for records management systems at a high-level of conceptualization. It does not discuss specific records management technologies. The same is true of ISO 30302:2022, *Information and documentation—Management systems for records—Guidelines for implementation*.

Characteristics and capabilities of systems and software to manage electronic records are covered in ISO 16175-1:2020, *Information and documentation—Processes and functional requirements for software for managing records—Part 1: Functional requirements and associated guidance for any applications that manage digital records*; ISO 16175-2:2020, *Information and documentation—Processes and functional requirements for software for managing records—Part 2: Guidance for selecting, designing, implementing and maintaining software for managing records*; and ISO 18829:2017, *Document management—Assessing ECM/EDRM implementations—Trustworthiness*. These international standards apply broadly to any software that captures and manages electronic records for business purposes, including RMA products and general-purpose content management applications as well as case management software, contract management software, project management software, and other special-purpose applications that create and maintain recorded information in support of specific business operations. While they do not deal exclusively with RMA software, the standards are nonetheless informative and useful for product evaluation. In the Sultanate of Oman, the National Records and Archives Authority (NRAA) uses international standards, in combination with its own National Procedures Guide for Electronic Documents Management, to test and certify records management software to be implemented by government agencies.

In the absence of an international standard that specifically addresses the evaluation and implementation RMA products, several organizations in the United States, Europe, and Australia have developed detailed guidelines for software to manage electronic records as official copies. Frequently cited examples are discussed below. While they have not been approved by national or international standard-setting bodies, these guidelines are widely recognized as de facto standards for records management applications. They have influenced the commercial development of RMA products as well as the evaluation and selection of RMA software by government agencies, businesses, and nonprofit entities. Although some of them have been discontinued, they remain useful reference sources for anyone interested in RMA applications.

DoD 5015.2-STD

US government agencies have played a leading role in the transition from paper to electronic recordkeeping. Their initiatives have highlighted the challenges associated with managing the lifecycle of electronic records. In the early 1990s, the US Department of Defense was criticized by Congress for failure to properly retain electronic records related to Gulf War Syndrome, an illness that affected soldiers who fought in the Persian Gulf War. That criticism led to the development of DoD 5015.2-STD, *Design Criteria Standard for Electronic Records Management Applications*:

- The initial release of DoD 5015.2-STD was issued by the Department of Defense in November 1997 as part of a business process reengineering effort for records management that began in 1993. It defined minimum functional requirements derived from federal statutes and regulations for commercially available electronic records management applications to be used by the Department of Defense.
- DoD 5015.2-STD was revised and reissued in 2002 to incorporate additional requirements related to classified federal records that require special treatment for reasons of national security. A 2007 revision, known as version 3, included provisions for transferring electronic records from one records management application to another or from federal agencies to the National Archives and for managing federal records associated with the Freedom of Information Act and Privacy Act.
- The Joint Interoperability Test Command (JITC), a unit of the Department of Defense that certifies technology products for military use, has tested and certified commercially available RMA software for compliance with DoD 5-15.2-STD and maintains a register of certified products. A given product could be certified for compliance with the standard's baseline, classified records, Freedom of Information Act, and/or Privacy Act requirements.
- DoD Manual (DoDM) 8180.01, *Information Technology Planning for Electronic Records Management*, issued in August 2023, has replaced DoD 5015.2-STD. It reduces the department's emphasis on narrow technical requirements and product certification. As of this writing, however, the register of certified products remains available on the JITC website.

DoD 5015.2-STD had a significant impact on electronic records management. Vendors of RMA software prominently advertised their products as certified for compliance with 5015.2-STD. They depicted 5015.2-STD as a de facto national standard that is equally applicable to government, companies, and nongovernmental organization. Some State Archives adopted the 5015.2 standard for RMA software acquired by state and local government agencies, and compliance with 5015.2-STD was often specified as a required or preferred feature in requests of proposals and bid invitations for RMA software. Even where the 5015.2 standard was not specifically referenced, many of its requirements were incorporated by excerpt or paraphrase into procurement specifications for records management software.

UERM Requirements

In January 2003, the US National Archives and Records Administration (NARA) endorsed the 5015.2 standard for selecting off-the-shelf software to store electronic records as official copies by federal agencies and to facilitate the transfer of permanent electronic records to the National Archives. The endorsement was repeated in 2008 following the release of version 3 of the standard, but it was rescinded in 2022. In 2017, NARA issued its own specifications, the Universal Electronic Records Management (UERM) Requirements, which identify high-level business needs for managing electronic records at all phases of the information lifecycle:

- Developed as part of the Federal Electronic Records Modernization Initiative, the UERM Requirements apply to records that originate in electronic form, including digital documents created by desktop applications, electronic messages, social media and website content, databases, and digital video and audio recordings.
- The UERM Requirements address six areas of the information lifecycle for electronic records: creation, maintenance and use, disposal, transfer, metadata, and reporting. These lifecycle management requirements specify mandatory and desirable functionality for the design and implementation of electronic recordkeeping policies and procedures by US government agencies, and they provide guidance for software developers and vendors of electronic records management applications and tools.
- The lifecycle management requirements apply to electronic records stored on-premises or by cloud service providers. The UERM Requirements also specify acceptable formats for transfer of electronic records to NARA. For each requirement, NARA specifies an author-

ity in federal laws and regulations, international standards, or guidance previously issued by NARA.
- Compared to DoD 5015.2-STD, UERM Requirements are shorter and less prescriptive. NARA worked with the General Services Administration to create a procurement category for electronic records management solutions to be acquired by federal government agencies.
- Vendors self-certify their products for UERM compliance without independent testing. At the time of this writing, over ninety vendors had certified their products as compliant with UERM lifecycle management requirements.

The UERM has been revised several times since its initial publication. NARA's move away from 5015.2-STD for electronic recordkeeping by US government agencies reflected waning interest in the standard within the broader records management community. A Google Trends analysis indicates that the number of web searches for 5015.2-STD in the United States peaked in early 2004 and has declined steadily and significantly since that time. Google Trends indicates a similar profile for web searches for records management software in general. Bibliographic surveys likewise indicated that electronic records management has lost research momentum in recent years, although this reduced research activity may be characteristic for a well-established topic that is already familiar to those interested it.

PROS 19/05

Like DoD 5015.2-STD, PROS 19/05, *Create, Capture, and Control Standard* is a proprietary standard developed by a government agency for its own purposes. PROS 19/05 defines principles and requirements for electronic records maintained by government agencies in the Australian state of Victoria, the country's most densely populated state:

- Issued in 2019 by the Public Record Office Victoria (PROV), the state's archival agency whose recordkeeping authority is defined by the Public Records Act 1973, PROS 19/05 is one component of PROV's recordkeeping standards framework, which also includes guidance for disposal, storage, operational management, and strategic management of recorded information maintained by state and local government agencies.
- PROS 19/05 is a multipart standard that incorporates provisions originally presented in the Victorian Electronic Records Strategy (VERS) for creation, capture, and preservation of digital records.

- VERS was an outgrowth of a 1996 consultant's report that examined the problem of preserving electronic records.
- The consultant's widely publicized recommendations were embodied in PROS 99/007, *Standard on the Management of Electronic Records*, which defined a format and metadata scheme for electronic records. As its most distinctive feature, PROS 99/007 required permanent electronic records to be converted to a long-term format called a VERS Encapsulated Object (VEO) for transfer to the Public Record Office Victoria, which has issued a technical specification for developers of systems and tools to construct VEOs.
- Like 5015.2-STD, VERS was supported by a testing and certification scheme for records management applications. The Public Record Office Victoria certified over four dozen products from twenty-two vendors for compliance with VERS, the predecessor of PROS 19/05. At the time of this writing, no products had been tested for compliance with PROS 19/05.
- Both the original VERS specification and PROS 19/05 are well documented by the Public Record Office Victoria, which makes ample information about them available online. Compared to the original VERS specification, PROS 19/05 is shorter, less restrictive, and easier for government agencies to understand and comply with.

Victoria government agencies must manage and retain public records in electronic form whenever possible. Electronic records must be created or captured in a format that is expected to remain accessible and usable throughout their retention periods. Permanent electronic records must be transferred to the Public Record Office in the VEO format as specified in PROS 19/05 S3, *Long Term Sustainable Formats Specification* and PROS 19/05 S2, *Minimum Metadata Requirements Specification*.

MoReq

The 5015.2-STD and PROS 19/05 standards were specifically developed for evaluation and certification of RMA products. By contrast, *Model Requirements for the Management of Electronic Records* (MoReq) is a generic specification for systems that manage electronic records.

- The initial MoReq version was developed by a team of consultants in 2001 for the DLM Forum, a nonprofit community of public archives and other parties active in records management. It was funded by the European Commission as part of their Interchange of Data Between Administrations (IDA) initiative.

- The DLM Forum issued a revised version, known as MoReq2, in 2008. The latest and apparently final version, MoReq2010, was formally introduced in 2011 under the title *Modular Requirements for Record Systems*. The revised title reflected future plans to broaden MoReq's applicability beyond general records management.
- Like its predecessors, MoReq2010 defines core functionality for effective management, access to, and retention of records. It is intended as an educational resource, a selection aid for organizations that want to acquire RMA software, and a guide for RMA software developers.
- A number of vendors of RMA software have supported MoReq and advertise their products as compatible with MoReq requirements. In 2008, the DLM Forum announced a program to accredit MoReq tests centers and certify RMA products and services for MoReq compliance but testing and certification never gained wide acceptance.
- In 2009, the MoReq Governance Board produced a roadmap that extended MoReq to include the legal, defense, finance, health, and other industry sectors with specialized records management requirements. This expansion was forecast to begin, with the assistance of industry experts, in 2012. In 2018, however, the DLM Forum announced that, after polling it membership, it will not initiate further development of MoReq.
- Unlike DoD 5015.2-STD and PROS 19/05, which were each developed for a single government agency, MoReq was conceived from the outset as an international specification that would be applicable to mainstream records management in government, businesses, and nonprofit entities throughout the European Union. Consequently, the MoReq2010 specification is much longer and more complicated than 5015.2-STD.

The various MoReq iterations have been translated and adapted for use in Asia, South America, and elsewhere. Apart from academic and archival communities, MoReq has attracted little attention in the United States. Unlike 5015.2-STD, it has had little impact on the development, acceptance, evaluation, or procurement of RMA products in the US market. A Google Trends analysis indicates that web searches for information about MoReq peaked in early 2004 worldwide but a reasonable level of interest was maintained through the introduction of MoReq 2010. In the United States, however, web searches for information about MoReq never reached the minimum level required for a Google Trends analysis.

FEATURES AND CAPABILITIES

While other technologies discussed in this book incorporate retention functionality as a standard or optional component, RMA software offers distinctive features and capabilities that are not replicated by other information governance products or services. Authorized users can designate records that warrant retention. Records can be retained in a centralized repository or managed in their original locations. Retention rules can be based on elapsed time or events. RMA software will identify records that are eligible for destruction or other disposition actions and temporarily suspend the destruction of records that are needed for legal proceedings. File plans and metadata allow authorized users to search for records when needed using a variety of retrieval methods. RMA administrators can control user privileges to ensure that retention functionality and retrieval capabilities are limited to authorized individuals or groups.

Declaring Records

RMA software is designed to manage official copies of an organization's records. Official copies are the subset of digital content that warrants retention for a specified period of time to satisfy legal and regulatory requirements, address operational needs, or preserve information of long-term significance. An organization must identify such content to differentiate it from extra copies, drafts, notes, and other items of trivial or transitory value. This process, termed record declaration, is the essential first step in managed retention of electronic records:

- Record declaration is a formal process. It must not be applied indiscriminately. Record declaration can only be performed by employees or other authorized persons who have declaration privileges. Declaration must be limited to records that are covered by retention guidance and properly considered official copies. A given record's status as an official copy that warrants managed retention must be confirmed by a knowledgeable person before it is declared.
- While declaration procedures vary from one RMA product to another, there are some commonalities. Authorized individuals can manually browse through shared drives, email servers, collaboration sites, and other storage repositories to identify and select individual or multiple files that are considered records. Alternatively, records may be declared through a policy or an automated workflow that routes records through an approval process. Some RMA software allows authorized individuals to declare records in batches. A given RMA implementation may use a combination of these methods.

- Records can be declared soon after they are created or at a later time, such as a specified number of days after the record was last modified and no further changes are reasonably anticipated. With some RMA software, a word-processing document, spreadsheet, presentation, email message, or other content can also be declared as a record from within its native application at the time it is created, received, or read.
- In most cases, record declaration is irreversible. Declared records cannot be undeclared or edited, and they cannot be deleted until their retention periods elapse. If a declared record needs to be revised, the modified version must be declared and saved as a separate record with its own metadata.
- Some RMA software allows designated users to override these restrictions—an RMA system administrator may be able to reverse the declaration of a record that was declared in error, for example—but this feature should be used sparingly. Multiple authorizations are typically required for such reversals to protect the integrity of the record declaration process.

Record declaration is a distinctive feature of RMA implementations. Other technologies discussed in this book have a broader scope that encompasses transitory content as well as official copies. An ECM repository, for example, may store multiple drafts of a report, legal brief, or other document, but only the final version will be declared as a record to be managed by RMA software. Email servers similarly contain many trivial communications that do not warrant continued retention as well as multiple copies of significant messages. Identification of records that need to be kept is an essential component of an effective record-retention program, but it is not the only one. Records managers typically establish policies for retention of drafts, information copies, and other documents that are not considered official copies and would not qualify for record declaration. In many organizations, transitory content outnumbers declared records. Such content is outside the scope of an RMA implementation, but it poses significant records management challenges. Without retention guidance, it will accumulate on shared drives, in filing cabinets, in offsite storage facilities, and in other repositories.

Centralized Repository vs. In-Place Retention

Once records that warrant continued retention are identified and declared, their storage location depends on the way an RMA product is designed. Some RMA products store declared records in a centrally managed repository; others support in-place management of declared records. Both approaches are compatible with either on-premises or cloud-based implementation:

- Traditional RMA architecture stores declared records in a centralized repository that is maintained by the RMA software itself. The RMA repository is sometimes described as a record center or archive. Declared records are transferred to the RMA repository from their original storage locations for retention, usually when elapsed time or events trigger the inactive phase of the information lifecycle.
- Records transferred to a centralized RMA repository are typically saved in folders or subfolders that are organized in accordance with the repository's file plan, which must be developed by someone who is familiar with the records and the business operations they support. As discussed later in this chapter, a repository's file plan may group declared records in folders that correspond to the business operations and types of records covered by an organization's retention schedule. A workflow script can be created to route records to the appropriate folders. Where disposition actions are based on elapsed time as discussed below, folders may be subdivided by year.
- The centralized repository model is used by ECM products that offer an optional records management module for organizations that want a single platform to manage both active and inactive information. Active content is maintained by the ECM application. When reference activity diminishes, declared records are transferred from the ECM repository to the RMA module, which functions as a back-end component for record retention. Alternatively, declared records can be transferred to the RMA repository from external storage locations.
- With in-place records management, RMA software applies record declaration and retention rules to official copies that remain in the locations where they are normally stored, which may be a shared drive, a collaboration site, an email server, an ECM repository, or another location. Adopting a federated model, some RMA products can manage records stored in multiple content repositories. A common portal identifies and provides access to declared records regardless of storage location, and RMA functions are initiated for all content repositories from a central dashboard. A unified file plan categorizes the records for retention and includes a link to the location where each record is stored.
- With the in-place approach to RMA implementation, declared records are typically intermingled in storage locations with drafts, notes, information copies, trivial email communications, and other digital content of transitory value that does not warrant managed retention. Those content items are ignored by RMA software.

Each of these RMA architectures has advantages and limitations. Advocates of centralized retention argue that a dedicated repository administered by a trained records management staff with a unified set of operating procedures can be more effectively and consistently controlled than multiple repositories with their own operating procedures administered by employees with varying levels of records management knowledge and interest. Advocates of the in-place retention model argue that it allows an organization to utilize the capacity and security of its own storage infrastructure and is less costly and complicated than migrating and consolidating electronic records in a centralized repository. Rather than moving records to a remote repository with its own file organization and retrieval procedures, the in-place approach keeps records in a location that is familiar and conveniently accessible to employees who may need them. The in-place approach may be preferred for records that contain personal information, trade secrets, or other confidential or sensitive content. The business units responsible for safeguarding such records may be reluctant to transfer them from their custody to a centralized repository that is managed by others, however secure that repository may be.

Transfer of declared records to a centralized retention repository and in-place retention of declared records are not mutually exclusive options. While most vendors are committed to one of these RMA architectures, some RMA products support both centralized and in-place records management, which organizations can combine as they see fit. Alternatively, some advocates of centralized retention have promoted a hybrid approach in which declared records remain in their original locations for a portion of their retention periods—one or two years, for example, when they are most likely to referenced—then they are moved into a centralized repository until their lifecycles are completed. This hybrid storage arrangement mirrors a common retention practice for paper records, which are filed in office areas while they are active then transferred to an offsite location until their retention periods elapse.

Metadata

Whether declared records are transferred to a centralized repository or managed in their original storage locations, RMA software allows authorized individuals or groups to define and create metadata for individual records or groups of records:

- As discussed later in this chapter, the determination of metadata requirements for a given collection of electronic records is part of the planning and configuration process for RMA software. The software itself gives the planner and system administrator considerable

flexibility. Metadata elements may be defined at the folder and/or individual record level. The number, type, and content of metadata elements will vary with the circumstances in which RMA software is used.
- RMA software imposes few limitations on the number of metadata elements or the acceptable types of metadata values. Metadata entry may be specified as mandatory for some elements, optional for others. Some metadata may be entered when a record is declared and the remainder completed at a later time.
- As with ECM implementations, RMA metadata is often entered manually by typing it. Alternatively, authorized individuals may select metadata from a displayed list of acceptable values. Certain metadata elements, such as a unique record identifier or the date a record was declared, may be generated automatically by RMA software. Metadata values may also be inherited from the folder in which a record is filed or transferred from an external application or database. Some RMA vendors and third parties have developed interfaces for transfer of records and metadata to and from ECM applications, email servers, and other external sources.
- RMA software may be able to extract specific metadata values from within certain records. When an email message is declared to be a record, for example, the sender, recipient, date, and subject can usually be captured automatically. Many word-processing files and spreadsheets contain embedded information about their creators and creation dates. Similarly, embedded metadata about the originator, creation date, location, and technical attributes may be captured when digital photographs are declared as records.

As previously noted, declared records cannot be changed, but authorized individuals or groups can add to, correct, or otherwise edit previously entered metadata for declared records. Where appropriate, however, RMA software can prohibit modification of specified metadata values. Where metadata is entered manually or captured from external sources, RMA software can validate it for format, completeness, or to confirm that metadata values fall within an acceptable range.

Retention Functionality

As its most distinctive and important attribute, RMA software manages the information lifecycle by tracking retention requirements for specific records and identifying those that are eligible for destruction or other disposition actions:

- All RMA software allows authorized individuals to specify retention periods for declared records. The retention period may be derived from an organization's retention schedule or from a blanket retention rule based on document type, such as the National Archives and Records Administration's Capstone approach, which specifies permanent retention for the email of senior federal employees and a shorter, uniform retention period for other email accounts.
- Depending on requirements, RMA users may specify retention periods at the folder or individual record level. If retention periods are assigned at the folder level, the same disposition action will be applied to all declared records in that folder. Similarly, a retention period specified for a given folder will be inherited by its subfolders and the records they contain.
- RMA software permits retention instructions that are based on elapsed time or specified events. With time-based retention, records are eligible for disposition after a fixed period of time from a specified cutoff date, such as six years from the last day of the year in which the record was created or received. With event-based retention, records are eligible for disposition after a specified event, such as a committee meeting or an educational program, occurs.
- In some respects, the distinction between time- and event-based retention is artificial. Most retention periods are based on a combination of time and event. Time-based retention actions are typically triggered by a chronological event, such as the end of a calendar year, fiscal year, or—for educational institutions—the school year. With event-based retention, disposition occurs a fixed period of time following a triggering event, such as six years after a case is closed, a contract is fulfilled, an insurance claim is settled, a project is terminated, an employee resigns or retires, a student graduates, or a hospital patient is discharged. RMA software can also close a folder to further filing after an event occurs; with some cases files, claim files, and other records, however, documents may continue to accumulate for a period of time following closure.
- With time-based retention periods, RMA software will automatically calculate a disposition date if the date that a record was created is included in the record's metadata. The disposition date will be recalculated if the retention period or retention instruction is changed. Disposition dates can likewise be calculated automatically for retention periods based on the date that a record was last opened or last modified. With email messages, disposition can be based on the date a message was received or last read.
- For event-based retention, with or without a time-based component, RMA software can be linked to an external resource, such as

a legal case management system or a contract database, that tracks the occurrence of specific events, such as the final resolution of a case or termination of a contract. Where this is not possible, implementation of event-based disposition requires manual intervention. An authorized individual must enter the date that the triggering event occurred. In most cases, this must be done by an authorized employee in the organizational unit that is responsible for the event—the attorney in charge of case or the manager of a project, for example.
- Managing event-based retention is one of the most challenging aspects of an RMA implementation. Entry of the occurrence date can be made a part of the close-out procedure for a case, project, or other event, but there is no assurance that this will be done for every event. If records will be transferred to a centralized RMA repository for retention, they can be kept in their original locations until the triggering event occurs, but that approach will still require the cooperation of knowledgeable employees in the organizational unit that is responsible for the event. As a further complication, delaying record declaration until after an event occurs is not practical where RMA software manages records in-place because the records, which are comingled with transitory content, might be inadvertently discarded.

To address this issue, some records managers have suggested eliminating event-based disposition whenever possible and replacing it with a time-based retention period based a reasonable estimate of the time required to complete an event. This is a workable solution for events that will be completed within one calendar year or fiscal year, but complicated projects, legal matters, or other activities may span multiple years. In such cases, a time-based retention period is difficult or impossible to estimate with confidence. An employee who is hired today may resign next week or retire in forty years. In many jurisdictions, healthcare providers must retain patient records for a specified number of years following the date of last treatment, but that date cannot be predicted for illnesses that require continuing care. Similarly, some pharmaceutical regulations require retention of certain manufacturing and testing records for a specified period of time after a drug is no longer sold or a medical device is no longer implanted in any patient, but that cannot be accurately predicted in advance. In situations of uncertainty, a long retention period—a reasonable portion of a human lifetime, for example—may be selected as a default, but this will result in over-retention of some records.

Disposition Actions

RMA software will identify folders or individual records with elapsed retention periods. When that occurs, the software will issue a notification or prepare a report listing records that are eligible for one of the following disposition actions:

- Destroy the records. The records will be deleted or otherwise destroyed in a manner that prevents their reconstruction by commonly used file-restoration software or other methods. Automatic destruction is possible, but many RMA implementations require a review to confirm that the records have no legal or operational value that warrants extending the retention period. The review should be conducted by someone who is knowledgeable about the records and can determine the organization's continuing need for them. At a minimum, the review must confirm that the records are not subject to a legal hold that suspends destruction until a lawsuit, arbitration, investigation, or other matter is resolved, as discussed below. Depending on the system, record destruction may require approval by multiple authorized individuals. When approval is obtained, RMA software will delete records that are stored in a centralized repository under its direct control. Where records are managed in-place, deletion may require the involvement of the administrator responsible for the content repository where the records are kept.
- Transfer the records to a designated repository. In government agencies, this disposition option typically involves the transfer of permanent records to the custody of an archival agency after a specified period of time. Copies of the records will be removed from the RMA software's control when the transfer is completed. Such transfers are rarely encountered in organizations that do not have an archival program for preservation of historically significant records, although some organizations may choose to retain historical records indefinitely in an RMA repository. In some cases, nonpermanent records may be transferred to a designated repository, including one managed by another RMA implementation, after a specified period of time or when a specified event occurs. As discussed above, RMA software that manages retention in-place may transfer nonpermanent records from a shared drive to a centralized repository when they are no longer needed for immediate or frequent reference. The 5015.2 standard requires an RMA product to be able to transfer records and metadata to other RMA installations.
- Delay disposition. In keeping with an organization's duty to preserve evidence that is relevant for pending or ongoing legal proceedings,

RMA software must have the ability to temporarily freeze or extend retention periods, thereby delaying destruction or transfer actions for specific records. Delayed disposition may also be applied to records that are needed for audits or business operations that have not been completed by the scheduled disposition date. The RMA system administrator will determine who is authorized to delay disposition and resume it. RMA software may provide a metadata field for an authorized individual to enter the reason why disposition is delayed and when it can be resumed. The metadata should be updated to include the dates when the delay was extended or resumption of disposition is authorized.

RMA software will generate and maintain documentation related to the destruction, transfer, or delayed disposition of records. For records that have been removed from the system, such documentation proves that a given record existed, that it was managed by RMA software, and that it was properly destroyed or transferred on a specified date. Without proof of proper disposition, an RMA administrator will not be able to explain the removal of a record that is requested for legal discovery, audits, or other purposes. RMA software may also give system administrators the option of retaining or removing metadata for records that have been destroyed or transferred. Removal of metadata is inadvisable where the metadata contains information about the disposition of a record.

Search and Retrieval

Unlike ECM applications, which support online search and retrieval of active records to support an organization's ongoing business operations, RMA software principally manages records that are in the inactive phase of the information lifecycle and are awaiting disposition when their retention periods elapse. While enhanced retrieval functionality is the principal business rationale for an ECM implementation, RMA software is designed to ensure compliance with legal and operational requirements for retention of recorded information. Retrieval functionality is a secondary but still important concern. In some RMA implementations, records are not declared until the projects, cases, events, contracts, or transactions to which they pertain are completed, but even inactive records may need to be retrieved when questions arise about business matters from the past:

- Where RMA software manages declared records in place, the search methods and retrieval mechanisms supported by the repository in which the records are saved apply to both active and inactive records. This is the case, for example, with declared records that are managed in an ECM repository or on an email server. Where declared records are saved in a separate RMA repository, however, RMA software must incorporate appropriate search and retrieval functionality. Even where records are managed in-place, RMA software can provide a unified search interface to access all associated repositories. This can compensate for the absence of effective retrieval mechanisms for records that are stored on shared drives or in other ungoverned repositories.

- Most RMA products provide search and retrieval capabilities that are comparable to the ECM functionality discussed in the preceding chapter. Authorized individuals or groups can browse through file plans, folder, and subfolders. Searches can be applied to any combination of metadata fields at the folder or record level. Metadata searches can be based on exact or partial matches, with or without search term truncation or wildcard characters in search terms. Boolean operators and relational expressions can be used to narrow or broaden searches.
- In response to a search specification, RMA software will display a list of retrieved records that correspond to the searcher's access privileges. If the listed records do not satisfy the searcher's information needs, the search can be modified. If the listed records are acceptable, authorized searchers can select one or more of them for display, printing, downloading, or transfer to an external source.
- A retrieved record will be displayed by launching its native application if it is available on the searcher's workstation. As time passes, however, the application that created a record may be discontinued or modified in a way that renders a previously saved record unreadable; the longer the retention period for a given record, the greater the likelihood that this will occur. This problem, which complicates the long-term retention of electronic records, has been recognized by records managers and archivists for decades. It can be minimized by saving electronic records in an obsolescence-resistant file format, such as PDF/A.
- If that is not possible, electronic records must be migrated to new file formats at predetermined intervals until their retention periods elapse, but RMA software generally prohibits the modification of declared records. Some RMA implementations do allow format conversions under tightly controlled conditions when approved by authorized individuals, but data migration becomes increasingly burdensome as the quantity of electronic records increases. As an alternative, RMA software may provide a multiformat viewer that will ensure the continued readability of digital documents if their originating software is discontinued or replaced. The viewer must

accurately depict the original appearance of digital documents. Newer viewers can support hundreds of file formats, including obsolete formats.

Access and Security

Because many RMA implementations store records that contain confidential business information and personal data, controlled access and security are paramount concerns:

- The RMA standards discussed in a preceding section require controlled access to declared records and their associated metadata. As with ECM applications, access is limited to authorized individuals or groups as determined by the RMA system administrator. Access privileges, which can be specified at the repository, folder, or record level, determine the specific data entry, retrieval, editing, retention, deletion, exporting, and other operations that a user is permitted to perform. Authorized users are identified by passwords or other security mechanisms, such as biometrics.
- Where declared records are stored in a centralized repository, RMA software controls all access. Records that are managed in place may also be accessible in their storage locations independent of RMA software. In that case, security is determined by local controls, which may be more or less stringent than those supported by RMA software. The 5015.2 standard specifies security requirements for records that contain classified information maintained by US government agencies.
- RMA software can track authorized and unauthorized actions, maintain event histories with dates and times, and generate audit logs for specific users, folders, and records, including failed access attempts. Audit logs and reports allow RMA administrators or other authorized individuals to review, reconstruct, and investigate suspicious searches, edits, deletions, or other events involving specific users, records, or metadata.

Physical Records Management

While most new records are created and managed digitally, many organizations continue to maintain valuable legacy documents and other non-electronic information in physical form. While RMA products were developed to manage retention of digital content, many of the requirements specified in the electronic records management standards discussed in a preceding section are applicable to paper documents, engineering drawings, maps, photographic records, computer disks and tapes, and audio- and video-recording media. RMA software offers some combination of the following capabilities for physical records management:

- RMA software can track the locations of physical records, which may be packed in boxes or stored in cabinets or on shelves in offices, file rooms, warehouses, or other repositories, either on-premises or offsite.
- Library-like circulation control functionality creates and maintains an audit trail and circulation history for all records that are removed from and returned to approved storage repositories by authorized users. Folders, boxes, or other items may be barcoded to simplify data entry and tracking. RMA software can prohibit unauthorized access to physical records just as it does for electronic records.
- As with electronic records, RMA software will calculate destruction dates based on predetermined retention periods. The software will identify records with elapsed retention periods, prepare notices of impending destruction for review by authorized persons, and maintain documentation to identify physical records that were destroyed.

These capabilities are a subset of the functionality supported by the inventory control software that is used by commercial record storage providers, but they may be sufficient for control of paper documents or other physical records that are stored in a small- to medium-size file room, warehouse, or another in-house repository. While it is not the strongest feature of RMA software and will rarely be the decisive capability that differentiates one RMA product from another, functionality for physical records management may appeal to government agencies, companies, and nonprofit organizations that want a single platform to manage retention of both electronic and physical records.

IMPLEMENTATION ISSUES

RMA software manages record retention and disposition, which are two of the eight Generally Accepted Recordkeeping Principles issued by ARMA International. Information governance recognizes carefully formulated retention guidance and systematic disposition of information assets as critical activities that must be based on formalized operating procedures rather than the discretion of individual employees. RMA software provide the technical functionality required to manage the retention of recorded information, but the development of retention guidance, supported by file plan and metadata scheme for organization and retrieval of digital content, is a nontechnical precondition for a successful RMA implementation.

Retention Guidance

Up-to-date retention guidance is a core component of a systematic records management program and a requirement for a successful RMA implementation:

- Retention guidance is typically provided at the record series level, where a series is a group of logically related records associated with a specific business or administrative function, operation, or activity. Retention guidance must specify the period of time, usually in years, that a record series included in an RMA implementation is to be kept to satisfy applicable legal, regulatory, operational, or historical requirements. Retention guidance must also identify the trigger event on which the retention period for a given record series is based. As noted in a preceding section, RMA software can accommodate retention periods that are based on elapsed time with or without a specified trigger event.
- Retention guidance is prepared by records managers in consultation with knowledgeable employees in the business units that create and use recorded information. Formulation of retention guidance requires legal research, an understanding of the role of information in an organization's business processes, and negotiation with business units and other interested parties to arrive at retention rules that satisfy the requirements of all stakeholders.
- Whether retention rules are being developed from scratch or existing rules are being updated, the development of retention guidance requires a focused initiative to identify records and obtain information about the need to retain them. Formulation of comprehensive retention rules can take longer than the technological aspects of an RMA implementation. In a large organization, it may be done in stages.
- As noted above, retention guidance is typically contained in a retention schedule that identifies record series maintained by all or part of an organization and specifies their retention periods. An organization's retention schedule may be supplemented by blanket retention policies that apply to specific types of record, such as email messages or social media content. RMA software is compatible with most approaches to retention scheduling—functional or program-specific, granular or aggregated—provided the retention rules are unambiguous—six years from the end of the fiscal year for purchase orders or

ten years following termination of employment for personnel files, for example.

An RMA implementation requires highly prescriptive, unambiguous retention rules that specify how long records must be kept and when they will be eligible for disposition. RMA software is not compatible with retention schedules that specify the minimum amount of time that records must be kept to satisfy applicable requirements but allow continued retention, at the discretion of record custodians, if a given record might conceivably be useful for a future business purpose. RMA software is similarly incompatible with flexible schedules that permit any retention period within a specified range—six to ten years after termination of a project, for example—at the discretion of the business unit managers or other decision-makers who are responsible for the records.

File Plans

Retention guidance is also a precondition for development of a file plan for an RMA implementation. File plans are not unique to RMA software. They are used to identify and categorize paper records as well as the digital content maintained by ECM applications, digital asset management applications, and other information governance technologies discussed in this book, but file plans for those implementations are primarily designed to organize records for convenient retrieval. They typically categorize records by the persons, events, activities, or subjects to which they pertain. While file plans for RMA implementations can also facilitate the retrieval of records when needed, that is not their principal focus. In keeping with the distinctive purpose of RMA software, the file plan for an RMA implementation categorizes electronic records for retention and disposition.

To accomplish this, an RMA file plan groups related records in a hierarchically arranged scheme that corresponds to the record categories and series identified in an organization's retention schedule. The detailed characteristics of the hierarchical arrangement will depend on whether the organization has a program-specific or a functional retention schedule. A program-specific retention schedule, sometimes described as a departmental retention schedule, identifies and provides retention guidance for record series that are maintained or controlled by a given department, division, office, or another program unit. Each program unit will have its own section in the organization's retention schedule and a top-level folder in the RMA file plan, which will include a second-level folder for each record series listed in program unit's retention schedule. For example:

Top-level folder: Student records
  Second-level folder: Course schedules
  Second-level folder: Academic transcripts
  Second-level folder: Health records
  Second-level folder: Guidance and counseling
  Second-level folder: Attendance records
  Second-level folder: Extracurricular activities

By contrast, a functional retention schedule categorizes record series by the business functions to which they pertain rather than by the individual program units that have the records in their custody or under their control. Examples of commonly encountered business functions include finance, human resources, facilities, and research and development. Records associated with a given functional category may be maintained by a single program unit or by multiple program units. In either case, the file plan will provide a top-level folder for each functional category. Second-level folders may be necessary for complicated categories. Tertiary subfolders, positioned at an appropriate location in the hierarchical arrangement, are provided for individual record series. For example:

Top-level folder: Student records
  Second-level folder: Academic records
    Third-level folder: Course schedules
    Third-level folder: Academic transcripts
    Third-level folder: Attendance records
    Third-level folder: Guidance and counseling
  Second-level folder: Nonacademic records
    Third-level folder: Health records
    Third-level folder: Extracurricular activities

Record series folders may include subfolders for the calendar year, fiscal year, or other chronological period on which the retention period is based. Record series with event-driven retention periods may include subfolders for individual cases, projects, contracts, or other matters. Some RMA software permits nesting of subfolders at multiple levels. Others restrict folder nesting to avoid overly complicated hierarchical arrangements. File plans rarely require more than four hierarchical levels for functional retention schedules and three hierarchical levels for program-specific schedules.

In any case, the folder hierarchy is important because retention periods are assigned to folders, and the retention period for a given folder is inherited by all folders and subfolders below it. With traditional retention schedules, retention periods are assigned at the record series level, but some organizations prefer an aggregated or "big bucket" approach that assigns retention periods at the category level. A retention period applied to a top-level or secondary-level folder in an RMA file plan flows down to all record series folders. In the above example, a ten-year retention period assigned to the second-level folder for nonacademic student records will be automatically applied to all tertiary-level folders in that category.

Metadata

ISO 23081-1:2017, *Information and documentation—Records management processes—Metadata for records—Part 1: Principles* defines metadata as information that permits the creation, management, and use of records through time and within and across domains. The same definition appears in ISO 15489-1:2016, *Information and documentation—Records management—Part 1: Concepts and Principles*. A carefully planned metadata scheme is essential for an effective RMA implementation, as it is for other information governance technologies discussed in this book:

- Metadata requirements for declared records are determined by meeting with knowledgeable stakeholders to discuss their needs and expectations and to review the ways that the records will be managed and used. Ideally, metadata requirements will be determined before RMA software is installed and tested. If necessary, however, most RMA products allow metadata elements to be added or modified postinstallation.
- While specific requirements will vary from one organization to another, certain metadata is necessary in every RMA implementation. Every declared record must have a unique identifier. RMA metadata must include sufficient descriptive information to conclusively identify a declared record, allow it to be retrieved by authorized users when needed, and enable RMA software to manage its lifecycle. An RMA implementation will also require technical metadata that indicates a record's file format, data compression and encryption algorithms, and other attributes that can affect the continued accessibility and usability of recorded information.
- The unique record identifier may be automatically assigned by RMA software or manually entered. Descriptive metadata may be contained in a folder label, a file name, or other title information; in a field specifically intended for description; or in a field for scope notes. To fulfill the distinctive purpose of an RMA implementation, metadata must include a record's retention period, sufficient information to allow RMA software to calculate the disposition date, and disposition instructions. As discussed above, certain technical

metadata may be embedded in word-processing documents, spreadsheets, digital photographs, and other declared records.
- Permanent records intended for transfer to archival custody may require metadata about copyright, trademark protection, or other intellectual property rights. Minimum metadata requirements for US government records to be transferred to the National Archives are based on ISO 15836-1:2017, *Information and Documentation—The Dublin Core metadata element set—Part 1: Core elements*, a widely adopted standard that defines fifteen metadata elements to describe information resources. Other archival agencies have developed similar requirements for records intended for permanent preservation, but such standards are less useful for nonarchival documents and administrative records with short retention periods.
- An RMA implementation may share some descriptive metadata with ECM applications and other technologies discussed in this book; a record's originator, the date created, the file format, external reference numbers, security classification, and privacy categorization are examples of commonly encountered metadata elements. The need for keywords, subject headings, or other metadata that will allow authorized users to search for records that deal with particular topics will depend on the nature of the RMA implementation.
- Subject searching is a useful and possibly essential capability where declared records will be transferred from their original storage locations to a centralized RMA repository for retention. While the transferred records are presumably inactive and awaiting disposition, they are not necessarily dormant. They may need to be retrieved, albeit infrequently, for audits, legal discovery, or when questions arise about the transactions or activities to which the records relate. This is most likely to occur if records are transferred to the RMA repository soon after the transactions, business operations, or other matters to which they relate are completed.
- Metadata that permits subject retrieval is less important where RMA software will manage records in place. Those records can be retrieved by whatever mechanisms are provided by their native applications or the locations where they are stored. This is the case, for example, where RMA software provides in-place management of declared records stored by an enterprise content management, digital asset management, or email archiving system. Those technologies typically provide excellent retrieval functionality that does not to be duplicated by RMA software.

Product Evaluation

As noted at the beginning of this chapter, RMA software is developed and sold by several dozen companies and their authorized representatives. RMA vendors range from specialized software developers with narrowly focused products that are marketed in selected geographical locations to large computer companies with broad product lines and worldwide operations. Criteria for evaluation and selection of RMA software are similar to those for other information governance technologies discussed in this book:

- Prospective purchasers want reliable, fully operational RMA products that will satisfy their functional requirements without excessive technical or administrative complications. They want to deal with a qualified, experienced, and stable vendor with an established, satisfied customer base and reference accounts with which it has some affinity—well-respected organizations in the same industry that have a similar number of employees, or that are known to be well managed, for example.
- The vendor must have the financial resources and technical expertise to support and enhance its products for the foreseeable future, an especially important consideration for RMA software that will manage records over years or decades. To simplify procurement and expedite contract approvals, an organization may prefer an RMA vendor that is already in its established supply chain and with whom is has a good working relationship.
- The number of RMA software developers, but not necessarily the number of RMA products, has decreased in recent years as computer companies and other suppliers have broadened their offerings or their markets by acquiring or merging with competitors. As evidence of this trend, 30 percent of the RMA products certified for compliance with the 5015.2 standard at the time this chapter was written were developed by companies that were subsequently acquired by a competitor. Some products have changed ownership and been rebranded multiple times. Such consolidation is typical of mature industries—RMA technology has been commercially available for four decades—but it can have an impact on product evaluation and selection.
- When a vendor acquires a competing RMA product, it may do so with the intention of phasing out its own presumably inferior product. Alternatively, the vendor may plan to phase out the acquired product and offer its own RMA software to the existing customers as a replacement. In either case, an RMA product will eventually be

discontinued. Postacquisition, the vendor may continue to sell both products for a period of time. It unlikely, however, that the vendor will allocate the same level of resources to maintaining, upgrading, and providing technical support for two RMA products that are functionally equivalent.
- When evaluating and selecting RMA software, planners and decision-makers will require an informed assessment of a given product's commercial viability, its importance as a revenue source, and the vendor's commitment to it. Unfortunately, even the most diligent research will not eliminate the risk that a product will be acquired and possibly discontinued by a competitor. Possible acquisition targets include RMA software developed by small companies with superior technical expertise but limited marketing resources and aging RMA products with a large installed base that an acquiring company can upgrade or replace.
- The development of RMA products has been guided by widespread acceptance of the standards discussed in preceding sections. Because standards-compliant products must support certain features and functions, prospective purchasers can have reasonable confidence that such products will offer the requisite records management capabilities. In this sense, prevalent standardization simplifies product evaluation. With respect to core functionality, there should be no significant difference among RMA products that comply with a given standard. Procurement decisions must consequently focus on criteria that are not covered by standards, such as the technical resources and expertise required for implementation and operation, ease of learning and use, postinstallation technical support, standards-compliant, price, and other characteristics that may make one functionally equivalent product a better choice than another.

Standards-compliant products in every field enjoy a presumption of functional acceptability, but standardization encourages conformity at the expense of innovation and competitiveness. If compliance with a specific standard is mandated in requests for proposal and bid invitations for RMA software procurements, the pool of available vendors will be limited and some highly functional products that warrant serious consideration may be excluded. Further, certification provides no assurance that an RMA product will remain commercially viable indefinitely. Some products that received perpetual certification for compliance with the 5015.2 standard are no longer actively marketed. In some cases, their developers have withdrawn technical support. On the other hand, some highly functional products with lapsed certification remain available.

Cost

As with other information governance technologies discussed in this book, the cost of an RMA implementation will vary with the number of user licenses; the greater the number of licenses, the lower the cost per user but the higher the total cost:

- While RMA products that comply with one or more the standards discussed in this chapter offer comparable records management capabilities, at least for core features and functions, there is considerable difference in the price of supposedly equivalent software from different suppliers. In a competitive bidding situation, price is often the decisive factor.
- The highest priced product in a competitive procurement can be more expensive than the lowest priced product by a factor of three or more. This differential is confirmed by pricing for RMA products that are available through the Federal Supply Schedule and other prenegotiated government contracts. Vendors that target enterprise-wide installations in large for-profit companies and government agencies generally have higher priced products than RMA software intended for small- to medium-size organizations.
- Apart from product pricing, the total cost of an RMA installation will depend on complications that may arise during software installation and configuration, as well as an organization's requirements for interface modifications, workflow programming, integration with external applications and databases, user training, and other customizations and support services. These costs will likely equal or exceed the cost of the RMA software itself. In some locations, an RMA software developer may provide these customizations and support services directly to customers.
- Alternatively, RMA customizations and supporting services are provided by an agent, reseller, or other third-party authorized by the software developer. Where this is the case, careful scrutiny of the third-party's qualifications is an important aspect of RMA software evaluation. Because additional RMA customizations and support services may be required in the years following the initial software installation, an organization can expect a long working relationship with the third-party provider.

RMA Alternatives

As noted in a preceding section, RMA software is often conflated and confused with enterprise content management. Both technologies support the storage, retrieval, and control of unstructured digital content and both emphasize their role in ensuring compliance with regulatory mandates and addressing an organization's business requirements, although RMA software's scope is limited to managing the lifecycle of inactive records while ECM products typically support a broader range of capabilities for capture, dissemination, and protection of active information.

Viewing RMA software as a subset of enterprise content management, some ECM applications have added records management modules as standard or optional components. Some ECM vendors have obtained records management capabilities by acquiring existing RMA software and integrating it into their product lines. This approach allows an ECM supplier to offer a comprehensive information governance solution; an ECM customer often has a need for lifecycle management functionality. Others ECM vendors have developed their own records management modules, which may be based on requirements specified in the RMA standards discussed above or modeled after the capabilities of existing RMA products. Less commonly, a few RMA software developers have expanded their products to incorporate ECM features and functions.

While acquired RMA components typically support a full range of record retention capabilities, other ECM-based records management modules may be limited to the basic retention functionality that many organizations want or need:

- Authorized users can declare records, which may be managed in place or transferred into a centralized repository. Once declared, a record will be locked so it cannot be modified, moved, or deleted. A record's metadata may likewise be locked. In some situations, record declaration can be reversed by a site administrator or other authorized persons.
- Authorized users can define retention policies and apply them to individual records, groups of records, or entire repositories. Retention periods can be based on elapsed time or events. While authorized users can specify any retention period from one day to indefinite, some ECM-based records management modules suggest common retention options—three, six, or ten years, for example—which customers can increase or shorten to satisfy their own recordkeeping requirements. Alternatively, a retention policy may be unmodifiable, in which case it can only be changed by removal or replacement.
- ECM-based retention policies prevent the accidental or intentional deletion of records before their retention periods elapse. When that occurs, records can be deleted automatically or manually, with or without review by authorized persons. Records with elapsed retention periods can also be migrated to another storage repository.

- An audit trail captures information about changes to or use of a record over time.
- Authorized persons can suspend destruction of records that are needed for litigation or other legal proceedings.

For organizations that are already using an ECM application, the addition of a records management module is the simplest way to implement retention capabilities for electronic records. An ECM-based records management module will cost less than a self-contained RMA product, and it will usually be easier to install and learn. However, multinational companies and other organizations with complex retention requirements may be better served by full-featured RMA software.

SUMMARY OF MAJOR POINTS

- RMA software tracks the retention of electronic records, identifies those with elapsed retention periods, and initiates their appropriate disposition, which may involve destruction of the records, transfer of the records to a designated repository, or prolonged retention to support pending or ongoing litigation, completion of audits, or unfinished business operations.
- Designed to manage the inactive phase of the information lifecycle for nonpermanent records, RMA software occupies a position on the IG technology spectrum between enterprise content management, which supports the active phase of the information lifecycle, and digital preservation products, which create and maintain an archival repository for digital content of enduring value.
- RMA software is developed and sold by several dozen companies and their authorized representatives. RMA vendors range from specialized software developers with narrowly focused products that are marketed in selected geographical locations to large computer companies with broad product lines and worldwide operation.
- Traditional RMA architecture stores records in a centralized repository that is maintained by the RMA software itself. The records are transferred to the RMA repository from their original storage locations for retention, usually when elapsed time or events trigger the inactive phase of the information lifecycle. With in-place records management, by contrast, RMA software applies retention rules to records that remain in the locations where they are normally stored. Some RMA products support both centralized and in-place records management, which organizations can combine as they see fit.

- RMA software permits time-based retention, in which records are eligible for disposition after a fixed period of time from a specified cutoff date; event-based retention, in which records are eligible for disposition after a specified event occurs; or retention based on a combination of time and events, in which records are eligible for disposition after a fixed period of time following the occurrence of a specified event.
- While RMA products were developed to manage retention of digital content, many of their features are applicable to paper documents, engineering drawings, maps, photographic records, computer disks and tapes, audio-recording media, video-recording media, and other physical records. Physical records management functionality may appeal to organizations that want a single platform to manage retention of both electronic and nonelectronic content.
- Up-to-date retention guidance is a core component of a systematic records management program and a precondition for a successful RMA implementation. It is also a precondition for development of a file plan for an RMA implementation.
- There is considerable difference in the price of supposedly equivalent RMA software from different suppliers. Apart from product pricing, the total cost of an RMA installation will depend on complications that may arise during software installation and configuration, as well as an organization's requirements for interface modifications, workflow programming, integration with external applications and databases, user training, and other customizations and support services.
- Some enterprise content management applications have added records management modules as standard or optional components. Compared to RMA software, these ECM-based components may be limited to essential retention functionality, which is all that many organizations want or need. For organizations that are already using an ECM application, the addition of a records management module is the simplest and least expensive way to implement retention capabilities for electronic records.

3

Digital Preservation Applications

Dictionary definitions equate preservation with the act or process of maintaining something in its original form or condition or keeping it safe from damage, deterioration, or other harm. This usage is well established; the *Oxford English Dictionary* cites examples that date from the fifteenth century.[1] The word "preservation" is often modified by an adjective that indicates the thing being preserved. Examples include architectural preservation for buildings and landmarks with historical significance or artistic merit, archaeological preservation for excavation sites and artifacts, environmental preservation for protection wildlife and ecosystems, infrastructure preservation to extend the life span of roads and bridges, and language preservation to prevent extinction of languages with a dwindling number of native speakers.

Broadly defined, digital preservation is concerned with maintaining the longevity of digital content, which is variously described as digital objects, digital materials, or digital assets. Definitions developed by professional associations and preservation groups provide additional information about the purpose and scope of digital preservation initiatives:

- The *Digital Preservation Handbook* issued by the Digital Preservation Coalition (DPC), a membership organization based in the United Kingdom, defines digital preservation as a "series of managed activities to ensure continued access to digital materials for as long as necessary."[2]
- The Society of American Archivists' *Dictionary of Archives Terminology* defines digital preservation as "the management and protection

of information to ensure authenticity, integrity, reliability, and long-term accessibility."[3]
- The terminology database developed for the InterPARES 3 Project, an international research initiative, defines digital preservation as "the specific process of maintaining digital materials during and across different generations of technology over time."[4]
- The National Digital Stewardship Alliance, a consortium of academic institutions and other organizations, defines digital preservation as a "series of managed activities, policies, strategies and actions to ensure the accurate rendering of digital content for as long as necessary, regardless of the challenges posed by media failure or technological change."[5]
- The American Library Association has developed three definitions that vary in length and detail. The most succinct defines digital preservation as a combination of policies, strategies, and actions that ensure access to digital content over time. The longest definition includes best practices for creation, integrity, and maintenance of digital content.[6]

Differences in wording aside, these definitions indicate digital preservation's essential attributes: It is an active process that involves policies, strategies, and planned actions to prevent the deterioration, loss, or alteration of valuable digital content and ensure its continued accessibility for an extended period of time. The Consultative Committee for Space Data Systems, which developed the Open Archival Information System reference model discussed later in this chapter, uses the phrase "long-term preservation," where long-term means long enough for digital content to be threatened by changing technologies and the changing requirements of user communities, a period that extends into the indefinite future.[7]

Like the records management applications discussed in chapter 2, digital preservation is concerned with digital content that is in the inactive phase of the information lifecycle. Unlike records management applications, however, digital preservation does not deal with all inactive information. Most inactive content will be discarded when its prescribed retention period elapses. Digital preservation is limited to content that will be retained permanently—that is, content for which a destruction date has not and cannot be specified, given general agreement about the content's long-term significance or uncertainty about its future usefulness. Such permanently valuable information constitutes a small subset of digital content that is created and maintained by government agencies, companies, and nonprofit organizations.

A digital preservation application is a software product that stores digital content in a reliable, secure repository where it will be maintained in stable, accessible condition for the foreseeable future. As discussed in subsequent sections, digital preservation applications will periodically inspect digital content for deterioration, format obsolescence, or other changes that may cause data loss or impact the content's continued usability. In the spectrum of information governance technologies, digital preservation applications occupy a position at the very end of the information lifecycle when records management operations end and archival involvement begins. As noted in chapter 2, a records management application might transfer permanent content to a digital preservation application for archival storage after a predetermined amount of time. A digital preservation application might also accept content from an enterprise content management application, email archiving system, digital asset management system, or other technologies discussed in this book.

HISTORY

While a records management application might retain any digital content indefinitely, the digital preservation applications discussed in this chapter are optimized for information that must be kept permanently. Concerns about the continued stability and future usability of digital data were expressed in the 1960s, but the need for a systematic approach to preservation of digital content was not widely discussed until the 1990s. Initial preservation concerns focused on two widely acknowledged problems: the limited stability of digital storage media and system dependencies that impact the continued readability of digital content. Digital storage media are subject to significant time-dependent degradation that makes them unsuitable for long-term preservation of information. With some digital storage media, stability problems that render content unreadable may arise within a decade. As an added complication, the hardware devices that read digital content recorded on specific storage media will eventually be discontinued by their manufacturers without a compatible replacement. Similarly, digital content is recorded in formats that depend on the continued availability of compatible software, which cannot be guaranteed.

Responding to these concerns, the earliest digital preservation initiatives converted digital content to nondigital form for storage on media with well-understood stability characteristics: paper, which has no hardware or software dependencies, and microfilm, which has limited hardware dependencies and no software dependencies. Such conversion involves time-consuming printing or microfilming and it sacrifices the retrieval advantages of digitally recorded information. Since the early 2000s, libraries and archival agencies, individually or in collaborative arrangements, have initiated studies and projects that examined the feasibility and practicality of preserving content in digital form. Various preservation methods have been employed, including transferring digital content from aging storage media to new ones at predetermined intervals to prevent the inevitable degradation of data in long-term storage; frequently checking digital content to detect degradation; migrating digital content to new media and file formats, as necessary, to address hardware and software obsolescence; storing multiple copies of digital content in dispersed locations to increase the likelihood that one of them will remain usable over time; keeping older technology in service to read digital content; using emulation software that replicates the functionality of outdated computing environments, thereby allowing digital content saved in obsolete file formats to be read; and using encapsulation, which packages digital content in a prescribed format with metadata that contains the information needed to interpret the content.

Each of these preservation methods had its advocates who explained and defended them in professional publications and conference presentations. The digital preservation applications discussed in this chapter employ some of these methods to maintain the integrity and usability of digital content. As discussed in subsequent sections, they monitor digital content for deterioration and obsolescence and apply corrective action as necessary to ensure its continued accessibility.

BUSINESS NEED

Unlike enterprise content management and records management, which principally deal with business information that supports decision making and transaction processing, digital preservation is most closely associated with the longevity and continued accessibility of scholarly, scientific, and artistic information. While digital preservation applications can be implemented by any organization, their principal market is the cultural heritage sector, which includes archives, libraries, museums, historical societies, ethnic awareness organizations, and research institutions. Many of these organizations are affiliated with government agencies, academic institutions, religious groups, charities, philanthropies, and other nonprofit entities that want to preserve their documentary heritage.

For-profit companies have shown less interest in or awareness of digital preservation applications, perhaps because few of them have archival programs. Most companies have some digital content, such as minutes of the meetings of governing bodies, that must be kept for long periods of time if not permanently, but those records are retained to satisfy legal requirements or for business reasons rather than for scholarly or scientific research. Companies may satisfy their preservation requirements for permanent records by retaining paper copies, if the quantity is manageable, or by saving them on a shared drive or in an ECM or RMA implementation, in which case their long-term stability and usability is not assured.

Digital preservation has been more extensively researched that other technologies discussed in this book, most of which support business operations rather than curatorial activities and scholarly research. Digital preservation concepts and initiatives are discussed in a large and growing number of studies, reports, journal articles, and other publications that analyze the challenges involved and evaluate alternatives for addressing them. Most of these publications were written by archivists, librarians, and academic researchers who are active in the preservation community. For cultural heritage organizations and for archival programs in companies and nonprofit entities, digital preservation applications address an important need. Archives, libraries, and other cultural heritage organizations view the continued stability and accessibility of significant information as a societal imperative. Safeguarding digital content of enduring value is a mission-critical obligation for them. Despite the size of their potential market—in the United States alone, there over 115,000 libraries and 35,000 museums—digital preservation applications are developed and marketed by a much smaller number of vendors than enterprise content management products and records management application software. Nonetheless, available products offer a full range of useful features and functions that will be discussed in subsequent sections.

STANDARDS AND GUIDELINES

A number of international standards and guidance documents address digital preservation requirements and methods at varying levels of specificity. These standards are well known and widely discussed by archives, libraries, and other cultural heritage organizations that maintain digital content. They play an important role in digital preservation initiatives, and they have strongly influenced the design, development, evaluation, and implementation of digital preservation applications.

OAIS Reference Model

ISO 14721:2012, *Space data and information transfer systems—Open archival information system (OAIS)—Reference model* defines a reference model for an archival system to preserve and provide access to digital content:

- A reference model provides a framework for understanding significant relationships among the entities of some environment and for the development of consistent standards or specifications supporting that environment. An Open Archival Information System preserves information and makes it available to a designated community of users. In this context, the term "open" indicates that the reference model and future enhancements are developed in open forums. It does not imply that preserved content will be open to the public, although that may be the case in some digital preservation implementations.
- ISO 14721 is the most influential and widely cited digital preservation standard. It is based on and closely aligned with a recommended practice developed by the Consultative Committee for Space Data Systems (CCSDS), a multinational organization that develops standards and practices for cooperating space agencies. The OAIS reference model is not limited to space data; it is applicable to any digital content that warrants long-term retention, where long-term extends into the indefinite future. The digital preservation applications discussed in this chapter conform to the OAIS reference model. Such conformance is essential for the cultural heritage market, where the OAIS reference model is well known and widely respected.
- As discussed later in this chapter, the OAIS reference model defines the purpose and characteristics of information packages that provide a structured framework for preservation, availability, integrity, and usability of digital content and its associated metadata. Among other preservation-related concepts, ISO 14721 addresses metadata requirements that support preservation, the importance of periodic validation of the integrity and authenticity of preserved content, and the need for data migration, emulation, or other preservation strategies to ensure the continued accessibility of digital content and metadata.
- ISO 14721 mentions the need for a certification standard to assess whether a given preservation repository conforms to the OAIS reference model and can be trusted to store and provide continued access to digital content. ISO 16363:2012, *Space data and information transfer systems—Audit and certification of trustworthy digital repositories* fulfills that need. A trustworthy repository is able to provide reliable access to preserved content for the foreseeable future. Like ISO 14721, ISO 16363 is based on a recommended practice issued by the Consultative Committee for Space Data Systems and on the Trustworthy Repositories Audit and Certification (TRAC) criteria and checklist developed by OCLC, RLG, and the National Archives and Records Administration. Drawing on the principles presented in ISO 14721,

it defines rigorous criteria for evaluating the organizational policies, technical characteristics, and managerial processes of repositories intended for reliable preservation of digital content.
- Among the criteria specified in ISO 16363, a trustworthy repository must have a strategic plan that defines its approach to preservation, a staff with appropriate skills and experience to support preservation functions, effective business processes to address the repository's continued financial stability, and policies and procedures to ensure that preservation functions will be properly implemented. For each criterion specified, ISO 16363 provides examples of ways in which conformance can be demonstrated. Even a cursory review of ISO 16363 indicates that attaining conformance will require significant effort. All aspects of an organization's digital preservation program must be thoroughly documented.
- ISO 16919:2014, *Space data and information transfer systems—Requirements for bodies providing audit and certification of candidate trustworthy digital repositories* specifies criteria and provides guidance for accreditation of entities that will audit and certify digital repositories for conformance to the OAIS reference model. The criteria and guidance are intended to ensure that audit and certification services are performed by properly trained, well-managed teams in a competent, impartial, and responsible manner, with proper attention to concerns about data security, privacy, and impartiality. ISO 16919 specifies prerequisite levels of work experience and education for team members.
- ISO 16919 is not a self-contained standard. It must be used in conjunction with ISO/IEC 17021-1:2015, *Conformity assessment—Requirements for bodies providing audit and certification of management systems—Part 1: Requirements*, a general international standard that specifies criteria for third parties that provide audit and certification services. As an extension of ISO/IEC 17021, ISO 16919 adds certain requirements that are specific to evaluation of trustworthy digital repositories.
- Several organizations offer audit and certification services based on ISO 16919. Alternatively, audit and certification services may be based on the CoreTrustSeal requirements, which were developed through an international collaboration of archives, libraries, and other nonprofit organizations with a strong interest in digital preservation. CoreTrustSeal, which is governed by its own standards and certification board, maintains an assembly of qualified volunteer reviewers. These services certify the digital preservation repositories implemented by libraries, archives, and other cultural heritage entities rather than the digital preservation applications discussed in this chapter. In this respect, digital preservation certification differs from certification of RMA products, which was discussed in chapter 2.

- As explained below, a Submission Information Package consisting of digital content and its associated metadata is a major component of the OAIS reference model. ISO 20652, *Space data and information transfer systems—Producer-archive interface—Methodology abstract standard* covers the relationship and interaction between the producer of a Submission Information Package and the archive where digital content and metadata will be preserved.
- ISO 20104, *Space data and information transfer systems—Producer-Archive Interface Specification (PAIS)* provides a standard method of defining the digital content to be transferred by an information producer to an archive. ISO 20652 and ISO 20104 are based on recommended standards developed by the Consultative Committee for Space Data Systems.

Other International Standards

Various international standards present requirements and guidance for preservation of digital content in specific situations. For example:

- ISO 19165-1:2018, *Geographic information—Preservation of digital data and metadata—Part 1: Fundamentals* presents principles and functional requirements for long-term preservation of geospatial information, a type of digital content that is not fully addressed by the OAIS reference model presented in ISO 14721. ISO 19165-2:2020, *Geographic information—Preservation of digital data and metadata—Part 2: Content specifications for Earth observation data and derived digital products* deals specifically with preservation of geospatial data from Earth-observing missions.
- ISO/IEC TS 22424-1:2020, *Digital publishing—EPUB3 preservation—Part 1: Principles* and ISO/IEC TS 22424-2:2020, *Digital publishing—EPUB3 preservation—Part 2: Metadata requirements* apply portions of the OAIS reference model to digital content published in the EPUB format and its associated metadata.
- IS/TS 21547:2010, *Health informatics—Security requirements for archiving of electronic health records—Principles* and ISO/TR 21548:2010, *Health informatics—Security requirements for archiving of electronic health records—Guidelines* specify requirements for an electronic archiving process to ensure the integrity, availability, confidentiality, and accountability of digital patient records, which may need to be preserved for one hundred years or longer.
- ISO/TR 15801:2017, *Document management—Electronically stored information—Recommendations for trustworthiness and reliability* and ISO 14641:2018, *Electronic document management—Design and operation of*

an information system for the preservation of electronic documents—Specifications provide requirements and practical guidance for preservation of digital documents, audio and video recordings, and other digital content that an organization creates and receives in the course of business operations.
- ISO/TR 18492:2005, *Long-term preservation of electronic document-based information* discusses a strategic framework and best practices for preserving the accessibility and authenticity of digital documents as evidence of business transactions and events. The guidance acknowledges that long-term preservation of digital documents will require the involvement of records managers, archivists, and information technology specialists.
- ISO 17068:2017, *Information and documentation—Trusted third-party repository for digital records* presents technological and operational requirements for a retention repository that will safeguard digital content entrusted to the repository's operator by a client. While the standard uses terminology from the OAIS reference model, the third-party repository is not necessarily intended for long-term preservation. It will protect digital content from business disputes related to its reliability, integrity, and accessibility as evidence until its retention period elapses.
- ISO/IEC 23681:2019, *Information technology—Self-contained Information Retention Format (SIRF) specification* proposes an approach to digital preservation that is modeled on the archival practice of packing related paper records in a labeled box. Digital content and metadata will be combined in a logical container. The proposed approach is designed to help archivists become comfortable with the digital domain. The stored content and metadata will be subject to fixity checking, file format conversion, and other preservation-related processing.
- ISO/TR 22299:2018, *Document management—Digital file format recommendations for long-term storage* provides guidance for selecting an appropriate digital file format for office documents, email, static web pages, audio recordings, and video recordings.
- ISO 19005 is a series of standards that specify technical characteristics and conformance levels for the PDF/A format, which preserves the static visual appearance of digital content independent of the applications or systems that create, store, or access it. PDF/A is a constrained version of PDF that eliminates features that are unsuitable for long-term archiving. ISO 19005-1:2005, *Document management—Electronic document file format for long-term preservation—Part 1: Use of PDF 1.4 (PDF/A-1)*, the original PDF/A standard, is widely discussed as an obsolescent-resistant file format for preservation of

digital documents. Other standards in the ISO 19005 series extend the capabilities of the PDF/A format.
- ISO 13008:2022, *Information and documentation—Digital records conversion and migration process* deals with planning issues, methods, and procedures for conversion of digital records from one file format to another and migration of digital records from one hardware or software platform to another. It notes that conversion and migration must be implemented in a managed way in order to preserve the usability, authenticity, reliability, and integrity of digital records over time.

Maturity Models

The OAIS Reference Model has influenced the development of maturity models that define the desirable characteristics of digital preservation programs. For example:

- The Digital Preservation Capability Maturity Model (DPCMM) is based on ISO 14721 and the trustworthy repository criteria presented in ISO 16363. It defines five stages of digital preservation ranging from nominal, where no digital preservation initiatives are undertaken and all digital content that warrants preservation is at risk, to optimal, in which digital preservation initiatives are successfully implemented and no digital content is at risk. Determination of a given organization's stage is based on fifteen technological and organizational components related to a digital preservation program's infrastructure and services.
- The Levels of Digital Preservation (LoP) Matrix developed by the National Digital Stewardship Alliance provides a tiered roadmap to assess the progress of a digital preservation program through five functional areas and four levels of capability. The functional areas are storage, integrity, control, metadata, and content. The lowest capability level consists of simple measures, such as creating backup copies and using antivirus tools, to protect digital content. At intermediate levels, a digital preservation program implements progressively more effective processes to ensure the long-term integrity and usability of digital content and metadata. At the highest capability level, a digital preservation program will implement proactive measures to respond to threats and adapt to technological changes that may affect the continued viability of digital content.
- The Digital Preservation Coalition Rapid Assessment Model (DPC RAM) identifies eleven elements that can be used to assess the scope and effectiveness of a digital preservation program. For each

assessment, the model defines five levels of attainment, ranging from minimal awareness to optimization. Six of the elements relate to organizational characteristics of a digital preservation program, including governance, structure, and staffing; policies, procedures, and strategies for operation of a digital archive; compliance with applicable regulations and legal obligations; information technology support; processes for continuous improvement; and engagement with the wider digital preservation community. Five assessment elements relate to service capabilities, including process to acquire and ingest digital content, ensure the integrity and usability of digital content in storage, processes for metadata management, and support for user access.

Developed by the digital preservation community, these maturity models have become influential industry norms that are widely referenced in professional publications and conference presentations. They support strategic planning, self-assessment, benchmarking, and gap analysis by defining and evaluating a digital preservation program's organizational viability and service capabilities at varying levels of effectiveness.

FEATURES AND CAPABILITIES

The OAIS reference model defines three information packages that establish a structured framework for the design, development, implementation, and operation of digital preservation applications. A Submission Information Package (SIP) consists of digital content and metadata that will be ingested and processed by a digital preservation application. An Archival Information Package (AIP) stores and preserves the digital content and its associated metadata. A Dissemination Information Package (DIP) makes digital content and metadata available to its intended audience, which the OAIS reference model terms "consumers."

An organization can assemble a digital preservation system from software obtained from different sources. A given digital preservation applications may be able to create and ingest Submission Information Packages, for example, but other applications must be acquired and implemented to preserve and retrieve digital content. By contrast, the digital preservation applications discussed in this chapter are full-featured products that support all aspects of the OAIS reference model. They provide a complete solution for preservation of digital content, although they may be enhanced by the integration of optional components from other suppliers.

Content Capture

The digital preservation process begins with creation and ingestion of a Submission Information Package. The digital content to be included in a SIP may be saved on a shared drive, included in an ECM or RMA implementation, maintained on offline media, stored in another repository, or obtained from an external producer. Authorized persons must assemble the content and its associated metadata in a form suitable for input to the digital preservation application.

Content capture is a complex process. Some aspects are similar to the importation of digital content by other technologies discussed in this book. Others are specific to digital preservation:

- The content items included in a digital preservation implementation may have been created or received in the regular course of business by the organization that operates a preservation application. This is the case with preservation applications operated by archival agencies that are responsible for the historically significant records of national, state, or local governments or with archival programs that play the same role in companies and nonprofit organizations. Alternatively, the digital content to be preserved may be obtained from a publisher or another external producer, such as a photographer who donates digital photographs of important events to a local historical society or a scholar who donates a personal collection of research materials to a university library.
- Like the ECM and RMA implementations discussed in preceding chapters, a preservation application can ingest digital content in several ways. Digital documents and other content items can be individually uploaded to a preservation application from the repository where they are stored. This may be done by manually browsing through the repository's directory or folder structure to select the files or folders to be included in a Submission Information Package. Alternatively, authorized users may be able to drag and drop individual files or folders into the preservation application. In either case, the capture process can be time-consuming and labor-intensive. To reduce manual effort and speed up the process, some preservation applications permit batch uploading of multiple files or bulk input of a large quantity of digital content. In some cases, a digital preservation application may be able to extract digital content or metadata from external systems.
- Where a preservation application functions as an institutional archive for a government agency, company, or nonprofit organization, the digital content to be preserved was typically created in the recent

past by widely available software and saved in a limited number of commonly encountered file formats. Often, the institutional archive can specify file format requirements for digital content to be transferred to its custody for preservation. In most cases, records created by obsolete software likely predate the period when the digital versions of documents were retained as official copies. Such records were probably printed for filing and retention in paper form. The digital versions may have been discarded; even if they were kept, they are probably unreadable due to media deterioration or format obsolescence.

- In other situations, a preservation application must be able to accept, identify, and process digital content that was created at various points in time by many different types of software and saved in a wide range of current and obsolete file formats. Cultural heritage organizations, in particular, have little control over the digital content they obtain from external sources. The personal papers of a famous author acquired by the special collections department of a university library, for example, may include word-processing files that contain drafts of published works and unpublished manuscripts. These files may have been created by software that was discontinued years or even decades ago. In such cases, a donor may be unable or unwilling to convert digital content to a format prescribed by the cultural heritage organization, which must either accept the digital content in the format in which it is offered or reject the donation.
- Digital preservation applications check content for viruses or other malware when it is uploaded. This is necessary to prevent contamination of the preservation repository. If a problem is detected, the content will be rejected or quarantined for remediation. Depending on the preservation application, malware detection may be performed by an internal scanning engine or through integration with third-party antimalware software. In either case, malware detection algorithms must be updated regularly to address emerging threats. Malware detection may impact the performance of a digital preservation application, especially when content is imported in bulk. In some digital preservation implementations, exclusions may be made for content that is known to be safe.
- A digital preservation application may also check incoming files for encryption or password protection, which can render content inaccessible in the future or require another layer of software to open or decrypt it. The tight security provided by digital preservation applications make these protections unnecessary in most situations.
- As previously discussed, digital content is subject to time-dependent degradation or other changes that can affect its accessibility and

trustworthiness. Fixity is a measure of a content item's stability. Digital preservation applications perform fixity checking of uploaded content at the bit level to ensure its continued integrity and authenticity. A mathematical algorithm calculates a checksum value that represents the content's state when it is ingested. Some digital preservation applications utilize multiple checksum algorithms. Calculated checksums, which are saved as metadata or elsewhere, provide a baseline for future detection of corruption, data loss, or unauthorized alterations that may compromise a content item's reliability and usefulness. When the content item is reexamined, any change will result in a different checksum value.

- Fixity problems may also be reflected in changes in file size, file count, or other characteristics. In some cases, baseline fixity values may be uploaded with digital content to allow detection of corrupted content items before they are added to a preservation repository. As with malware detection, fixity checking may impact the performance of a digital preservation application when large quantities of content are being uploaded.
- Retaining duplicate content in a preservation repository can increase storage costs and cause confusion when duplicate items are retrieved. Some digital preservation applications will identify duplicate content during the ingestion process. Duplicate files may be detected by comparing checksums, content, metadata, file size, or other characteristics. Potential duplicates are flagged for manual review. There could be situations in which duplication is warranted, as when the same digital document is included in two folders that relate to different business operations or activities. Copies of a winning project proposal submitted in response to a procurement solicitation, for example, might be included in a contract file and in a project file, where they are accompanied by different documents that establish a context for understanding and interpreting the proposal. Each copy may be used by different people for different purposes.
- When content items are uploaded, digital preservation applications identify their file formats and check them for obsolescence. To identify the file format, the preservation application may analyze the file's internal structure as well as information contained in the file header, filename extension, and embedded metadata. The file format is matched against an authoritative database of known formats to conclusively identify it and determine whether it is obsolete or in danger of obsolescence. The file format database may be incorporated into the digital preservation application or it may be an external resource such as PRONOM, a comprehensive technical registry of software products and their associated file formats and versions.

PRONOM is maintained in the United Kingdom by the National Archives, which has also developed an open-source software tool for automated batch identification of file formats. Similar tools have been developed by other organizations.
- When an obsolete file format is detected, a digital preservation application may be able to convert it into a currently viable format, assuming that this can be done without comprising the digital content's usability and trustworthiness. The format conversion is typically documented in logs and in the converted file's metadata. Alternatively, the original file may be preserved with an indication of the format's obsolescence. Emulation software may be available to read it.

Preservation vs. Access Copies

Whether or not format obsolescence is detected, some digital preservation applications automatically generate preservation versions and access versions of uploaded content. The preservation and access versions do not necessarily replace the original content. They are created for different purposes:

- The preservation version, sometimes described as a preservation master, is a storage copy. In terms of the Open Archival Information System model, it is intended for inclusion in the Archival Information Package. The access version is a reference copy. It relates to the Dissemination Information Package component of the Open Archival Information System model.
- The preservation copy is intended specifically and exclusively for long-term retention. Designed to address concerns about the continued viability of digital content, the preservation copy's file format must be nonproprietary, well documented, widely supported by available software, and unlikely to become obsolete in the foreseeable future. Preservation in perpetuity may not be possible, however, for all characteristics of digital content. Some compromises may be necessary. Long term, for example, a cultural heritage organization may be committed to preserving the textual content of a digital document but not necessarily its exact appearance.
- The access copy is intended for rapid downloading and convenient viewing by an untrained user community equipped with a broad range of workstations. Access versions may have lower resolution images that are acceptable for display and optimized for transmission within available bandwidth constraints. Access versions may also have personal data and confidential content redacted.

File Plans and Metadata

As with other technologies discussed in this book, file plans and metadata are essential for retrieval of digital content, to support preservation processes, and other operations. Many of the file plan and metadata concepts and issues discussed in the preceding chapters apply to digital preservation applications:

- Like ECM and RMA software, digital preservation applications support customer-defined file plans consisting of a structured framework of folders and subfolders nested to multiple levels. Much of the digital content maintained by archives and libraries is unique. A digital preservation file plan must be tailored to the requirements of a specific content collection, and it must be scalable to accommodate new categories and subcategories as needed. Development of a well-designed file plan from scratch for a given content collection will likely require many person-hours of effort for planning, review, testing, and implementation.
- A digital preservation application may be able to replicate an existing directory structure of folders and subfolders when uploading content from a shared drive or from an ECM or RMA repository. This directory structure can be modified to reorganize folders, add or delete categories and subcategories, and relabel folders where necessary. As a potentially helpful resource, some digital preservation applications offer prebuilt file plans or preconfigured templates for specific content types, industries, or organizations. These prebuilt file plans can be customized to address local requirements.
- Metadata may be prepared in advance and uploaded with the digital content to which it pertains. Alternatively, metadata for individual content items can be entered or added by authorized persons after the content is uploaded. Metadata can be entered for files or folders. To facilitate data entry, digital preservation applications provide formatted screens with labeled fields, dropdown menus or picklists for selection of metadata values, and other features supported by ECM applications, RMA software, and other technologies discussed in this book. A metadata scheme must be expandable to accommodate new metadata elements.
- Metadata requirements for digital preservation are more complicated than those encountered in ECM and RMA implementations. Most organizations require a combination of descriptive metadata, which supports retrieval of digital content; administrative metadata, which supports preservation processes; technical metadata, which documents the structure and format of digital content; and rights

metadata, which documents the intellectual property rights and access restrictions that apply to digital content.
- Most organizations adapt their metadata schemes from an existing reference model. The Dublin Core, as discussed in chapter 1, provides an excellent starting point for selecting metadata elements for a particular content collection. The Dublin Core metadata set is sufficiently adaptable to work in a broad range of digital preservation environments involving a variety of content types. The Metadata Object Description Schema (MODS), which was developed by the Library of Congress, provides a larger set of metadata elements intended specifically for describing digital content maintained by libraries, archives, and other cultural heritage organizations.
- Organizations can modify these reference models to address special requirements. Metadata elements can be added. Digital preservation applications imposes few limitations on the number of metadata elements or the acceptable types of metadata values. Metadata entry may be specified as mandatory for some elements, optional for others. Unnecessary metadata elements can be eliminated.

Storage and Preservation

In the Open Archival Information System reference model, the Archival Information Package is the collection of digital content and metadata that is imported by a digital preservation application. An Archival Information Package is derived from a Submission Information Package:

- The Archival Information Package includes the digital content and its associated metadata along with contextual information about the content's historical, cultural, and intellectual significance. To establish the Archival Information Package, the digital preservation application verifies file formats, performs fixity checks, creates preservation copies and access copies, adds preservation metadata, and otherwise processes the Submission Information Package for long-term storage and preservation.
- Digital preservation applications store Archival Information Packages in a designated archival repository, which may be implemented on-premises or operated by a cloud provider. While some historical documents, photographs, and genealogical resources managed by a digital preservation application may be of general interest, most archival records, historical manuscripts, and other cultural heritage materials are preserved for possible future access by a limited audience of highly specialized researchers. Some Archival Information

Packages are subject to privacy or other restrictions that may prohibit their use for decades from the time they enter an archival repository.
- Recognizing that much archival content will be infrequently consulted, some digital preservation implementations utilize tiered storage arrangements that allow an organization to balance accessibility and cost based on the characteristics of a given Archival Information Package. A tiered storage arrangement provides two or more level of data storage that differ in performance and cost. Where a digital preservation application is installed on premises, tiered storage will be configured by an organization's information technology unit, which may contract with a cloud-based service to provide certain storage tiers. With cloud-based digital preservation applications, two- or three-tiered storage arrangements may be a standard feature or an optional component. The customer selects the content to be stored in given tier based on the anticipated need to access the content.
- An active access tier, the most responsive and expensive storage category, is typically reserved for high-priority Archival Information Packages that will be subject to frequent retrieval and need to be immediately accessible by authorized users, including an organization's employees as well as researchers or the general public. The active access tier may store digital content on solid state drives or low latency hard drives.
- An intermediate access tier stores Archival Information Packages that need to be conveniently available but do not require immediate retrieval. Conventional hard drives, which offer reasonable retrieval speed but are less expensive than the high-performance drives used in the active access tier, are the dominant storage medium for this tier.
- A cold storage tier combines economical storage with delayed retrieval for Archival Information Packages that will rarely be accessed or where access is prohibited until a future date. Lower performance hard drives or offline media are used for storage in this tier. An Archival Information Package can be transferred from tier to tier as access requirements change.
- A digital preservation application must provide effective mechanisms to confirm the continuing readability and usability of digital content and to alert responsible parties when problems or concerns are detected. To maintain the integrity and authenticity of digital content, preservation applications check Archival Information Packages at regular intervals to detect data corruption in storage. As discussed above, possible integrity issues are identified by fixity checks, which are usually based on comparison of AIP checksums to base-

line values calculated when Submission Information Packages were prepared. Any deviation suggests a problem that requires further investigation and, if warranted, corrective action, such as restoration of uncorrupted content from backup copies.
- Digital preservation applications also monitor Archival Information Packages for file format obsolescence. Depending on the preservation application and an organization's requirements, format monitoring may be performed annually or at shorter intervals. If the preservation application detects a file format that is obsolete or at risk of becoming unreadable or unusable, the content item will be migrated to a sustainable format. This may be done automatically or with manual intervention. In either case, the migration must be documented and the content item's metadata updated to indicate that migration was performed.
- If migration is not possible, as might happen with proprietary formats that cannot be accurately mapped to a replacement format or where legal restrictions prohibit format conversion, a digital preservation application may use emulation software to maintain the accessibility and functionality of an obsolete file format. By simulating an outdated computing environment, emulation software allows an organization to run applications that can read obsolete file formats, but that approach can involve significant technical challenges and high costs. Accurate replication of an older computing environment may not be possible in every case. Even if it works, emulation may be a short-term solution to the problem of file obsolescence. Over time, emulation software may itself become obsolete. To remain usable and maintain compatibility with changes in an organization's computing environment, emulation software will require continuing updates or periodic replacement, which may not be sustainable indefinitely.
- Creation of exact copies of digital content for storage in multiple locations or on multiple computer platforms is widely considered an effective data preservation strategy. Some cooperating libraries have implemented peer-to-peer digital preservation systems in which the same digital content is replicated by multiple participants for retention at their own locations. The participants may, in turn, create their own backup copies for offsite storage.
- Among its advantages, replication of digital content ensures continued accessibility and recoverability if data corruption is detected. A corrupted copy can be replaced by an exact replica made from an undamaged copy. A replication-based preservation strategy also facilitates integrity-checking and detection of data corruption by comparison of copies. Some cloud-based digital preservation ap-

plications store multiple copies of Archival Information Packages in geographically dispersed locations.
- Some digital preservation applications support a data escrow capability to ensure long-term availability of digital content and its associated metadata in the event that a given preservation application is discontinued, the vendor ceases operation, or other problems arise. Data escrow is handled by a trusted third party who maintains a copy of preserved content and metadata. Access to escrowed data is limited to authorized employees of the organization that deposited it. Some data escrow providers comply with the previously cited ISO 16363 standard for trusted digital repositories.

Access and Retrieval

Digital preservation applications store Archival Information Packages in a centralized repository that supports both preservation and retrieval operations. In the Open Archival Information System reference model, a Dissemination Information Package makes digital content and selected metadata from one or more Archival Information Packages available in response to a retrieval request submitted by an authorized user, subject to applicable access restrictions:

- A Dissemination Information Package must be suitable for its intended audience. The Open Archival Information System reference model uses the phrase "designated community" to denote the stakeholders and users for whom digital content is preserved. Identifying the audience for specific digital content and understanding its requirements and expectations for access to digital content is an essential aspect of a digital preservation implementation. A cultural heritage organization may have multiple designated communities for its preserved digital content.
- The designated community for a given Dissemination Information Package may be employees of the organization that has implemented the digital preservation application or scholars, researchers, educators, students, writers, government agencies, or others who are interested in specific digital content. As previously noted, there is a limited designated community for the specialized digital content preserved by many cultural heritage organizations. That audience may be well educated and knowledgeable about the information resources available in their areas of specialization. Their work may require access to large quantities of digital content over a period of months or years.

- Some materials preserved by cultural heritage organizations may appeal to a broad designated community that does not have well-defined research objectives. Certain digital preservation implementations are designed for internet access by the general public, but those implementations are typically limited to a subset of digital content preserved by a cultural heritage organization. A variety of examples implemented by libraries and archives are available online. The designated community for such content includes many users who lack specialized subject knowledge or research skills. The search interface intended for public access must be usable with little or no instruction. Such a large and varied community of users contrast sharply with an ECM or RMA implementation, which is principally accessed by an organization's employees or another closed user group.
- Most organizations designate a system administrator who is authorized to set up user accounts, modify menus and screens, define user privileges, and otherwise configure a digital preservation application based on organization's access policies. Access control lists define user privileges at the repository, subrepository, folder, subfolder, or content item levels. Authorized users can have full or partial access privileges for importing, retrieving, moving, duplicating, viewing, printing, downloading, sharing, or deleting preserved content and its associated metadata. Digital preservation applications use the customary combination of usernames and passwords to verify identity. Some applications support multifactor authentication and other access control methods for greater security.
- An organization can broaden, narrow, revoke, or otherwise redefine access privileges as circumstances warrant. Some Archival Information Packages may be subject to access restrictions that were imposed when digital content was submitted. Those restrictions may be modified or removed as time passes. Restrictions on retrieval of trade secrets or other proprietary content, for example, may be in effect when an Archival Information Package is created but no longer applicable decades later. Similarly, data protection restrictions on dissemination of personal information may elapse after a reasonable portion of a human lifetime. Restrictions related to copyright or other intellectual property rights may likewise be removed when the period of protection expires.
- Digital preservation applications support metadata searches based on keywords, phrases, or numeric values via a web interface that can be customized for users with varied knowledge and search experience. Search statements can include Boolean operators, relational expressions, and other retrieval capabilities discussed in preceding chapters. Some digital preservation applications support wildcard

searches and fuzzy searches, which are based on inexact matching of search terms and metadata values. Full-text searching of textual content is a standard feature with most digital preservation applications.
- Like ECM applications and RMA software, digital preservation applications respond to searches by displaying a list of retrieved content, from which the searcher can select one or more items for viewing. Search results may be sorted alphabetically, chronologically, by popularity, by presumed relevance, by size, or by other criteria.
- As previously explained, digital preservation applications create access copies of digital content for inclusion in Dissemination Information Packages. Preservation copies are not used for retrieval. Unlike ECM applications, a digital preservation application does not display content by launching its native application, which is less likely to be available as time passes. Instead, a multiformat viewer is provided for display of access copies. The file formats supported and specific display capabilities vary from one digital preservation application to another. Some digital preservation applications also support external viewers.
- Some digital preservation applications support federated searches to retrieve content from multiple archival repositories maintained by cooperating organizations or from external sources, such as an RMA repository or digital asset management system operated by the organization that implements a digital preservation application. Searchers must be authorized to access the federated repositories.
- Most digital preservation applications maintain audit logs that track all actions, operations, and events that involve or affect preserved content or metadata, including format conversions, fixity checking, addition or removal of digital content or metadata, replication of digital content or metadata, and transfer of digital content or metadata between storage tiers. Audit logs also track access to specific content, including failed attempts. An audit log can be used to troubleshoot access issues, to highlight matters that may require further investigation, and to respond to security incidents, trace their source, and assess their impact.

IMPLEMENTATION ISSUES

As with ECM applications and RMA software, implementation of a digital preservation application begins with the selection of a product with appropriate technological features and functionality. Rigorous product evaluation based on a clear understanding of an organization's requirements is essential, but technology is just one component of a digital preservation implementation. An appropriate governance mechanism must provide the leadership, planning, and coordination necessary for a successful implementation. The cost of a digital preservation application and the advantages and limitation of on-premises installation versus cloud-based software must be considered. Finally, planners and decision-makers must assess factors that affect the sustainability of a digital preservation implementation.

Product Evaluation

Digital preservation products can be divided into two groups: commercial software and open-source applications. Commercial digital preservation software is developed and sold by for-profit companies. Open-source applications may be developed by for-profit companies or by cultural heritage organizations, library and archival consortia, foundations, and other nonprofit organizations. Criteria for evaluation and selection of digital preservation applications in both groups are similar to those for other information governance technologies discussed in this book:

- Even though their potential market is huge—tens of thousands of libraries, archives, museums, historical societies, and other cultural heritage organizations worldwide maintain digital content that must be preserved for future generations—digital preservation applications are developed and sold by a small number of companies and nonprofit entities. Compared to ECM applications or RMA software, there is less competition, and prospective customers will have fewer products to choose from, especially if a completely preconfigured system is desired.
- As their principal advantage, open-source digital preservation applications are free to use. There are no upfront charges or annual licensing fees, which is appealing for cultural heritage organizations with limited budgets, but open-source applications can be more difficult and time consuming to install, configure, and maintain than commercial products. Open-source digital preservation applications offer a limited set of built-in capabilities and will often require considerable customization to address an organization's requirements. Some open-source applications have a community of developers who are experienced with such customization, but expert support services from the application's developer or consultants may be needed.
- For a fully operational digital preservation implementation, an organization may need to integrate an open-source application with open-source components from other suppliers. An open-source

application may be able to process Submission Information Packages and create Archival Information Packages, for example, but additional open-source products are needed for storage, retrieval, file format validation, fixity checking, and other preservation-related operations. Assembling a digital preservation application from components obtained from multiple suppliers will require a high level of technical expertise and extensive involvement by an organization's information technology unit. This makes open-source applications a poor choice for small cultural heritage organizations with minimal or no in-house computer staff.
- Commercial digital preservation applications, by contrast, offer a well-developed, fully integrated set of features and functions, although they are not necessarily plug-and-play products. Some customization may be needed during the initial implementation or thereafter. When expert advice and assistance are required during the implementation process and after the application is operational, open-source suppliers cannot match the knowledgeable technical support services provided by commercial vendors.
- A cultural heritage organization considering a commercial digital preservation application needs a qualified, experienced, and stable vendor with an established track record of satisfied installations in cultural heritage organizations with a mission, collections, and user community similar to its own. To evaluate a vendor's qualifications, an organization must obtain information about its financial stability and likely continued viability as evidenced by the company's latest financial statement or other appropriate documentation and the number digital preservation installations the vendor has successfully completed and the types of customers.
- To merit serious consideration, a digital preservation application must be actively marketed commercially available in a fully operational general-release version at the time of procurement. Experimental, developmental, or near-release products are unacceptable for digital content that warrants long-term preservation. A cultural heritage organization must have reasonable assurance that a given digital preservation application will be subject to continuing development to add new capabilities or improve existing ones. This is important because an application for long-term preservation of valuable digital content will be expected to remain in service for the foreseeable future.
- A digital preservation application intended for on-premises installation must be fully compatible with an organization's existing resources, including its computing and networking infrastructure and the technical capabilities of the employees responsible for im-

plementation and operation of the application. This concern is less significant for cloud-based digital preservation applications, but a cultural heritage organization's staff must have sufficient technical knowledge to communicate with the cloud provider. Whether cloud-based or installed on premises, a digital preservation application must comply with the customer's information security and backup protection protocols and practices.
- Over time, a digital preservation application will serve a progressively larger user population and store an increasing quantity and variety of digital content. A digital preservation application must be able to accommodate this expanded deployment. It must permit the future addition of user licenses, and it must not impose impractical limits on the number, size, or other characteristics of digital content it can accommodate.

Preservation Governance

A digital preservation project of limited scope and duration may be undertaken by a small library, historical society, museum, or other cultural heritage organization or as a pilot implementation by a larger organization. Such projects typically deal with a focused collection of digital content and are managed by a designated employee based in an existing department. The project manager, possibly assisted by a small team, is responsible for project planning, administration, and execution.

By contrast, a digital preservation implementation involving multiple content collections and ongoing initiatives will be administered by a dedicated organizational unit that has an archival or curatorial mission and a staff with appropriate preservation knowledge and skills. In libraries and archival agencies, digital preservation may be integrated into a multimedia program that is also responsible for preservation of paper documents, photographs, motion picture films, analog audio and video recordings, and other nondigital objects.

Preservation departments and project managers are responsible for day-to-day execution and administration of digital preservation activities and operations. As a governance mechanism, many organizations establish an advisory committee to provide planning, oversight, and coordination of digital preservation initiatives:

- The advisory committee's membership should reflect the multidisciplinary nature of digital preservation. Committee members must represent the interests and expertise of archivists, librarians, curators, or other stakeholders who are responsible for acquiring digital content, ensuring its continued reliability and accessibility, and making it available to users. The advisory committee should also include knowledgeable representatives from the parent organization's top management, which authorizes resources for digital preservation, as well as from an information technology unit, which will provide technical support for a digital preservation implementation, and a finance unit, which will provide budgetary support and oversight.

- The advisory committee will need the occasional participation of a legal representative who can address issues and concerns related to intellectual property rights, agreements with originators and donors of digital content, contracts with vendors of digital preservation products, and other matters related to acquisition and use of digital content. The legal representative will also advise about access restrictions to comply with laws, regulations, or donor agreements that mandate confidentiality of proprietary information or privacy of personal data. External experts can provide guidance about best practices and address preservation issues that require special knowledge or experience.
- The advisory committee will be responsible for short- and long-term strategic planning within the context of a mission statement that affirms the digital preservation program's commitment to responsible stewardship of digital content. To comply with ISO 16363, a digital preservation program must have a documented strategic plan that states the program's goals and objectives and specifies the types of preservation services to be provided. A digital preservation program must also have a documented contingency plan to fulfill its preservation commitments in case the program changes its scope or ceases operation. The advisory committee must ensure that these plans are aligned with the mission, values, and strategic priorities of its parent organization.
- The advisory committee will review and approve policies that support the program's mission and preservation plan. According to ISO 16363, a digital preservation program must have a collection policy that specifies the types of digital content to be acquired and preserved, staffing policies that specify required skills and expertise to fulfill preservation responsibilities, transformation and migration policies to address degradation or obsolescence of digital content, access policies that specify the types of digital content that will be available to designated communities of users and under what conditions, and a risk management policy that addresses technical or operational failures that may affect preserved content. An organization may need different versions of these policies for different types of digital content.

- The advisory committee will monitor the progress and effectiveness of digital preservation initiatives and recommend adjustments or improvements as warranted. The advisory committee will also review any proposed expansion of the digital preservation program or changes in its scope. As time passes, a digital preservation application may need to be upgraded to accommodate larger quantities of digital content or to meet the needs of a broader user community. The advisory committee will evaluate requirements, benefits, and costs for additional user licenses, customizations, and other capabilities to be added to the digital preservation implementation.
- The advisory committee will identify the digital preservation's staffing and technology requirements and advocate for the resources that the program needs to fulfill its mission. The advisory committee will work with the program's management to promote its benefits and accomplishments and to obtain funding for new preservation initiatives from internal and external sources. In some organizations, the advisory committee evaluates the digital preservation program's budgetary allocations and expenditures to confirm alignment with the program's objectives and priorities.
- The advisory committee may authorize audits or reviews to confirm a digital preservation program's compliance with applicable laws and regulations, to determine the program's conformance with international standards and best practices, or to assess the program's maturity level using one of the models discussed in a preceding section. Program audits or reviews may be initiated in response to issues or concerns raised by committee members, stakeholders, preservation staff, or users. Alternatively, they be conducted as part of routine programmatic assessments or continuous improvement initiatives. The advisory committee will define the objectives and scope of the audit or review, which may be limited to specific preservation activities or operations. The audit or review may be performed by an internal audit team or by preservation experts with audit experience.
- Meeting minutes and other records of the advisory committee's deliberations, decisions, and recommendations should be kept for accountability and transparency. This information may be needed for future review and evaluation of specific preservation activities or issues. Documentation about past decisions is also important for continuity for the committee's work as membership changes.

Cost

As with other information governance technologies, the actual cost of a digital preservation application can only be determined by obtaining a firm quotation for a specific product based on a detailed statement of requirements. Most organizations will incur a combination of infrastructure, software, and services costs that vary with the scope and complexity of a given digital preservation implementation:

- Digital preservation applications are available as commercial and open-source products for on-premises installation on an organization's own servers or as a cloud-based service. Subject to minor variations, the on-premises and cloud-based versions of a given application provide equivalent functionality, but they differ in their start-up costs, ongoing charges, ease of implementation, and scalability.
- Compared to an on-premises installation, the cloud-based approach offers faster implementation because the digital preservation application is preinstalled, tested, and fully operational on the cloud provider's servers. An on-premises digital preservation application must be properly installed and configured. This will involve significant time and effort by an organization's information technology staff, which may require training from the digital preservation application's developer. Even then, installation support services from the developer or a qualified consultant may be required.
- An on-premises installation of a commercial digital preservation application will require the upfront purchase of server and user licenses. An organization may also need new or upgraded servers and networking components as well as a specific operating system and database management system, although some organizations avoid this requirement by selecting a digital preservation application that is compatible with its existing computing environment. If an on-premises installation does not need to increase its data storage capacity when a digital preservation application is initially implemented, it will likely need to do so eventually to accommodate an increasing amount of digital content and metadata. Additional servers and networking components may likewise be needed to accommodate a growing user community.
- As previously noted, open-source digital preservation products are free to use, which give them an advantage over commercial applications in on-premises installations that have limited access to capital funds for server and user licenses, but an organization may still incur start-up costs for new or upgraded servers, storage devices, and networking components. Compared to commercial applications, open-source products may be more difficult and time-consuming to implement. Software installation, configuration, testing, customization, and integration with open-source components obtained from multiple suppliers may require hours of technical assistance by an

organization's information technology unit or the paid services of external consultants.
- With cloud-based digital preservation services, start-up costs are minimized or eliminated. Cloud customers pay an annual subscription fee that will depend on the number of user licenses, the amount of data to be stored, and other factors. A customer's infrastructure expenditures are limited to personal computers, which an organization may already own, and a reliable internet connection with effective security protection. The cloud service provides all required servers, storage devices, and system software and is responsible for upgrading its computing environment to improve performance or increase storage capacity when needed.
- Cloud services substitute ongoing charges for start-up costs. An on-premises digital preservation implementation will incur annual charges for software maintenance and technical support. An organization must repair or replace malfunctioning servers or other system components at its own expense. Cloud service providers are responsible for maintaining their own computing infrastructures and installing software fixes and upgrades when required. Technical support charges are included in the annual subscription fee paid by cloud customers. An on-premises installation must perform regular backup operations for recovery of digital content and metadata that may be lost or damaged. Backup copies must be stored in a secure offsite location. Cloud providers are responsible for backing up their systems and secure storage of backup copies.
- Cloud services are scalable on demand. An organization can start with a pilot implementation of limited scope at a relatively low cost and increase the number of user licenses and the amount of data storage as digital content is added. By contrast, scalability is more complicated with an on-premises installation. New servers and storage devices may be needed, and some downtime may be experienced while the expanded system is being installed and tested.

Sustainability Concerns

As applied to digital preservation implementations, sustainability refers to an organization's ability to ensure the continued integrity and accessibility of digital content without depleting its financial resources or harming the environment. With respect to sustainability, digital preservation programs faces two significant challenges: maintaining digital content in stable, usable form requires a perpetual commitment to periodic media migration and format conversion, and the amount of digital content to be preserved is growing at an accelerating rate. The pyramidal effect of these challenges—burdensome preservation actions that must be repeated indefinitely for an ever-increasing quantity of information—has been recognized for years.

The scholarly and societal benefits associated with digital preservation are widely acknowledged, but they come at a monetary and environmental cost. As discussed in the preceding section, digital preservation implementations may incur significant start-up costs as well as ongoing expenditures for computing processing and storage, IT support, and staff. These costs will increase over time and continue indefinitely. Most libraries, archives, and other cultural heritage organizations must operate within moderate to severe budgetary constraints. Money spent on preserving digital content is not available for other services and activities. Like all technology-based initiatives, digital preservation is energy-intensive. Energy consumed by preservation activities impacts the environment and also increases the cost of digital preservation. These problems and some proposed solutions have been widely discussed in the digital preservation community:

- The simplest way to reduce costs and energy consumption is to preserve less digital content. It is neither necessary nor feasible to preserve everything. Rigorous appraisal of digital content for historical, cultural, or societal significance is required to determine whether it truly merits permanent preservation. When making preservation decisions, an assessment of the long-term financial impact and environmental consequences of preserving specific digital content must be weighed against the content's long-term value and the potential loss to scholarship or society if the content is not preserved. Acknowledging that specialized archival materials may not be consulted for many years, some preservation specialists have suggested deferring the digitization of paper records until they are requested by researchers unless the records are in danger of physical deterioration.
- Whenever possible, digital content in unusual or obsolete formats should be converted to a sustainable format at the time it is acquired, thereby minimizing the need for future format conversions. As previously discussed, PDF/A, which is specifically designed to minimize future format conversions, is a good choice for many digital documents.
- A cost-sensitive, environmentally aware preservation program should prioritize energy efficiency over performance. Price and electrical consumption should be important selection criteria for servers, storage devices, personal workstations, and other computing components for on-premises operation of digital preservation applications. Access time is rarely an important consideration for preserved con-

tent. With tiered storage configurations, as discussed in a preceding section, a digital preservation implementation can sacrifice retrieval speed to reduce cost and energy consumption.
- To reduce storage and bandwidth requirements, a digital preservation implementation can create lower resolution copies of document images and video content for online access and store high-resolution preservation copies offline. Some preservation specialists have suggested limiting high-resolution preservation copies to the most valuable digitized documents or video content.
- As discussed in a preceding section, a cloud-based digital preservation application can be less expensive than an on-premises in some situations. Some cloud service providers have taken steps to address environmental sustainability concerns to a greater degree than a digital preservation operation can achieve in-house. A growing number of cloud providers have increased their reliance on renewable energy.
- Operating costs and energy consumption can be reduced by limiting preservation processing for certain types of digital content. Media migration, file format conversions, and computationally intensive fixity checks can be eliminated or performed at less frequent intervals. The number of backup copies produced for offsite storage might also be reduced.

The combination of perpetual commitment and a growing quantity of content is unique to digital preservation. While perpetual commitment also applies to preservation of nondigital information, paper documents and microfilm have long stable life spans that rarely require media migrations and format conversions, and the quantity of paper and microfilm records created by government agencies, businesses, nonprofit organizations, and individuals is not increasing significantly, if it is growing at all. As discussed in chapter 2, most content is now created and received in digital form, but only a small percentage of that content is printed for filing and retention.

SUMMARY OF MAJOR POINTS

- Digital preservation involves policies, strategies, and planned actions to prevent the deterioration, loss, or alteration of valuable digital content and ensure its continued accessibility for an extended period of time.
- Digital preservation is concerned with digital content that is in the inactive phase of the information lifecycle. Unlike records manage-

ment applications, however, digital preservation does not deal with all inactive information. It is only relevant for content that warrants permanent retention.
- Digital preservation is most closely associated with the longevity and continued accessibility of scholarly, scientific, and artistic information. While digital preservation applications can be implemented by any organization, their principal market is the cultural heritage sector, which includes archives, libraries, museums, historical societies, ethnic awareness organizations, and research institutions.
- Archives, libraries, and other cultural heritage organizations view the continued stability and accessibility of significant information as a societal imperative. Safeguarding digital content of enduring value is a mission-critical obligation for them.
- A number of international standards and guidance documents address digital preservation requirements and methods at varying levels of specificity. The Open Archival Information System (OAIS) reference model specified in the ISO 14721 standard has strongly influenced the design, development, evaluation, and implementation of digital preservation applications.
- The OAIS reference model defines three information packages that establish a structured framework for the design, development, implementation, and operation of digital preservation applications. A Submission Information Package (SIP) consists of digital content and metadata that will be ingested and processed by a digital preservation application. An Archival Information Package (AIP) stores and preserves the digital content and its associated metadata. A Dissemination Information Package (DIP) makes digital content and metadata available to its intended audience.
- Maturity models support strategic planning, self-assessment, benchmarking, and gap analysis by defining and evaluating a digital preservation program's organizational viability and service capabilities at varying levels of effectiveness.
- Digital preservation applications are available as commercial and open-source products for on-premises installation on an organization's own servers or as a cloud-based service. Commercial digital preservation applications are developed and sold by for-profit companies. Open-source applications may be developed by for-profit companies or by cultural heritage organizations, library and archival consortia, foundations, and other nonprofit organizations.
- Open-source digital preservation products are free to use, but they may be more difficult and time-consuming to implement than commercial digital preservation applications.

- As a governance mechanism, many organizations establish an advisory committee to provide planning, oversight, and coordination of digital preservation initiatives. The advisory committee is responsible for short- and long-term strategic planning within the context of a mission statement that affirms the digital preservation program's commitment to responsible stewardship of digital content. The advisory committee will also review and approve policies that support the program's mission and preservation plan.
- Most organizations will incur a combination of infrastructure, software, and services costs that vary with the scope and complexity of a given digital preservation implementation. Cloud-based implementations may be preferable for organizations that lack the capital funds and information technology support required for on-premises installation and operation of digital preservation software.
- Digital preservation faces significant sustainability challenges, both financially and environmentally. Digital preservation requires burdensome preservation actions that must be repeated indefinitely for an ever-increasing quantity of information.

NOTES

1. *Oxford English Dictionary*, s.v. "preservation (n.)," July 2023, accessed August 29, 2024, https://doi.org/10.1093/OED/1113136140.

2. *Digital Preservation Handbook*, second edition (Glasgow, Digital Preservation Coalition, 2015), accessed August 29, 2024, https://www.dpconline.org/handbook.

3. *Dictionary of Archives Terminology*, s.v. "digital preservation (n.)," accessed August 29, 2024, https://dictionary.archivists.org/entry/digital-preservation.html.

4. InterPARES Project Terminology Database, s.v. "digital preservation (n.)," accessed August 29, 2024, http://www.interpares.org/ip3/ip3_terminology_db.cfm.

5. National Digital Steward Alliance Glossary, accessed August 29, 2024, https://ndsa.org/glossary/.

6. American Library Association, LibGuide, Preservation: Digital Preservation, https://libguides.ala.org/libpreservation/digitalpreservation.

7. Reference Model for an Open Archival Information System, Recommended Practice (Washington, DC, Consultative Committee for Space Data Systems, June 2012), accessed August 29, 2024, https://public.ccsds.org/pubs/650x0m2.pdf.

4

✣

Email Archiving

The problems of email management have been widely recognized and much discussed since the late 1990s when email began replacing other forms of business communication in companies, government agencies, and nonprofit organizations. Until then, email usage was limited to brief, often informal communication among an organization's employees and, less commonly, with external entities. As a management tool, email was initially promoted as an alternative to telephone calls for brief exchanges of information where the called party was unavailable or immediate interaction with the called party was not required. Attachments were either not permitted or restricted in size. Most email messages contained information of transitory value that did not warrant retention after they were read and acted upon. Messages that contained information of continuing value were printed for filing with other documents pertaining to the same matters. Organizations imposed few rules for retention of older messages in their email systems. Mailbox owners could keep or delete them at their discretion.

As the number of email users and the volume of message traffic increased, that approach to email management became untenable. By the early 2000s, email was rapidly becoming the most voluminous category of recorded information in many organizations. Supplanting much paper-based correspondence and virtually eliminating intra-office memoranda, email assumed an integral and indispensable role in many business processes and operations. Organizations adopted it as a fast and reliable way to disseminate policies and procedures, announce decisions and accomplishments, authorize specific actions, approve payments and other financial transactions, interpret the terms and conditions of contracts, communicate with customers and suppliers, and address other business matters that must be fully documented.

As email's prominence and importance increased so did concern about its impact on business efficiency and cost. Some employees received dozens or even hundreds of messages each day. Message sizes increased as well, due to the greater length needed to address serious business matters and the inclusion of large attachments. The large and increasing quantity of email highlighted the need to delete obsolete messages to reduce storage requirements and maintain an acceptable level of system performance. As the quantity of saved messages increases, email databases may malfunction, the reliable operation of email servers may be compromised, and backup operations become more difficult to complete in the time allotted. To encourage employees to purge irrelevant messages and large attachments, some organizations imposed capacity limits on individual mailboxes, but there was growing apprehension that such limits would lead to the inadvertent destruction of messages needed for regulatory compliance or legal discovery, thereby exposing an organization to fines or other penalties.

Email archiving addresses these concerns. With the best-known archiving method, inactive email messages and attachments are moved from user mailboxes to an alternative storage location. The transfer may be performed manually or automatically when certain conditions are met. Alternatively, incoming and outgoing email may be automatically captured in a separate archival repository when it is sent or received, allowing inactive messages and attachments to be deleted from user mailboxes when they are no longer needed. In either case, email archiving may be done to manage mailbox content within predetermined capacity limits, to reduce mailbox clutter by removing older messages that are not consulted regularly, to make messages accessible when an email system is not available, to preserve messages of former employees, or for other reasons.

Email archiving is not a new concept. Popular email platforms have long incorporated simple archiving functionality. Mailbox owners can manually transfer selected messages and attachments from an inbox folder to a designated archive folder. Such transfers are intended for messages that the mailbox owner has read and answered but wants to keep for possible future reference. Removing these messages from the inbox will make it easier to identify unread messages or those that require further action. This archiving process can help mailbox owners manage their inboxes but it does not reduce the overall mailbox size. The archive folder is part of the user's mailbox. Messages in the archive folder remain accessible and searchable. They can be moved back to the inbox or deleted at any time. With some email platforms, an archived message will be automatically returned to the inbox if someone responds to it.

By contrast, the email archiving applications discussed in this chapter maintain messages and attachments in an external repository that is optimized for email storage and retention. The messages are accompanied by its date, time, sender, recipient(s), and other metadata. Message content and metadata are typically archived in their original file formats, although they may subsequently be converted to a different format for data migration or preservation purposes.

Like the records management and digital preservation applications discussed in preceding chapters, email archiving is principally intended for messages that are in the inactive phase of the information lifecycle, but archived messages remain retrievable and usable by authorized persons. Access privileges are typically synchronized with the mailbox from which message and attachments are archived.

As will be discussed in a later section, email archiving applications can also manage the retention of messages and attachments, but archiving and retention are not equivalent concepts. Email archiving is a housekeeping operation that maintains messages in an alternative storage location outside of the email system. Email retention, by contrast, is a policy-based activity that specifies the period of time that messages must be kept, wherever they are stored. Email archiving systems are not necessarily implemented in the context of an email retention policy. Some email archiving implementations merely allow messages to be offloaded from email servers. Others aggregate selected messages in a single repository for a specific purpose, such as litigation support. To provide a complete "solution" to the problem of email retention, an email archiving application must be a managed resource implemented in conjunction with comprehensive, coherent email retention rules.

HISTORY

Email archiving applications were introduced in the early 2000s. The initial products were widely praised and proved immediately attractive to large companies, government agencies, and other organizations with many email users and growing accumulations of unmanaged messages and voluminous attachments. As happened with other technologies discussed in this book, some developers of first-generation email archiving applications were acquired by larger computer and software companies that integrated them into their existing product lines, added new features and functions, and broadened their markets to include medium-size companies and nonprofit organizations. A period of strong customer interest and rapid growth followed.

By the mid-2010s, however, the market for email archiving applications had begun to mature. A Google Trends analysis indicates that searches for the phrase "email archiving" peaked between 2004 and 2007, followed by a steady and significant decline, as prospective customers acquired products that presumably met their needs and had no interest in exploring the technology further. By the early 2020s, the number of email users and volume of message traffic began to level off, albeit at a high level, as some organizations turned to alternative communication technologies, such as instant messaging, collaboration platforms, and specialized messaging services. This trend is expected to continue. Young people entering the workforce often prefer informal interactions with their peers via mobile apps. Having limited interest in and experience with email in high school or college, they are likely to limit its use to formal business communications.

Nonetheless, email continues to accumulate in formidable quantities. Vendors continue to promote and enhance their email archiving products, but the number of new installations is likely to grow slowly or decrease slightly. Most organizations that intend to implement an on-premises email archiving application have already done so. As part of a cloud-first strategy, a growing number of organizations have transitioned from on-premises email servers to cloud email services to simplify their information technology operations, reduce costs, facilitate access by remote workers, or for other reasons. While on-premises email archiving can coexist with cloud-based email, most cloud email services offer email archiving as a standard feature or optional component. Where an organization prefers on-premises email servers for security, control, customization, or other reasons, it may use a cloud-based email archiving services for long-term storage of messages that warrant continued retention.

BUSINESS NEED

Whether implemented on-premises or obtained from a cloud provider, a systematic approach to email archiving provides significant legal and operational benefits:

- Email archiving can improve the performance of on-premises email installations and simplify backup operations. Storing older messages and attachments in an archival repository rather than users' mailboxes will enable email servers to operate more efficiently and minimize capacity-related malfunctions. Reducing the quantity of

messages stored on email servers will facilitate the completion of backup operations within an allotted time window.
- Email archiving can reduce storage requirements and costs for a given quantity of messages and attachments. As will be discussed later in this chapter, most email archiving applications utilize compression, single instance storage (de-duplication), and other optimization technologies to store messages and attachments more compactly than is possible on with some email servers. While the cost of computer storage has decreased steadily and significantly, so has the amount of digital content to be stored. Storage costs remain a factor in most information technology budgets, and email must compete with other information for available capacity. It also important to note that the purchase price of storage components is only one part of the total cost to storage a given quantity of digital data. Direct and indirect costs associated with the use and maintenance of storage components must also be considered. Examples include, but are not limited to, the cost of installation, testing, and deployment; charges for repairs and maintenance contracts; labor costs for operation and technical support; the cost of floor space and utilities; data backup and disaster recovery costs; the cost of migrating data to replacement devices; and administrative overhead costs.
- For mailbox owners, periodic transfer of email to a separate archival repository eliminates the need for time-consuming review and purging of messages to comply with mailbox capacity limits. Email client software will also operate more efficiently with smaller mailboxes. Removal of older email makes it easier to identify messages that require further action.
- Email archiving supports compliance with email retention mandates. This is a frequently cited reason for email archiving implementations in financial services, pharmaceuticals, healthcare, transportation, and other highly regulated industries. Messages and attachments that must be kept for periods of time specified in laws and regulations can be designated for automatic transfer to a secure archival repository where they will be stored until their legally mandated retention periods elapse. Retention rules can prohibit deletion of archived email before that time. This safeguard gives email archiving applications a significant advantage over retention of messages in user mailboxes where they are subject to inadvertent or intentional deletion.
- Legal holds, which address an organization's duty to preserve evidence, may be imposed on email that is identified as relevant for litigation, government investigations, or other ongoing or pending legal proceedings. Legal holds suspend destruction of relevant mes-

sages and attachments until legal proceedings are resolved, but they can be difficult to enforce where email is scattered in multiple inboxes. Taking a single-silo approach, an email archiving application provides a secure, managed repository for messages that are subject to legal holds. Holds can be applied to archived email at the folder or item level, thereby providing a documented chain of custody and avoiding adverse inferences associated with inadvertent destruction of email. Archived messages will be retained and protected from destruction until all applicable legal holds are released.
- The single-silo approach also simplifies identification and production of email in response to discovery orders and, in government, freedom of information requests. With a fully indexed email archive, multiple mailboxes can be searched simultaneously and quickly to locate relevant messages and attachments, thereby reducing the time and cost to complete these burdensome operations. Some organizations create folders within an archival repository to aggregate email that is subject to discovery for specific legal proceedings.
- When employees retire or resign, their email accounts are typically closed but their mailboxes continue to reside on the organization's email server, where they may remain indefinitely. Over time, the continuing accumulation of closed mailboxes can have an adverse impact on server performance and storage costs; in many organizations, the inactive mailboxes of former employees outnumber active ones. Transferring closed mailboxes to an email archive will store messages and attachments in a secure location until their retention periods elapse and give authorized users access to the email of former employees when needed.
- Most organizations have an email usage policy that forbids the creation of messages with abusive, racist, sexist, defamatory, obscene, or criminal content. Incoming messages with such content must be deleted immediately upon receipt. In conventional email installations there is no way to enforce these rules, but messages and attachments aggregated in a centralized repository can be screened for inappropriate content. Messages and attachments can also be screened for inappropriate disclosure of personal data or confidential business information.

STANDARDS AND GUIDELINES

Despite the importance of email for business operations, standardization bodies and professional organizations have issued few standards and guidelines for email management, and none have developed standards for email archiving:

- Electronic mail is mentioned in various international standards, but none deal specifically and exclusively with email management. ISO/IEC 2382-32:1999, *Information Technology—Vocabulary—Part 32: Electronic Mail*, which defined selected terms related to email, has been withdrawn and replaced by ISO/IEC 2382-32:2015, *Information Technology—Vocabulary*, which includes email-related definitions along with those for other information technologies. ISO/IEC 2382-32 is the source for email-related definitions presented in ISO 5127:2017, *Information and documentation—Foundation and vocabulary*.
- Two older standards developed by ARMA International remain useful for information governance specialists and records managers. ANSI/ARMA 19-2012, *Policy Design for Managing Electronic Messages* specifies requirements for organizational policies to manage email as records throughout the information lifecycle. ANSI/ARMA TR02-2007, *Procedures and Issues for Managing Electronic Messages as Records* addresses issues pertaining to security, compliance, appropriate use, and other matters related to electronic messages and attachments.
- Several publications issued by the National Institute of Standards and Technology address email security management practices and controls. NIST SP 800-45, *Guidelines on Electronic Mail Security* provides guidelines and recommendations for email administrators and information security specialists who are responsible for installing, configuring, and maintaining secure email servers and clients. NIST SP 800-177, *Trustworthy Email* provides recommendations for technologies to detect and prevent malicious email messages. NIST SP 1800-6, *Domain Name System-Based Email Security* presents guidance for secure exchange of messages across organizational boundaries.
- *Commentary on Email Management: Guidelines for the Selection of Retention Policy* was issued in 2007 by the Sedona Conference, a nonprofit group that develops guidance for legal and policy issues. It was published in volume 8 of *The Sedona Conference Journal*.

FEATURES AND CAPABILITIES

Email archiving applications import messages that are created and received by mailbox owners. The messages are stored in a separate repository that is optimized for that purpose, where they are organized and indexed for access by mailbox owners and other authorized users. Email archiving applications support a full range of retrieval capabilities to identify messages that are needed for a given purpose. Retrieved messages can be viewed, printed, downloaded, or returned to their originating mailboxes. As one of its most important features, an email archiving application can manage the lifecycle of archived messages as determined by an organization's retention rules. It can identify messages and attachments that are eligible for destruction and ensure the continued retention of those that need to be kept for legal, operational, or historical reasons.

Direct Transfer to an Email Repository

Depending on the email archiving application, messages and attachments can enter an archival repository by direct transfer from user mailboxes or through real-time capture of inbound and outbound email. With the direct transfer approach, mailbox owners can manually archive messages and attachments as needed to manage mailbox size within defined capacity limits. Mailbox owners select the messages to be transferred to an archival repository. They can archive individual messages or folders containing multiple messages at any time. In many email archiving installations, however, transfers are performed automatically based on predefined rules and schedules:

- Messages and attachments may be transferred automatically from user mailboxes to an archival repository at a predetermined time following creation or receipt. The transfer interval is typically based on operational considerations and the information needs of mailbox owners. Messages and attachments may remain in user mailboxes for sixty to ninety days, for example, then transferred to the archival repository. Some systems may archive unread email after a shorter period of time than messages that have been read. Alternatively, read messages may be archived shortly after the mailbox owner responds to them. Short archival intervals may also be applied to messages where the mailbox owner is the recipient a copy rather than the primary recipient.
- Automatic archiving of messages may be triggered when mailbox capacity reaches a predetermined level. As previously discussed, large mailboxes can degrade the performance of email servers and clients. Email system administrators consequently prefer short intervals for offloading of messages from mailboxes to an archival repository, but this may conflict with the information needs of mailbox owners who want to keep recent messages on hand for fast access. In the capacity-based approach to archiving, a mailbox owner's messages will be retained on an email server as long as mailbox capacity remains below the level at which archiving is automatically initiated.

Mailbox owners can delay archiving by manually purging obsolete messages, preferably in compliance with an organization's email retention rules.
- With some email archiving applications, automatic transfer of messages from user mailboxes to an email archiving application can be limited to messages with specific characteristics—for example, messages sent to or received from designated email addresses, messages with attachments larger than a given size, messages that contain or do not contain certain words in the subject or body, or messages that have attachments with specific file extensions. Alternatively, transfer rules can exclude messages with specific characteristics—for example, messages with attachments identified by MP3, WMA, or other music file extensions in organizations that are not involved in the entertainment business. Such attachments are likely to be associated with personal email.
- As its principal advantage, automatic transfer ensures consistent archiving of messages without the participation and cooperation of mailbox owners, which is an important consideration where email is archived for compliance with regulatory requirements. By contrast, manual transfer give mailbox owners control over the archiving process, which some employees may prefer. High-value messages can be archived immediately to protect them from inadvertent deletion between archiving intervals. Messages that may be needed for future reference can be kept in users' mailboxes. Personal email, unfiltered spam, and work-related messages without continuing value can be deleted rather than archived, which will occur if the messages are not deleted before the next archiving interval.
- The two transfer methods are not mutually exclusive; some email archiving applications permit manual transfers between automatic archiving intervals. Regardless of method, messages and attachments transferred to an archival repository are removed from email servers, but they remain accessible to mailbox owners and, depending on the circumstances, other authorized persons. In some email archiving implementations, shortened versions of transferred messages, termed stub files, are left in users' mailboxes as pointers to their archived counterparts.

Real-Time Message Archiving

As an alternative to transfer of messages from user mailbox, some email archiving applications save copies of incoming and outgoing messages, including intra-domain messages, in an archival repository. While direct transfer is applied to messages that were sent or received in the past, real-time capture occurs automatically at the time messages are sent and received:

- Archiving may occur at the email gateway, the point where messages enter and leave an organization's network. Incoming and outgoing messages are captured by the email archiving application before they are delivered to their intended recipients, which may be a user's mailbox or an external addressee. Alternatively, archiving may be integrated with an email server's journaling function, which automatically records all inbound and outbound messages in a specially designated mailbox from which they are forwarded to an email archiving application. This may occur either immediately or at scheduled intervals. Following the transfer, the archived messages will be deleted from the journal mailbox.
- In some implementations, all incoming and outgoing messages are archived. Alternatively, archiving may be limited to messages that are sent to or received by specific mailboxes. In either case, real-time capture does not affect users' mailboxes, which may still be subject to capacity limits. Users can delete messages at any time, however, with assurance that they have been archived.
- Messages received from external domains are typically processed by filtering software that identifies likely spam, messages that may contain viruses or other malicious content, messages that are sent to or received from email addresses that are suspicious or otherwise prohibited, messages with unacceptably large or inappropriate attachments, or messages that are returned to the sender as undeliverable. Such messages will not be archived. Some organizations also apply filtering software to identify and block outbound messages with confidential or inappropriate content.
- Real-time email capture ensures that all messages falling within a defined scope will be archived. Incoming and outgoing messages are available immediately in the archival repository, which provides a single source for email searches. Because incoming messages are archived before they are transferred to their intended recipients, they cannot be altered or deleted by mailbox owners.
- These are important considerations where an email archiving application is implemented for compliance with recordkeeping regulations or to preserve or retrieve email with evidentiary value for litigation, government investigations, or other legal proceedings. Where messages and attachments are transferred from user mailboxes, either manually or after a prescribed period following creation or receipt as described above, the archival repository may not contain all messages needed for a given purpose and significant

messages may be altered or deleted, intentionally or inadvertently, during the prearchiving interval.
- Compared to applications that transfer messages from mailboxes to an email archive, real-time email archiving can be more difficult to set up and maintain. It also imposes a significant burden on an organization's email infrastructure. By contrast, automatic transfer of messages from mailboxes can be scheduled during off-peak hours when there is a lower level of email traffic. As its principal limitation, however, real-time capture may archive insignificant messages—including unfiltered spam—that would have been discarded by mailbox owners in compliance with an organization's retention rules.
- As an additional, potentially significant limitation, the real-time capture approach cannot replicate folders created by mailbox owners to organize messages by date, topic, or other parameters. Messages are moved into folders after they are sent or received, at which point real-time capture has already occurred. Where messages are archived by direct transfer from user mailboxes, folder structures are replicated in the archival repository. As discussed below, mailbox owners create folder to organize messages by the matters to which they pertain, thereby facilitating searches for messages that deal with specific topics.

Message Storage

While a short text-only message may require a few kilobytes of storage, email attachments can add a megabyte or more to the storage requirement. To address the voluminous quantity of messages, large size of many email attachments, and changing needs of current and prospective customers, email archiving applications must provide scalable storage capacity at a reasonable cost:

- Hard drives are the most common storage devices for archived messages, but some email archiving applications offer tiered storage arrangements that allow customers to optimize storage resources by balancing their accessibility requirements and storage costs based on the value of archived messages. Where rapid retrieval is essential, high-value messages and attachments can be stored on relatively expensive solid-state devices or high-performance hard drives. Mid-performance hard drives, the workhorses of the digital storage industry, are suitable for messages that must be conveniently available without unreasonable delay, while a low-cost cold storage tier is provided for inactive messages that are awaiting deletion when their retention periods elapse.

- Tiered storage of email is compatible with the information lifecycle concepts discussed in preceding chapters. Like other types of recorded information, email loses its value over time. Messages are most likely to be retrieved when the matters to which they pertain are under active consideration. Those messages should be kept in users' mailboxes. Email archiving is principally intended for inactive messages that rarely require urgent retrieval. Consequently, the highest cost storage tier should be used sparingly, if at all. Mid-performance storage is adequate for most archived messages.
- Some email archiving applications support a write-once storage option for compliance with financial industry regulations that require retention of email on media that cannot be erased, overwritten, or otherwise altered. Such media include nonerasable hard drives and optical disks. Regulations in other industries require storage of digital communications on media that are durable and resist alteration or deletion but are not necessarily nonerasable. Write-once storage can also be used to ensure the integrity of email that is subject to court-ordered discovery for legal proceedings.
- To attain a reasonable market share, email archiving applications must be compatible with popular email platforms. Some email archiving applications store messages in file formats, such as MSG or EML, that can be read by widely utilized email clients. Others store messages in a proprietary file formats that require conversion or add-on components to be read by popular email clients. Some email archiving applications can convert messages and attachments to PDF files for long-term preservation, submission to regulatory authorities, or delivery to other organizations that may not have access to compatible email clients.
- As noted above, some email archiving applications place stub files, also described as shortcuts, in users' mailboxes as placeholders for messages that have been transferred to an archival repository. Stub files give mailbox owners convenient access to messages they have archived. A stub file contains the subject, names of senders and recipients, and other information sufficient to identify a message plus links to the full message in the email archive. When the link is selected, the corresponding message, with any attachments, will be retrieved, perhaps with a slight delay. It may be displayed directly from the email archive or returned to the user's mailbox for viewing.
- Stub files are smaller than the messages they represent, but they do occupy space and can affect the performance of email clients, which may be degraded as the number of stub files increases. Mailbox owners can delete stub files manually at any time without affecting archived messages. In some email archiving installations, stub files

are deleted from user mailboxes automatically after a predetermined period of time. As a potential problem, stub files can pose migration issues if an email archiving application is replaced.
- Removal of message and attachments from user mailboxes will save space on an email server. Email archiving applications use several techniques to optimize storage resources in an archival repository and simplify backup operations. Data compression can significantly reduce the space required to store a given quantity of messages. Compression will not compromise a message's integrity or impair its usability. The email archiving application automatically decompresses messages for viewing or return to users' mailboxes. The resulting cost savings usually outweighs the computational resources required for compression and decompression.
- The level of compaction attainable in a particular email archiving implementation depends on the compression algorithm employed and the characteristics of the information being compressed. Data compression is generally more effective for long textual documents than for short ones. Consequently, its advantages may be greater for attachments than for messages, which are often short. Some attachments, such as image files, may be compressed at their source, in which case further compression during the archiving process will have little impact.
- Compression is often combined with single-instance storage, also known as duplicate detection or de-duplication, to achieve an even greater reduction in storage requirements for archived messages. Information copies of messages are routinely sent to multiple recipients, some of whom have little or no continuing interest in the message after it is read. Nonetheless, many of those copies are saved in recipients' mailboxes, from which they will eventually be transferred to an archival repository. Where incoming and outgoing messages are captured in real-time, all copies will be archived. Where multiple copies of the same message are archived, only one copy is saved in the archival repository. Pointers link that copy to the individual mailboxes where the message originally resided. This de-duplication process is transparent to mailbox owners. Like compression, single-instance storage requires computational overhead, but it can reduce storage costs and simplify backup operations, especially for multiple copies of messages with lengthy attachments.
- As an optional capability, some email archiving applications encrypt messages for storage or for transfer to or from an archival repository. Email systems are frequent targets of data breaches. Encryption may be useful or necessary for archived messages and attachments that require safeguards beyond password protection, network access con-

trols, and other measures designed to prevent unauthorized access to the email archive. Examples include messages and attachments that contain personally identifiable information, protected health information, payment card information, log-on credentials for computer applications, or proprietary business information, such as financial data, contracts, purchase orders, revenue projections, strategic plans, and product specifications, any of which may be contained in the text of an email message or, more commonly, in attachments.
- Encryption can be applied to all archived messages or limited to messages and attachments that are subject to special security requirements. Such messages may be identified by their senders, recipients, or other parameters. Encryption does not interfere with indexing, searching, display, or printing of archived messages. Messages are decrypted when retrieved by authorized persons. Some computational overhead is involved but this usually trades off favorably against the greater security the encryption can provide.

Organization and Metadata

An email archiving application adds value to an organization's email installation by maintaining an organized repository of indexed messages and attachments for searching and retrieval by authorized users:

- Folders enable mailbox owners to categorize and manage the messages they send and receive. Unlike ECM applications and RMA software, which define a folder taxonomy for an entire repository, email folder taxonomies are created at the mailbox level rather than the repository level. Folders created for a given mailbox apply to that mailbox only. An email archive may contain hundreds or thousands of folders.
- Email clients typically provide default folders for the mailbox owner's inbox, sent items, drafts in progress, archived messages, and deleted items. Some mailbox owners create additional folders to group messages pertaining to particular projects, events, activities, customers, topics, or other matters. Folders may also be created for particular types of messages, such as inquiries, complaints, orders, and invoices. Some mailbox owners create folders for messages that require an urgent response or follow-up action, for messages with sensitive content requiring additional security measures, or to separate personal email from work-related messages.
- As previously noted, email archiving applications that transfer messages from a user's mailbox to an archival repository can preserve the mailbox's folder structures. With such applications, organization

of messages in the archival repository mirrors the email system with which it is associated. Each mailbox maintained by an organization's email server has a counterpart in the archival repository, assuming that the mailbox is designated for archiving by the email system's administrator. If the mailbox owner has organized messages into folders, those folders will be replicated in the mailbox's archival counterpart.
- By contrast, email archiving applications that utilize the real-time capture approach cannot replicate folders created by mailbox owners to organize messages by date, topic, or other parameters because incoming messages are archived before they are received by mailbox owners. Mailbox owners may object to the elimination of folders that they have created to organize archived messages, even where metadata and full-text indexing provide equally effective approaches to message retrieval.
- Indexing of archived email may be based on message metadata, such as the sender's name or email address; the names or email addresses of recipients, including recipients of copies; the date the message was sent or received; or words in the subject line. Indexing can also be based on subject headings or other index terms that are assigned to messages by mailbox owners before they are archived. Alternatively, some email archiving applications allow authorized users to add index terms to archived messages. One or more index fields can be defined for this purpose. ISO 15836-1:2017, *Information and Documentation—The Dublin Core metadata element set—Part 1: Core elements*, which was discussed in preceding chapters, provides a useful starting point for selection of index fields for archived messages.
- As a standard or optional supplement to metadata, most email archiving applications support full-text indexing based on words in a message's subject line, in the body of the message, and in attachments, assuming that the attachments contain character-coded text as opposed to images or other graphical information. In this respect, the functionality of email archiving applications surpasses the capabilities of email clients, which may support full-text indexing of subject lines and the body of messages but do not index the complete text of attachments.
- Email archiving applications may perform full-text indexing in real-time or during off-peak hours to avoid interfering with other archive-related operations, although off-peak indexing prevents searches for messages that are archived between indexing intervals. As the quantity of email increases, performance of an email archiving system may be degraded during index updates. To minimize this problem, some email archiving installations allow users to limit full-

text indexing to designated messages or attachments that are needed for specific purposes, such as project management, internal investigations, early case assessment, freedom of information requests, or response to court-ordered discovery.
- Some email systems support an automatic categorization module as an optional component. Automatic categorization, also known as automatic classification, uses pattern-matching algorithms, word clustering, word frequencies, word proximities, synonym lists, and other linguistic and statistical concepts and tools to automatically organize email into topical folders based on the subject content or other characteristics of archived messages. Like full-text indexing, automatic categorization analyzes a message's content and identifies words for indexing purposes; but unlike full-text indexing, which creates index entries for all words except those designated for exclusion, automatic categorization evaluates rather than extracts words.
- An automatic categorization module compares new messages to previously categorized messages and assigns them to folders based on the words they contain or do not contain. Typically, the categorization decision is based on a word in the subject line and body of a message, although attachments might be analyzed as well. The ability to accurately categorize messages depends on several factors, including message content and the nature and complexity of the topical categories to which messages must be assigned. Email archiving applications increasingly incorporate machine learning and pattern-recognition algorithms but accurate categorization of messages remains a challenge, as it can be with manual filing of documents. A given mailbox may have dozens of topical folders. Some messages deal with multiple topics that are covered by several different folders; others may have new or ambiguous content that does not appear to match any existing folder.

Access and Retrieval

Email archiving applications enable authorized users to search for and retrieve archived messages and attachments with designated characteristics or that deal with specific matters:

- Access privileges for archived messages are assigned by system administrators based on organizational policy. In most implementations, mailbox owners have access to their own messages; they may be limited to read-only access to prevent alteration or deletion of archived messages. This limitation is essential for organizations that rely on email archiving to comply with recordkeeping laws

and regulations or to preserve messages that are relevant for legal proceedings.
- Read-only access privileges may be assigned to persons or groups. An organization's legal department, for example, may be given cross-mailbox access privileges to respond to discovery orders, to conduct investigations, or for other purposes. Department supervisors may have access to archived messages of employees who report to them. Project managers may have access to archived messages of team members.
- Authorized users can view a hierarchical display of folder icons that represent individual mailboxes. Subfolders are included where present. Well-organized folders facilitate browsing through collections of related messages, but browsing is less efficient than index searches. To locate a given message, an authorized user must open individual folders and subfolders and examine their contents.
- Searches for archived messages can be based on metadata or full-text indexing. Metadata searches can retrieve messages sent by or to specific mailboxes, messages that were sent or received on a specific date or range of dates, messages that are larger or smaller than a designated size, messages with or without attachments, or messages having attachments of a designated type, which is identified by the file extension. Full-text searches can be limited to specific parts of an email message, such as the address field, the subject line, the text of the message itself, or the text of attachments.
- Most email archiving applications support the search capabilities discussed in preceding chapters, including single-word searches, phrase searches, root-word searches, wildcard characters in search words, proximity operators, relational operators, and Boolean operators. Retrieved messages can be sorted by sender, date, subject, or other fields.
- Depending on the implementation, archived messages can be accessed by an email client, through a browser-based interface, or via mobile apps intended for smartphones and tablets. If an email client is used, mailboxes and archived messages can be searched simultaneously. Subject to appropriate security and access controls, some email archiving applications support cross-mailbox searching, which allows multiple mailboxes to be searched simultaneously, and federated searching, which permits simultaneous searching of multiple email archives and, in some cases, external information repositories.
- Mailbox owners and other authorized persons can use an email archiving system's search capabilities to retrieve messages for display, printing, downloading, response, forwarding, or—if permitted—return to an originating mailbox. Most email archiving applications

maintain audit logs that track access, deletion, exporting, changes in access privileges, and other actions related to archived messages. The audit logs can be searched by the name of the user, the type of action, and the date and time interval when the action occurred.

Retention of Archived Messages

As discussed above, the information lifecycle concept applies to archived email. As with other types of recorded information, the business value of email varies inversely with age. An archived message is most likely to be retrieved while the transactions, operations, activities, or events to which it pertains are under active consideration. As time passes and those matters are resolved or cease to be of active interest, the message is less likely to be retrieved. If enough time passes, the message may no longer be needed, although certain messages may have long-term operational or historical value that warrants continued retention or permanent preservation.

Archiving older messages can improve the performance of an organization's email servers and clients, but indefinite retention of large quantities of obsolete messages can degrade an email archiving application's retrieval and backup operations, complicate software upgrades and migration to a replacement application, and increase storage costs and the potential for system malfunctions. For many organizations, systematic management of the information lifecycle is an important motive for implementing an email archiving application. Among their most valuable features, email archiving applications can implement an organization's retention rules for messages and attachments:

- Retention periods for archived messages can be saved as metadata. Depending on the system, retention periods may be calculated from the date a message was created, the date the message was last modified, or the date the message was archived. Messages and attachments will be deleted or otherwise removed from the archival repository when their retention periods elapse.
- Email archiving applications are compatible with schedule-based retention periods or a uniform retention period. With the schedule-based approach to email retention, an organization's record retention schedule is the authority for retention decisions about archived messages. The retention schedule specifies how long records related to a specific business operation, activity, event, person, or other matter must be kept. Retention periods may be applied to individual messages or entire folders. A topical folder for messages related to a

contract, for example, may be retained for six years after termination of the contract if that is what the retention schedule specifies.
- Schedule-based retention is consistent with three-quarters of a century of records management practice, but it is impractically labor intensive and time-consuming to apply to the large quantity of email that organizations send and receive daily. Mailbox owners must consult the retention schedule to determine how long each message or folder of messages must be kept.
- With the uniform retention approach, a predetermined retention period applies to most archived messages with exceptions allowed for certain messages that need to be retained for a longer or shorter amount of time as determined by legal, operational, or historical considerations. The uniform retention period may range from three to ten years, depending on an organization's requirements; the longer the uniform period, the fewer the number of required exceptions.
- Exceptions may be based on the role of the mailbox owner or the nature of the message. Some organizations retain the messages of senior officials or high-level decision-makers indefinitely. Messages that promulgate official policies, interpret the terms and conditions of contracts, relate to capital projects, or deal with important legal matters may need to be kept longer than the uniform retention period.
- Email archiving applications that transfer messages from mailboxes to an archival repository are compatible with schedule-based or uniform retention. A uniform retention period is the only workable method where incoming messages are archived in real-time. Such messages are archived before they are received by mailbox owners. If the schedule-based approach is used, messages must be marked for retention or deletion by mailbox owners or other authorized persons after they are archived.
- An email archiving application can be configured to delete messages automatically when their retention periods elapse, but authorized users can manually override deletion and extend the retention period for selected messages. An email archiving application will document the destruction of specific messages and maintain an audit trail that logs all retention actions.
- Whether schedule-based retention or uniform rules are used, an email archiving application will temporarily suspend the destruction of messages and attachments that are considered relevant for litigation, government investigations, arbitrations, mediations, or other legal proceedings or for financial audits or reviews by tax agencies, public accounting firms, government officials, or other external authorities. Holds can also be placed on messages that must be retained

for compliance audits, quality reviews, operational audits, information system audits, safety audits, internal investigations of possible legal or policy violations, or other internal control processes.
- The retention capabilities of email archiving applications resemble those supported by the RMA software products discussed in chapter 2. If desired, messages can be exported from an email archiving application to an RMA repository for retention with other records pertaining to the same matters. Alternatively, archived messages of long-term value can be exported to a digital preservation application for permanent retention. But RMA software and digital preservation applications lack some of the email management functionality discussed in this chapter. In particular, they do not support real-time capture of incoming and outgoing messages, the automatic transfer of messages to an archival repository at predetermined intervals, and single instance storage to eliminate duplicate messages.

Other Capabilities

While email archiving is not a new technology, developers of email archiving applications are continually adding features and functionality to address customers' requirements and keep their products competitive. Examples include the following capabilities, which may be supported as standard features or optional components:

- Government regulations in some countries specify recordkeeping requirements for certain non-email communications. Regulations aside, many organizations want to preserve non-email messages that contain information of legal, operational, or historical significance. To address these requirements, developers of email archiving applications have expanded their products to accommodate a variety of digital communications beyond traditional email, including SMS text messages, instant messages, messages and posts from social media and collaboration platforms, transcribed voice mails and video conferences, and fax transmissions.
- Some email archiving applications can screen email messages and attachments for problematic content, such as social security numbers, bank account numbers, credit card numbers, protected health information, and other personal or sensitive data. Content screening can also identify messages and attachments that contain suspected viruses, obscene expressions, menacing or defamatory words, racial epithets, ethnic slurs, sexist comments, and other statements that may violate antidiscrimination laws or an organization's code of conduct. Messages and attachments flagged by content screening

algorithms are set aside for review prior to archiving. Some real-time archiving applications will stop outgoing messages that are marked for internal use only.
- Some email archiving applications support a caching capability that creates a local copy of archived items on a shared drive or on a mailbox owner's laptop or desktop computer. This feature is useful when the server on which the archival repository resides will be offline for scheduled maintenance, when a mailbox owner is traveling and cannot access the archival repository, when network connections are disrupted, or when an email archiving application is otherwise unavailable. The local copy may provide faster access to archived messages in locations with bandwidth constraints. The local copy is synchronized with its counterparts in the archival repository. When a message is added to or deleted from the repository, the local copy will be updated accordingly. The local copy also serves as a backup for restoration of the archival repository, but the number of cached messages is limited by the capacity of local storage devices. Controls and safeguards for the local copy must be equivalent to security protection supported by the archival repository.
- Email archiving applications can generate various statistical and operational reports about an organization's email traffic and archiving activity. Examples include the number of messages archived by specific mailboxes or in total during a specified time period, the amount of storage space occupied by archived messages, the amount of storage space occupied by archived attachments of a specified type, the number of archived messages deleted or forward to external recipients during a specified time period, and comparative analysis of archived messages by originating source, size of attachments, or other characteristics.
- Most email archiving applications can archive tasks, contacts, calendars, notes, and other non-message items created by email clients. Some applications can also be set up to archive word-processing documents, spreadsheets, presentations, and other non-mail files that are transferred from network or local drives. These items can be indexed for retrieval by assigned metadata or full-text, and the email archiving application's access and retention controls can be applied to them. This would appear to place electronic archiving systems in direct competition with the RMA products discussed in chapter 2, but email archiving systems do not provide the same level of retention functionality for such electronic records. They do not support event-based retention periods or version control. Unlike RMA products, email archiving applications are not certified for compliance with DoD 5015.2-STD or other records management standards. As noted

above, however, RMA software does not support the broad range of message management capabilities provided by email archiving applications. The two technologies should be viewed as complementary rather than competing information governance tools.
- Some email archiving applications can import and export message and attachments as PST files, a proprietary file type developed by Microsoft to remove older messages from mailboxes where capacity limits would otherwise force their deletion. Email archiving applications can identify existing PST files on local or network drives and migrate them into an archival repository for access by mailbox owners and other authorized persons. Migrated PST files are subject to the same retention rules as other archived messages. Some email archiving applications can also export selected messages in the PST format to provide offline access when the archival repository is unavailable, but many organizations prohibit the creation of new PST files when an email archiving application is fully operational. Because older messages are stored in an archival repository, mailbox owners have less need to create PST files for mailbox management.
- As noted above, some email archiving applications incorporate machine learning, pattern recognition, and other artificial intelligence algorithms for automatic categorization of messages. Developers of email archiving applications increasingly use AI-supported capabilities to differentiate their products. These capabilities include detection of security threats and data leaks in archived messages, identification of archived messages and attachments that may be contaminated by malware, enhanced retrieval capabilities to improve the relevance of search results, storage optimization based on email access patterns, and selective archiving of messages that are likely to be needed for future reference. Some email archiving applications use artificial intelligence to create summaries of messages in email chains and to translate archived messages into different languages.
- Email archiving applications can be integrated with external applications, including enterprise management applications, RMA software, customer relationship management systems, enterprise resource planning applications, human resources information systems, project management systems, and collaboration platforms. Depending on the application, integration may be achieved through application programming interfaces that allows external systems to communicate with an email archiving application, middleware that can route data between email archiving applications and external systems, plug-ins that supply prebuilt connections to specific external systems, or webhooks that allow email archiving applications to

send notifications to external systems when certain events, such as archiving of new messages, occur. File transfers can also be used to deliver archived messages to external systems.
- As the email archiving market has matured, replacement systems account for an increasing share of new installations. Some email archiving vendors offer capabilities to simplify and support the migration of archived email from competing products. Documentation, compatibility guides, and training webinars draw on their experience migrating email for new customers. Technical assistance is available to address questions and issues that may arise while a migration project is being planned or to help with problems that may occur when email is being migrated. Some vendors provide prebuilt tools and utilities to import messages from specific platforms. Application programming interfaces and software development kits may also be offered for organizations that require customized migration. Some vendors offer professional services, either directly or through authorized representatives, to manage the migration process.

IMPLEMENTATION ALTERNATIVES

Most of the evaluation and selection criteria discussed in other chapters are relevant for email archiving products. An email archiving application must be compatible with an organization's email system and offer the features and functions that the organization requires. It must be a commercially viable product sold by an experienced, financially stable vendor. It must have a proven history of reliably operational implementations and effective technical support. Its installed base should include organizations with requirements that are similar to those of the prospective customer. Email archiving procedures must be easily initiated by properly instructed nontechnical employees. The application must provide a user-friendly interface that is convenient to use on a day-to-day basis. The application must be scalable to accommodate an expanded user base and an increased quantity of stored messages without an adverse impact on performance.

An email archiving system is a computer application. It may be sold as software for installation and operation on an organization's own computers, packaged as an integrated configuration of hardware and software components, or offered as a cloud-based, hosted application, which is usually sold as a subscription service. As discussed in the following sections, each type of implementation has advantages and limitations.

On-Premises Implementation

An on-premises email archiving implementation offers significant advantages, but organizations that want to install and operate email archiving applications on their own servers must address a combination of technical and operational requirements and challenges:

- Proponents of on-premises email archiving cite the advantage of direct control over the archiving installation, including selection and scaling of the server configuration, storage capacity, network infrastructure, and other system components to satisfy an organization's performance requirements and expectations.
- An on-premises email archiving implementation allows an organization to customize and streamline user interfaces by changing screen layouts and menus, simplifying navigation elements, highlighting frequently used operations, removing features that are not needed, adding help screens and tutorials, changing the interface language, and incorporating the organization's own logos, colors, or other branding. These customization can create a better user experience and ensure accessibility by all mailbox owners and others who may need to access archived messages.
- An on-premises implementation will ensure that the email archiving application is compatible with the organization's security requirements and protocols, including encryption of archived messages, malware scanning software, firewalls, and intrusion detection and prevention systems. An on-premises installation also gives an organization direct control of the physical location where the application operates.
- An on-premises implementation gives an organization control over data backup and recovery, including the frequency of backup, storage location of backup copies, and encryption of backup copies.
- An on-premises email archiving implementation also enables an organization to ensure compliance with country-specific retention requirements, data residency requirements, and restrictions on cross-border transfer of email messages that contain personally-identifiable information.
- An on-premises implementation provides complete control over the integration of email archiving with an external application, whether it is custom-developed or a commercially available product. Cloud-based email archiving services offer prebuilt connectors and other tools to simplify integration with popular commercial software, but fewer tools are available to support integration with applications that an organization has developed for its own use. If both email

archiving and the external application operate in-house, data can be exchanged faster than with a cloud-based email archiving service that transfers data over the internet.
- As discussed below, cloud-based email archiving services have minimal start-up costs. By contrast, an on-premises implementation involves significant capital expenditures for email archiving software and equipment to operate it. While some email archiving vendors have adopted subscription pricing to better compete with cloud services, some organizations prefer to purchase a perpetual license for email archiving software for a one-time fee. This will reduce their long-term costs, but the perpetual license fee does not include the continuing cost of annual contracts for software upgrades and technical support.
- An organization undertaking an on-premises implementation may need to purchase a new server or upgrade an existing server on which the email archiving application will operate. The organization must also buy or upgrade storage devices for the email archive and network components to ensure reliable access by mailbox owners. Over time, additional infrastructure upgrades may be needed to accommodate a growing quantity of archived email and users. An organization may also incur additional costs for operating system and database licenses that the email archiving application requires.
- Installation, testing, operation, and maintenance of an email archiving application will require time and effort by an organization's information technology staff, who may require vendor-supplied training to get the application up and running. Depending on the size and complexity of an organization's email environment, an on-premises implementation may not be fully operational for weeks or months after the archiving application is installed. Postinstallation, additional staff involvement will be necessary to perform troubleshooting and make any modifications required to keep the application operating reliably.

Email Archiving Appliances

An email archiving appliance, also known as email archiving server, is a self-contained configuration of computer hardware and preinstalled software designed for simplified on-premises deployment and high performance archiving of messages and attachment:

- As their principal advantage, email archiving appliances are designed for rapid implementation. As an alternative to installation and operation of an email archiving application on an organization's

own server, an email archiving appliance can be fully operational with a few days or less after it is delivered. Email archiving software is preinstalled on, fully integrated with, and optimized for the appliance's hardware components.
- An email archiving appliance's hardware components include a server and data storage devices—usually fault-tolerant hard drives. Some appliances also include tape backup components. Most vendors have a scalable product line with multiple models that vary in processing speed, storage capacity, and the number of users supported. Processing power, storage capacity, network bandwidth, and other factors impact performance. In large organizations with a high-volume input and retrieval activity, multiple archiving appliances can be clustered for improved performance, redundancy, high availability, and convenient upward scalability.
- An email archiving appliance can be installed by the vendor, an authorized reseller, or an organization's own information technology staff. An email archiving appliance typically requires a larger capital expenditure than on-premises installation of email archiving software on an organization's own servers, but some organizations may prefer the ease of implementation that an all-in-one configuration offers.
- Because it is preconfigured and ready to deploy when delivered, an email archiving appliance may be a good choice for small organizations with limited information technology staff or for organizations of any size that are interested in a plug-and-play on-premises archiving solution. An email archiving appliance will need some information technology support, however, for postinstallation software patches and upgrades, hardware replacement, performance optimization, storage expansion, and general troubleshooting.
- In a large organization with a complex information technology infrastructure, installation of an email archiving appliance may require considerable time and effort, particularly if customizations, migration from an existing email archiving system, or integration with external applications are involved.
- Email archiving appliances may be sold by developers of email archiving software as well as by providers of cloud-based email archiving services that want to offer their customers an on-premises solution for all or part of their archived messages. Where bandwidth is constrained, an email archiving appliance can be used in a hybrid on-premises/cloud implementation where large quantities of messages and attachments will be captured locally for access during the workday and uploading to a cloud provider during off-peak hours.

Cloud Services

As an alternative to installation and operation of email archiving software on an organization's own computer system, some email archiving vendors offer cloud versions of their on-premises products. Other vendors offer email archiving exclusively as a cloud service. Interest in cloud-based email archiving is driven by increased adoption of cloud computing as an alternative or supplement to in-house data centers in general and to cloud-based email services as a replacement for on-premises email servers in particular.

Cloud-based email archiving has the customary technical and administrative advantages of other cloud-based services discussed this book:

- Compared to an on-premises implementation, cloud email archiving can be deployed more rapidly with less involvement by information technology staff or consultants. Servers, storage devices, and network components do not need to be purchased, installed, configured, and tested. The electronic email archiving application is pretested and fully operational on the provider's cloud servers, but the organization must integrate with its email platform and define email archiving rules, identify authorized users, establish retention policies, and specify other operating parameters.
- A cloud-based email archiving implementation involves minimal start-up costs. Cloud customers pay a monthly or annual subscription fee based on the number of users, the quantity of storage required, the specific capabilities required, and the desired level of customer support. Capital expenditures for new or upgraded computing equipment, network components, and other information technology infrastructure are eliminated. An organization does not need to purchase email archiving software, but some cloud providers charge a one-time setup fee for new customers. Additional charges will accrue if email must be migrated from another cloud provider or an on-premises archiving implementation. While most cloud services can be accessed by web browsers, some providers require special client software to take advantage of all available archiving functionality.
- Cloud-based email archiving services are immediately scalable. An organization can add or remove users or increase storage capacity to address changing requirements. Cloud providers can allocate or reduce resources for a given customer on demand without disrupting archiving services.
- Hardware and software upgrades, which may be difficult and costly in on-premises archiving implementations, are handled by cloud-based email archiving services without customer involvement.

Cloud providers monitor performance and upgrade their archiving platforms regularly to increase processing power, expand storage capacity, fix software defects, and incorporate software enhancements. These improvements are implemented in the background or during off-peak hours to ensure that email archiving services remain accessible. Customers are typically notified in advance if scheduled maintenance will cause disruptions.
- Customers connect to cloud-based email archiving services via the internet. The global reach of cloud-based archiving is well suited to organizations with a geographically dispersed workforce. This include multinational organizations as well as any government agency, company, or nonprofit entity whose employees work remotely all or part of the time. Many cloud-based email archiving providers serve a worldwide customer base from multiple data centers located in different parts of the world. This allows cloud-based email archiving to satisfy many data residency regulations that require in-country storage and retention of email. An on-premises email archiving implementation is necessary, however, in countries where the cloud provider does not have a physical presence or reliable internet connections are not available.
- As noted in other chapters, some organizations have adopted a cloud-first policy that prioritizes cloud services over on-premises computing when planning information technology initiatives. In keeping with that policy, many organizations have replaced their on-premises email applications with a cloud-based email service. An organization can have cloud-based email with on-premises email archiving, but a cloud-based archiving service may be preferable. Some cloud-based email services include archiving capabilities. A single service for email and archiving simplifies monitoring and management of email activities. Users may benefit if a combined services offers a consistent interface.
- Some organizations prefer on-premises installation and operation of email archiving for security and privacy, but cloud-based archiving providers have made extensive investments in security measures to protect archived email and prevent unauthorized access to or alteration of messages and attachments. They employ data encryption, multifactor authentication, regular security audits, malware detection, and other electronic safeguards. Data centers that host email archiving services are protected by round-the-clock security personnel and surveillance. These precautions are comparable to those of the best on-premises archiving implementations.
- For backup protection and disaster recovery, some cloud-based email archiving services replicate messages and attachment in

real-time across multiple, geographically dispersed data centers. Backup copies are encrypted and validated regularly for continued reliability.

Hybrid Implementations

On-premises installation and cloud-based email archiving are not mutually exclusive implementation options. They can be combined to take advantage of the distinctive attributes of each approach. For example:

- Incoming and outgoing messages can be captured in real-time by an on-premises email archiving application and forwarded to a cloud-based archiving service for storage, retrieval, and retention. Copies may be kept by the on-premises archiving application for a predetermined period of time following transfer to the cloud service then deleted to keep local storage requirements at a manageable level. The cloud implementation, which is more readily scalable than an on-premises installation, will be expanded as necessary to store a growing quantity of archived messages.
- Copies of messages that are archived by an on-premises application may be forwarded to a cloud-based email archiving service for backup and accessibility when the on-premises implementation is unavailable. Unlike the preceding example, messages are not deleted from the on-premises archive following transfer to the cloud. Copies are kept in both locations. In addition to ensuring continuous access to archived email, redundant storage will decrease the likelihood that messages needed for regulatory compliance or to support mission-critical operations will be damaged or inadvertently deleted. This approach may also be useful for organizations with geographically dispersed offices or remote workers who are unable to connect to the on-premises email archiving application but can access the cloud provider via the internet.
- A hybrid approach may be useful in organizations with multiple on-premises email archiving installations that operate independently in geographically dispersed divisions, branches, subsidiaries, or affiliated enterprises. Archived messages from each application can be transferred to a cloud-based service, which will function as a unified email archive to support information sharing and collaboration by related entities. Single-instance storage detects and consolidates duplicate messages from multiple sources.
- To test the technology and develop operating procedures, an organization may use a cloud-based email archiving service for a pilot implementation, then transition to an on-premises archiving instal-

lation for an enterprise-wide rollout, at which point cloud-based archiving will be discontinued. Cloud email archiving, which offer rapid deployment with a minimal capital investment, are well suited to pilot implementations. Alternatively, an on-premises pilot implementation may transition to and ultimately be replaced by a cloud-based email archiving service.
- An organization may utilize a cloud-based service as its primary email archiving platform, but operate an on-premises archiving application for selected email, such as messages the must retained for regulatory compliance or messages that are subject to legal holds for litigation.
- To support hybrid implementations, some vendors of email archiving software offer a cloud-based service that utilizes the same archiving application as their on-premises installation product line. A single interface provides access to both on-premises and cloud-based archival repositories.

SUMMARY OF MAJOR POINTS

- Email archiving applications maintain messages and attachments in an external repository that is optimized for email storage and retention. The messages are accompanied by its date, time, sender, recipient(s), and other metadata. Message content and metadata are typically archived in their original file formats, although they may subsequently be converted to a different format for data migration or preservation purposes.
- A systematic approach to email archiving can improve the performance of on-premises email installations, simplify email backup operations, reduce storage requirements and costs for a given quantity of messages and attachments, support compliance with email retention mandates, facilitate the preservation of email needed for legal proceedings, and provide other legal and operational benefits.
- Depending on the email archiving application, messages and attachments can enter an archival repository by direct transfer from user mailboxes or through real-time capture of inbound and outbound email.
- Email archiving applications must provide scalable storage capacity at a reasonable cost to address the voluminous quantity of messages, large size of many email attachments, and changing needs of current and prospective customers.
- Email archiving applications use several techniques to optimize storage resources in an archival repository and simplify backup opera-

tions. Data compression can significantly reduce the space required to store a given quantity of messages. Single-instance storage, also known as de-duplication, stores one copy of messages that are sent to multiple recipients.
- As an optional capability, some email archiving applications can encrypt messages for storage or for transfer to or from an archival repository. Encryption may be useful or necessary for archived messages and attachments that require safeguards beyond password protection, network access controls, and other measures designed to prevent unauthorized access to the email archive.
- An email archiving application adds value to an organization's email installation by maintaining an organized repository of indexed messages and attachments for searching and retrieval by authorized users. Indexing of archived email may be based on metadata or the full-text or messages and attachments.
- Access privileges for archived messages are assigned by system administrators based on organizational policy. In most implementations, mailbox owners have access to their own messages, they may be limited to read-only access to prevent alteration or deletion of archived messages.
- Mailbox owners and other authorized persons can use an email archiving system's search capabilities to retrieve messages for display, printing, downloading, response, forwarding, or—if permitted—return to an originating mailbox. Most email archiving applications maintain audit logs that track access, deletion, exporting, changes in access privileges, and other actions related to archived messages.
- Email archiving applications can implement an organization's retention rules for messages and attachments. Email archiving applications are compatible with schedule-based retention periods or a uniform retention period. Messages and attachments will be deleted or otherwise removed from the archival repository when their retention periods elapse.
- An email archiving applications may be sold as software for installation and operation on an organization's own computers, packaged as an integrated configuration of hardware and software components, or offered as a cloud-based, hosted application, which is usually sold as a subscription service.
- An on-premises email archiving implementation offers significant advantages, but organizations that want to install and operate email archiving applications on their own servers must address a combination of technical and operational requirements and challenges.
- Some email archiving vendors offer cloud versions of their on-premises products. Other vendors offer email archiving exclusively

as a cloud service. Interest in cloud-based email archiving is driven by increased adoption of cloud computing as an alternative or supplement to in-house data centers in general and to cloud-based email services as a replacement for on-premises email servers in particular.
- On-premises installation and cloud-based email archiving are not mutually exclusive implementation options. They can be combined in hybrid implementations to take advantage of the distinctive attributes of each approach.

5

✣

Digital Asset Management

Citing usage from the early nineteenth century, the *Oxford English Dictionary* defines an asset as "an item of value owned."[1] Other dictionary definitions similarly equate assets with valuable resources owned by an organization or individual. ISO 55000:2024, *Asset management—Vocabulary, overview, and principles* extends the definition to encompass things or entities that have potential or actual value to an organization, including tangible assets such as equipment, inventory, and other physical property as well as brands, intellectual property rights, use rights, licenses, and other intangible assets. The ISO 55000 standard further defines asset management as a coordinated activity to realize value from an asset.[2]

ISO/IEC 19770-1:2017, *Information technology—IT asset management—Part 1: IT asset management systems—Requirements* defines a digital asset as "an IT asset expressed electronically in a digital format" and IT asset management as a coordinated activity to realize value from an IT asset, including software assets and digital information content assets, which are files or other digital entities that contain information.[3] This definition of digital assets is broadly applicable to word-processing files, spreadsheets, email messages, digital images, web pages, and other digital content that has legal, operational, or historical value to a government agency, company, or other organization. Similarly, the above definition of asset management might apply to the digital content managed by ECM applications, RMA software, digital preservation applications, and email archiving systems discussed in preceding chapters, but digital asset management (DAM) has a narrower focus and distinctive purpose that distinguish it from other technologies.

While DAM applications can manage any digital information, they are principally intended for storage, cataloging, indexing, retrieval, distribution, and protection of digital assets with visual and audio content. These digital assets are sometimes characterized as "rich media assets," a phrase that emphasizes their multimedia content in marked contrast to textual documents. Examples of rich media assets include photographs, video recordings, logos, illustrations, animation, three-dimensional models, product imagery, podcasts, webinars, and recorded music, voice, and sound effects. In companies, government agencies, cultural institutions, and other organizations, these digital assets are important and, in some cases, revenue-generating resources that must be safeguarded and tightly controlled. They may support publishing and broadcasting, film and video production, educational programs, marketing initiatives, public relations campaigns, customer support activities, or other operations. Digital assets may have intrinsic monetary value if an organization can sell or license digital assets for authorized use by others. By contrast, most office documents, email messages, and other business records have little if any marketable value. Sale of business records that contain personal data or trade secrets is typically prohibited by law unless the consent of all affected parties is obtained.

Like ECM applications with which it shares many characteristics and capabilities, DAM technology is principally intended for content that is in the active phase of the information lifecycle, the period when a digital asset must be conveniently available and readily retrievable. The active phase of the information lifecycle begins when a digital asset is created or collected and ends when the asset is no longer needed to support ongoing operations or activities. Like the active phase of business records, which is often aligned with the completion time for transactions, projects, or other operations, the duration of the active phase for a given digital asset depends on the asset's purpose, content, audience, production quality, and other factors. A podcast that deals with current events, for example, will likely have a short active life. Similarly, animation or product photographs created for an advertising campaign may be needed for a few weeks to several years, depending on the campaign's success and the product's continued commercial viability. On the other hand, some digital assets, like corporate logos, can remain in use for decades, while digital images of art works from a museum's collection may be needed indefinitely to respond to requests from researchers, publishers, and others.

DAM applications provide little, if any, built-in support for managed retention of digital assets that are in the inactive phase of information lifecycle. As noted in a later section, digital assets can be timestamped with the date of last usage, which can be used to identify aging assets that might be deleted, but manual review will be necessary to confirm obsolescence. Time-based retention periods or expiration dates can be included among the metadata for assets stored in a DAM repository, but a workflow script would have to be written to identify and purge assets with elapsed retention periods. Otherwise, inactive digital assets will remain in a DAM application until they are manually removed or replaced. Inactive digital assets with continuing legal, operational, or historical value can be transferred to an archival repository managed by RMA software or a digital preservation application.

HISTORY

DAM applications became commercially available in early 1990s. Before that time, organizations stored their small but growing collections of digital assets on file servers, local hard drives, or optical disks, possibly accompanied by a simple database or spreadsheet that served as an online catalog. As with other technologies discussed in this book, the first DAM applications were developed by specialized start-up companies whose founders recognized the technology's potential. Some of these start-ups were subsequently acquired by larger computer and software companies interested in offering a broader range of technologies to their current and prospective customers. Compared to other technologies discussed in this book, however, the digital asset management industry has seen less acquisition and consolidation. DAM software developers that remained independent have since been joined by new entrants. All DAM vendors have continued to improve and expand their product offerings.

At the outset, DAM applications were niche products intended for media-intensive enterprises with growing collections of digital photographs, video recordings, and audio files that were rapidly replacing slides, photographic negatives, photographic prints, analog videotapes, audio cassettes, and other nondigital media. Early adopters were publishers, broadcasting companies, film studios, and music producers, well as the marketing firms, advertising agencies, professional photographers, and graphic designers that provided them with promotional and creative services. Interest in DAM technology expanded in the early 2000s to include museums, libraries, archives, historical societies, and other cultural heritage organizations with large collections of digital images as well as corporate communications departments, creative teams, product managers, sales teams, and marketing departments that needed to manage product images, promotional videos, multimedia presentations, and other digital content. By the 2010s, the market for DAM applications had broadened to encompass a variety of digital assets maintained by a wide range of companies, government agencies, educational institutions, healthcare providers, and nonprofit organizations.

Digital asset management is not the only technology that deals with digital audio-visual assets. In broadcasting companies, film production facilities, television studios, and the music recording industry, DAM applications compete or coexist with Media Asset Management (MAM) systems. Both technologies can handle large media files and have some overlapping features, but they differ in purpose and functionality. MAM systems provide highly specialized capabilities to manage, convert, and deliver video and audio assets. MAM implementations tend to be closely integrated with an organization's media production, editing, and distribution processes. To support those operations, they provide automated video transcoding, live feed recording, audio waveform visualization, captioning management, and other advanced video and audio features that most DAM applications do not offer.

DAM applications, for their part, have evolved to support a broad range of business operations and content types, including textual as well as audio-visual assets. As such, they overlap the capabilities of some other technologies discussed in this book. Organizations use DAM applications to store, retrieve, control, and distribute an increasingly diverse array of digital content, including product designs and specifications, customer support materials, user manuals, training materials, survey results, and licensing agreements. Some organizations also use DAM applications for storage and retrieval of office documents, spreadsheets, source code files, and web and app development files, but other technologies are better suited to such digital content.

Reflecting this expanded usage, revenues of DAM vendors have increased significantly in the past decade. Market researchers predict strong growth as the quantity and importance of digital assets increase, advanced features enhance the usefulness of DAM products, prospective customers become aware of the technology's capabilities, and cloud-based implementations make DAM applications accessible to smaller organizations that lack the technological expertise and start-up funds needed for an on-premises installation. Based on a Google Trends analysis of web searches for the phrase "digital asset management," worldwide interest in DAM concepts and technology has remained steady since 2010.

BUSINESS NEED

The business case for digital asset management is based on the technology's advantages for organizations that maintain audio-visual content and related materials. As the principal source of these advantages, a DAM application creates and maintains a centralized repository, sometimes described as an asset library, as a single, authoritative resource for efficient storage, reliable retrieval, and systematic control of an organization's digital assets:

- In the absence of a DAM implementation, few organizations have an enterprise-wide catalog of their digital asset. Uncoordinated assets maintained by individual divisions or departments in multiple storage locations may be organized in different ways, assuming that they are organized at all, which makes them difficult to find when needed. Assets needed for a given purpose may be maintained in several or many local repositories, which must be identified and searched individually. By contrast, a centrally managed DAM repository can be organized and indexed for convenient, comprehensive retrieval of specific content when needed.
- A centralized DAM repository is typically limited to the latest versions of an organization's approved assets—that is, audio-visual content that has been reviewed by designated stakeholders for quality, legal compliance, usage rights, and other attributes. Unapproved assets are excluded. Superseded versions will be clearly identified as such. Alternatively, they may be removed from the DAM repository or rendered inaccessible, thereby preventing their use.
- A centralized DAM repository simplifies collection of information about the use of digital assets for specific purposes, integration of digital asset management with external applications, backup operations, and recovery of digital assets that may be damaged or lost due to disastrous events, careless handling, user error, equipment or software malfunction, or other causes.
- A centralized DAM repository can have a uniform folder taxonomy for digital assets. Consistent metadata standards and indexing processes can be applied to digital assets at the folder or item level. Assets created by multiple departments can be searched simultaneously. A single searchable repository with uniform categorization and retrieval procedures simplifies user training.
- Decentralized repositories with inadequate safeguards against improper use can compromise the strategic and commercial value of proprietary images, logos, copyright-protected assets, and other intellectual property. DAM applications incorporate security features that prevent unauthorized access to and distribution of digital assets. An audit log that tracks access to and use of specific assets provides information for security reviews and investigations.
- A DAM application can track usage rights, permissions, expiration dates, and restrictions for licensed digital assets that have been legally obtained or purchased under specific terms and conditions.

- As discussed in a later section, a DAM application allows authorized users to download digital assets to external applications for further processing. Alternatively, many DAM applications provide content creation tools that allow digital assets to be incorporated into documents, posted social media sites, added to web pages, or otherwise used to support business operations.
- A DAM application's centralized repository promotes enterprise-wide resource sharing. Assuming appropriate network connections, authorized users have access to digital assets at any time from any location. This is a particularly important benefit where geographically dispersed teams in different time zones will collaborate on advertising campaigns, new product launches, media production, package design, and other projects involving digital assets.
- DAM applications support workflow functionality that simplifies the review, approval, utilization, and distribution of digital assets. DAM applications can also import data from and exchange data with content management, customer relationship management, product management, brand management, and other applications that maintain digital content.

STANDARDS AND GUIDELINES

There are no international standards that deal specifically with digital assessment management, but ISO standards pertaining to other business operations and technologies may contain useful guidance for DAM implementations. More directly relevant are guidelines and best practices developed by professional groups, particularly those concerned with management of visual materials and their associated metadata maintained by cultural heritage organizations:

- The Digital Asset Management System Open Specification was issued in 2020 by *Digital Asset Management News*, a publication that provides reports and opinions about industry developments. The specification delineates basic, intermediate, and advanced features and capabilities of DAM applications in twenty functional areas. It updates and expands a list of ten core characteristics issued in 2014 by the DAM Foundation, a nonprofit organization that is no longer in existence. *Digital Asset Management News* has posted the specification online as a Word document, which can be reviewed and edited by vendors, consultants, end-users, and others. *Digital Asset Management News* has also issued the SimpleDAM API Protocol for interoperability between DAM applications and external systems.

- A DAM maturity model was issued under a Creative Common license in 2012 by the DAM Foundation and the Real Story Group, a technology analysis firm. Like its counterpart for other activities, the model is a useful tool for evaluating DAM initiatives. It specifies competency levels and evaluative criteria for the systems, processes, content, and staff involved in a DAM implementation.
- The VRA Core is a metadata standard developed by the Visual Resources Association, a multidisciplinary nonprofit group, for the description of paintings, drawings, sculpture, photographs, and other visual resources. The VRA Core is hosted by the Library of Congress, which maintains a registry of cultural heritage organizations that have implemented it for their collections.
- Categories for the Description of Works of Art (CDWA) is a set of best-practice guidelines developed by the Art Information Task Force with funding from the J. Paul Getty Trust. It specifies core and extended metadata categories for describing cultural heritage objects at varying degrees of specificity and exhaustivity.
- The Dublin Core metadata set, which was discussed in preceding chapters, is sufficiently adaptable to work with a variety of visual materials and other digital assets. The Metadata Object Description Schema (MODS), which was developed by the Library of Congress, provides a larger set of metadata elements intended specifically for describing digital content maintained by libraries, archives, and other cultural heritage organizations.
- The IPTC Photo Metadata standard, issued by the International Press Telecommunications Council, defines core and extended schemas for description and rights management for digital images created by cameras and scanners. It is widely used by new agencies, photographic agencies, museums, libraries, and other organizations.
- ISO 55001:2024, *Asset management—Management systems—Requirements* presents recommendations for establishment, implementation, maintenance, and improvement of asset management systems and methods in general. ISO 55001:2018, *Asset management—Management systems—Guidelines for the application of ISO 55001* provides examples to align asset management initiatives with organizational objectives.
- ISO/IEC 19770-1:2017, *Information technology—IT asset management—Part 1: IT asset management systems—Requirements*, which was cited at the beginning of this chapter, is one of a series or international standards that deal with management of computer hardware and software assets, including digital information content assets. The principles and recommendations presented in other ISO 19770 series standards can be applied to DAM implementations, although they are not explicitly covered. Examples include ISO/IEC 19770-3:2016,

Information technology—IT asset management—Part 3: ISO/IEC 19770-4:2017, *Entitlement schema; Information technology—IT asset management—Part 4:* ISO/IEC 19770-11-2020, and *Information technology—IT asset management—Part 11: IT asset management systems—Requirements for bodies providing audit and certification of IT asset management systems.*

- ISO/IEC 15938-5:2003, *Information technology—Multimedia content description interface—Part 5: Multimedia description schemes,* also known as the MPEG-7 standard, presents a common set of descriptors for visual and audio content, including genre, summaries, color, texture, motion, object shape, and sound properties.
- ISO/IEC TS 22424-1:2020, *Digital publishing—EPUB3 preservation—Part 1: Principles* and ISO/IEC TS 22424-2:2020, *Digital publishing—EPUB3 preservation—Part 2: Metadata requirements* provide recommendations and guidance for electronic publications in the EPUB format, an open standard that may be encountered in DAM implementations.
- ISO 14721:2012, *Space data and information transfer systems—Open archival information system (OAIS)—Reference model* and other standards discussed in chapter 3 are relevant for DAM applications implemented in the context of digital preservation. Many digital preservation initiatives involve art works, photographs, sound recordings, and other audio-visual materials maintained by museums, libraries, archives, and other cultural heritage organizations. Some digital preservation applications support digital asset management functionality as a standard or optional feature.
- Several standards address digital asset management in the context of blockchain technology. IEEE 2418.10-2022, *Standard for Blockchain Based Digital Asset Management* defines a framework, processes, and functional roles for a DAM implementation based on blockchain concepts, which are secure, prevent unauthorized modification or deletion of digital assets, and support digital rights management. IEEE 3207-2022, *Standard for Blockchain Based Digital Asset Identification* defines data structures and formats for identification of digital assets in blockchain systems.

FEATURES AND CAPABILITIES

Of the information governance technologies discussed in this book, digital asset management most closely resembles enterprise content management; indeed, several ECM products can be configured with an optional digital asset management module, and some DAM vendors promote their content management capabilities. Both technologies are designed for management of unstructured digital content that is in the active phase of the information lifecycle, but DAM and ECM applications differ in the capabilities they provide and the business functions they support. As noted in chapter 1, ECM applications can manage a broad spectrum of digital content, but most ECM implementations involve storage and retrieval of office documents and other business records. ECM applications can store and retrieve an organization's audio and visual recordings, but ECM is not the best technology for organizations with complicated image-processing and rights-management requirements. By contrast, DAM applications are optimized for storage, retrieval, and control of visual and audio content. While there is some overlap with ECM functionality, DAM applications support distinctive features and capabilities that are described in the following sections.

Asset Capture

DAM applications are not designed to create digital assets; they collect, store, and manage content that is created by desktop publishing applications, graphic design software, video and audio production systems, three-dimensional modeling software, digital cameras, document scanners, and other applications or devices. The content may be created in the regular course of business activities by the organization that implements a DAM application or acquired from external sources. Asset capture is the process of importing this content from its current storage location into a centralized repository managed by a DAM application. DAM software developers continue to refine and expand the available methods for capturing digital assets:

- Individual digital assets or groups of assets can be manually uploaded into a DAM application by dragging and dropping them from shared drives or other storage locations into specific folders or subfolder within a DAM-managed repository. A file browser can be used to navigate through the directory of a shared drive, local drive, or other storage resource to select the assets to be uploaded. DAM applications are compatible with uploaded assets in a broad range of formats for images, video, audio, and text.
- Manual selection is appropriate for uploading a few assets at a time. To reduce labor requirements and expedite the capture process where large numbers of digital assets are involved, files can be uploaded in batches from designated directories or subdirectories on network servers, personal computers, or cloud-based repositories. Where voluminous quantities of assets are involved, most DAM applications can connect to an FTP server.

- Some DAM applications will continuously or periodically check for new digital assets on FTP servers or other designated storage locations and automatically upload them. Connectors may be available to upload assets from designated cloud storage providers.
- Some DAM applications allow authorized users to upload digital assets by emailing them as attachments to a specific mailbox.
- DAM applications increasingly support mobile apps that will upload photographs, video recordings, and audio recordings directly from smartphones and tablets.
- Some DAM applications allow an organization to create automated workflows for control of the uploading process and for review and approval of uploaded assets. These workflows can accelerate uploading of large quantities of digital assets, promote consistency, and minimize manual intervention for asset capture.
- Whatever capture method is utilized, a DAM application monitors the uploading process for network malfunctions, upload interruptions, unsupported file formats, invalid file names, incomplete files, oversize files, duplicate assets, versioning conflicts, files infected by malware, or other problems that require intervention and corrective action. Image files will be examined for acceptable resolution. Some DAM applications can convert rejected files to acceptable formats.
- Like the digital preservation applications discussed in chapter 4, some DAM applications will perform validation checks on uploaded assets using checksum verification or other mathematical algorithms to identify content that may have been corrupted during the upload process. Some DAM applications can also monitor incoming digital assets for copyright violations or other rights management issues.
- Some DAM applications allow organizations to create subrepositories for different purposes, asset types, or user groups. Each subrepository can have its own rules and restrictions for acceptable asset sources, uploading permissions, supported file formats, data validation, de-duplication, and other aspects of the capture process. Automated workflows can be customized for different subrepositories or asset types.

File Plans and Metadata

File plans and metadata support the management, control, and retrieval of digital assets maintained by a DAM application. Many of the file plan and metadata concepts and issues discussed in preceding chapters apply to DAM implementations:

- File plans organize and categorize digital assets in a structured, consistent manner to facilitate access by authorized users. DAM applica-

tions support customer-defined file plans consisting of a hierarchical framework of folders and subfolders nested to multiple levels. Digital assets might be organized by type, by the products or activities to which they relate, by the department that created them, by date, or in another way that will enable them to be located with needed.
- As an example, a file plan for digital assets related to an organization's marketing campaigns for specific products might have the following structure:

    Top-level folder: Product name
       Second-level folder: Print materials
       Second-level folder: Email marketing
       Second-level folder: Website advertising
       Second-level folder: Social media content
          Third-level folder: Instagram
          Third-level folder: Facebook
          Third-level folder: X
       Second-level folder: Video-sharing platforms
          Third-level folder: YouTube
          Third-level folder: TikTok
       Second-level folder: Events
          Third-level folder: Conferences and trade shows
          Third-level folder: Webinars

- A file plan must be tailored to the requirements of a specific collection of digital assets, and it must be sufficiently flexible and scalable to permit the addition or removal of categories and subcategories as needed. Some DAM software developers or other providers offer prebuilt file plans for the digital assets associated with specific industries or business operations. An organization can adapt and edit these file plans to suit its purposes.
- DAM applications support customer-defined metadata at the folder, subfolder, or asset level. Specific metadata elements will vary for one DAM implementation to another, depending on the types of digital assets involved and an organization's retrieval and control requirements. Most DAM implementations involve a combination of descriptive metadata, which supports retrieval of digital assets; administrative metadata, which supports a DAM application's control and management processes; technical metadata, which documents the structure and format of digital assets; and rights metadata, which documents the intellectual property rights and access restrictions that apply to digital assets.
- Many organizations adapt their metadata schemes from an existing reference model. The metadata standards discussed in a preceding section provide an excellent starting point for selecting metadata

elements for a particular collection of digital assets. Organizations can modify these reference models to address special requirements. Metadata elements can be added and unnecessary elements eliminated. DAM applications impose few limitations on the number of metadata elements or the acceptable types of metadata values. Metadata entry may be specified as mandatory for some elements, optional for others.
- Rights metadata, which plays a critical role in many DAM implementations, ensures that digital assets are used in a manner that complies with applicable laws, licensing agreements, and organizational policies. Examples of right metadata include the identity of the individual or organization that holds the property rights to a digital asset; information about the type, scope, terms, and conditions of licenses that specify how, where, and when an asset can be used, including any applicable restrictions; expiration and renewal dates for licensing arrangements; and information about permissible sublicensing.
- Metadata values can be entered manually or extracted automatically from information contained in the digital assets themselves. Authorized users can key-enter metadata values for each folder, subfolder, or asset after it is uploaded into a DAM application.
- Some digital assets contain embedded metadata values, which a DAM application will identify, extract, and match to the appropriate metadata fields. A digital photograph, for example, contains information about the creator, date and time of creation; the geographic location where the photograph was taken; the image format, the image size, and the image resolution; and certain camera characteristics, such as the brand and model, the lens used, the focal length, and the shutter speed. Music files contain information about the artist, song, release year, genre, and the album on which it appears. Digital video files contain information about the bit rate, frame rate, creation date, codec, and recording device used.
- Some graphic design software, image editing tools, and other applications that produce digital assets can add metadata to an asset as part of the creation or editing process. Alternatively, metadata can be automatically imported from an external application. To support this, most DAM applications provide optional connectors or other software tools for integration with external resources, although some integrations may require customizations that take time and effort to develop.
- DAM applications increasingly incorporate machine learning, computer vision, and other artificial intelligence technologies that can extract metadata values from nontextual assets by identifying objects,

people, scenes, or logos in images or videos and by detecting specific speakers or sounds in audio recordings. Voice recognition can be used to transcribe audio recordings into searchable text. Artificial intelligence can also use sentiment analysis to determine the emotional tone of customer surveys, feedback forms, product reviews, social media posts, chat transcripts, voice mail messages, recorded interactions with customers, and other textual or audio assets. Steady and significant refinement of these artificial intelligence capabilities is expected.

Search and Retrieval

For many organizations, the ability to quickly locate digital assets needed to support business operations is a prime motive for a DAM implementation as it is for other information government technologies. As an alternative to time-wasting searches for assets that are scattered across multiple storage devices, a well-planned DAM implementation maintains a unified collection of digital assets in a comprehensive, centralized repository that is optimized for effective searching by authorized users:

- Digital assets can be retrieved by manually browsing through the folders and subfolders maintained in a DAM repository or by searching the metadata values associated with folders, subfolders, or individual assets. If a DAM application maintains multiple subrepositories, authorized users may be able to search them simultaneously. Some DAM applications support simultaneous searching of multiple DAM installations.
- DAM applications provide a full range of retrieval commands. Authorized users can search specific metadata fields for words or phrases, asset types, the date an asset was created or last modified, or other values. Subject to variations from one DAM application to another, search statements can include Boolean operators, relational expressions, truncated search terms, and other retrieval capabilities discussed in preceding chapters. Some DAM applications support wildcard searches and fuzzy searches, which are based on inexact matching of search terms and metadata values. Full-text searching of document assets may also be supported.
- As a distinguishing feature, DAM applications make effective use of artificial intelligence functionality to support retrieval capabilities that are tailored to visual assets. Authorized users can search for images with a specified color profile, resolution, aspect ratio, or other characteristics. Video recordings can be searched by resolution, bit rate, duration, or visual content. Some DAM applications can con-

vert the spoken words in video or audio recordings to searchable text.
- DAM applications can use image recognition, face recognition, feature extraction, and other artificial intelligence tools to retrieve assets that are visually similar to a given asset or to search for assets that depict specific scenes, people, or objects. In addition to supporting retrieval operations, this capability can be used to locate duplicate images for review and possible deletion. It can also detect images that resemble copyright-protected assets.
- DAM applications respond to searches by displaying a list of retrieved content, from which the user can select one or more items for viewing. Search results may be sorted alphabetically, chronologically, by file types, by presumed relevance, by size, or by other criteria.
- Authorized users can display retrieved assets as thumbnail images or in larger sizes for preview and selection for full display or downloading. DAM applications include built-in viewers for widely encountered asset types and file formats. Compatible viewers for other file formats may be available from third parties.
- In contrast to other technologies discussed in this book, retrieved assets are more likely to be downloaded for further processing than viewed within a DAM application. A given search might retrieve dozens of digital assets. Preview images enable authorized users to examine retrieved assets without opening individual files. Users can identify assets that meet their requirements and eliminate others, thereby limiting unnecessary downloading of irrelevant assets or those with confidential or copyright-protected content. Preview images also allow users to compare similar assets or different versions of a given asset. Because preview images are smaller than their full-size counterparts, they can be displayed quickly. This is especially useful for large assets, which can be time-consuming to view or download in their entirety where bandwidth is limited.
- Authorized users can zoom in or pan around to examine preview images. Some DAM applications support advanced playback controls for preview of video assets. Some DAM applications allow users to rotate preview images of three-dimensional models.
- Following preview, authorized users can download selected digital assets for modification, annotation, enhancement, or other processing by graphic design software, video and audio editing tools, 3D modeling software, animation software, desktop publishing software, office productivity applications, web content management platforms, learning management systems, project management applications, and customer relationship management systems, among

other applications. Downloaded images may be incorporated into presentations, publications, or marketing materials; included in web pages or post on social media sites; or distributed to customers, business partners, or other external organizations via email attachments or physical media.
- Previewed assets might also be downloaded for internal communication or review or for offline reference in locations where the DAM application is inaccessible. Authorized users of DAM implementations in cultural heritage organizations may download photographs, images of artworks, or other digital assets for research or study.
- Some DAM applications allow authorized users to transform retrieved images for preview or downloading without leaving the application. Depending on the application, images can be resized, cropped, enhance, rotated, mirror-reversed, reformatted, converted to grayscale, upscaled, or downscaled. Colors can be changed, background removed, and unwanted objects erased. These modifications allow a DAM application to make images available for different purposes without storing multiple versions.
- Some DAM applications allow authorized users to annotate preview images or downloaded assets. Watermarks can be applied to specific assets to signify ownership, incorporate a logo or other trademark, label copies as unofficial, identify copyright-protected content, prevent unauthorized reproduction or distribution of downloaded assets, identify images intended for preview only, embed metadata in asset previews, or for other purposes. With some DAM applications, organizations can customize the size, position, opacity, and other characteristics of watermarks.
- A DAM application may include an embedded player with playback controls for preview of audio assets. Some DAM applications can provide waveform visualizations that depict an audio asset's characteristics. A transcript preview may be available for nonmusical voice recordings.
- As an alternative to downloading, DAM applications increasingly provide content creation tools that allow authorized users to incorporate retrieved assets into presentations, brochures, marketing materials, web pages, social media posts, blogs, newsletters, and other documents without leaving the application. Preformatted templates ensure that the resulting documents are consistent with an organization's brand management guidelines for page layouts, logos, color palettes, fonts, and other characteristics. An organization can customize the templates to meet its requirements. These integral content creation tools are intended for ease of use by employees with little or no design experience. While their editing and formatting capabilities

are less advanced than those offered by external applications used by professional graphic designers, they can produce polished output that is acceptable for many purposes.
- Similarly, some DAM applications include built-in tools for video editing. Authorized users can alter a video recording's bitrate, resolution, and other technical properties; add captions, subtitles, and chapter markers to video recording; merge two video recordings for cohesive playback; combine selected sections from multiple video recordings; create previews of long video recordings; shorten a video recording to a specified duration; excerpt video recording to create promotional clips or trailers; and optimize a video recording for playback on a specific device or where bandwidth is constrained.
- With some DAM applications, application programming interfaces can establish a connection with external data sources. This federated retrieval functionality allows authorized users to search content repositories maintained by ECM applications, records management applications, digital preservation systems, email archiving systems, or other external sources. The effectiveness of such federated searches may be limited by variations in the search functionality, metadata schemes, security controls, and other characteristics of individual repositories.

Access and Security

Recognizing the value of an organization's digital assets, DAM applications provide safeguards to ensure the security, integrity, reliability, confidentiality, and controlled availability of digital content and its associated metadata:

- Access privileges are assigned by a DAM administrator based on a given user's need-to-know, as determined by the user's supervisor, department head, team leader, or another person who is knowledgeable about the nature of the assets to be accessed and the user's assigned duties. Access restrictions may be imposed by an organization's legal department, compliance officer, information security team, or other stakeholders who are responsible for the protection digital assets and intellectual property rights. Access privileges may be restricted, for example, based on a user's geographic location if necessary to comply with local data privacy regulations or licensing agreements. Access privileges may be refused for remote workers where network security is inadequate.
- User privileges can be defined at the repository, subrepository, folder, subfolder, or asset levels. User privileges typically flow down

from folders to subfolders to individual assets unless an exception is specified. Access controls can be based on predefined roles, which may restrict user privileges. A predefined read-only role, for example, may allow a user to search for, preview, and download digital assets but not move, modify, or delete them. Predefined user roles can be applied to individuals or groups.

- Organizations can broaden, narrow, revoke, or otherwise redefine access privileges as circumstances warrant. Access restrictions for particular assets may increase of decrease when specific events occur. Some users may be given temporary access to certain assets until a particular project or task is completed.
- DAM applications provide reliable mechanisms to authenticate users who are allowed to access content and verify their specific privileges. The customary combination of username and password is typically used to verify a given user's identity, but some DAM applications also support multifactor authentication. Access privileges can be integrated with an organization's existing user authentication mechanisms. A DAM application may use session timeouts, automatic termination of idle sessions, and other security measures to prevent unauthorized access to digital content.
- To further protect intellectual property rights and prevent unauthorized use of licensed or copyright-protected items, some DAM applications encrypt digital assets and metadata for storage or transmission. With end-to-end encryption, assets and metadata are encrypted from the moment they are uploaded until they are decrypted by an authorized user for viewing.
- To support collaboration or information dissemination, most DAM applications allow authorized users to share digital assets with advertising agencies, marketing consultants, freelance designers and photographers, business partners, resellers, third-party developers, clients, attorneys, and other external parties who do not have user privileges. Depending on the application, this may be accomplished in several ways. With some DAM applications, authorized users can create a public portal that gives external stakeholders access to selected assets for a limited period of time. Alternatively, selected assets can be embedded in a public website. A shareable link can allow external parties to access to the latest versions of specific assets or collections without signing into the DAM application. A system administrator can set up temporary guest accounts that give external users access to specific assets, possibly with restrictions on editing, downloading, or other capabilities. With these methods, DAM applications can track the use of shared assets, which is not possible where assets are emailed to external parties.

Other Capabilities

A given DAM application may support the following capabilities as a standard feature or optional component:

- Digital assets are often modified to create new versions, which do not necessarily supersede their predecessors. Multiple versions of a given asset may serve different purposes. The versions may differ in content, quality, color palette, size, or other characteristics, depending on the asset's intended audience, the device on which it will be used, or other factors. An artist, graphic designer, or photographer may also save different versions of an asset to document the creation process and trace the development of the asset over time. Most DAM applications can track the various versions of a given asset to allow authorized users to compare them, determine which is the most recent, and rollback to a previous version where appropriate. A DAM application's versioning functionality may also track changes to the metadata and user privileges associated with specific assets over time.
- When an asset requires modification, an authorized user must check it out of the DAM repository to prevent its retrieval by others until the modification is completed and the new version is checked back in. The check-out process also prevents the simultaneous modification of a given asset by multiple users. A checked-out asset is typically downloaded for modification by an external application that provides the requisite editing functionality. Following review and approval of the modifications, the new version will be checked into the DAM repository and the original asset will either be removed or marked as superseded. Where minor adjustments to a given asset are needed, some DAM applications provide built-in editing tools that allow authorized users to modify a checked-out asset from within the application itself. These built-in editing tools might also support collaborative modification of a given asset by geographically dispersed users.
- Most DAM applications support a lightbox function that allows authorized users to assemble collections of retrieved assets. The lightbox function takes its name from the illuminated enclosure used by photographers. Lightbox collections may be created to provide convenient access to frequently used assets, to support specific projects or tasks, for use in presentations, for sharing selected assets with others, for review and approval of specific assets, for bulk downloading or distribution of selected assets, or for other purposes. Creation or removal of a light box collection does not affect the assets stored in a DAM repository. A given lightbox collection may be publicly acces-

sible or limited to designated individuals or groups. Public lightbox collections are typically restricted to view-only access. Based on defined privileges, individual assets in a private lightbox collection may be copied, edited, annotated, downloaded, or sent others. The creator of a lightbox collection can manually add or delete assets at any time. With some DAM applications, lightbox collections may be automatically updated based on specified search criteria when new assets are added to a DAM repository.
- Integrations allow a DAM application to receive assets and metadata from or transfer digital content to an external system. Application programming interfaces permit customized integration with content creation tools, graphic design software, video and audio recording and editing applications, ECM applications, file sharing services, product information systems, digital marketing systems, electronic commerce sites, social media platforms, or other sources. Some DAM vendors offer prebuilt integrations with popular business applications and online services, including those that specialize in marketing and sales support. These integrations may be based on work previously performed for other customers. Prebuilt integrations may also be available from third-party developers. Customized integrations may be developed by an organization's information technology staff, by a DAM vendor, or by a consultant or contractor. The degree of difficulty in implementing such integrations will vary with the DAM application and the external resources involved.
- In multinational organizations, a DAM application can be linked to a content delivery network (CDN) for transmission of digital assets to authorized users. A CDN provides a network of interconnected servers that store copies of the assets at geographically distributed points of presence. A given point of presence serves users within its vicinity. CDN links, which may be implemented through a prebuilt integration or an application programming interface, offload transmission of requested assets from the server on which the DAM application operates to one closer to the requester. As their principal advantage, CDN links offer fast delivery to a geographically dispersed user community, providing a consistent experience regardless of the user's location.
- Most DAM applications allow organizations to create automated workflows that facilitate and expedite the uploading and processing of digital assets. Workflow scripts can route newly captured assets to appropriate stakeholders for review and approval, monitor delays in the review and approval process, detect and reject unacceptable assets, convert incoming assets to different file formats, detect duplicates and updated versions of existing assets, identify and notify

management about assets with expiring license agreements, and distribute selected assets to individuals, groups, or external parties, including social media platforms. Workflow scripts can also exchange data between a DAM application and an external system, assuming that appropriate integration is in place. Depending on the complexity of the asset management processes to be automated, a workflow script may be written by a trained employee, by the DAM vendor, or by a contractor or consultant who specializes in workflow implementations. As with ECM applications, a workflow script must be carefully planned, properly configured, and thoroughly tested before it is rolled out and monitored for potential problems and needed improvements once it is operational.

- A DAM application can apply timestamps to identify the date and time that a given asset was created or uploaded, modified, superseded by a new version, viewed, and downloaded. Timestamps can also indicate the expiration date for licensing agreements, the date when a given asset should be posted on a social media site, or the date that a given asset should be removed from a DAM repository. Timestamps can trigger automated workflows that will release a given asset for public access or other purposes, purge obsolete assets, or transfer them to an archival repository for retention.
- Like some other technologies discussed in this book, DAM applications maintain an audit log of capture, modification, retrieval, printing, downloading, and deletion events involving specific users, assets, and metadata. The audit log provides a comprehensive historical record of user interactions with specific digital assets. It identifies the date, time, user, and type of interaction (upload, alter, view, annotate, download, etc.) in sufficient detail to determine the circumstances in which the interaction occurred. The audit log also identifies unauthorized access attempts, which may indicate a security breach. Administrators can use the audit log to troubleshoot specific problems and to analyze how, when, by whom, and for what purpose the DAM application is being used.
- The audit log can be used to generate reports that enable an organization's management and system administrators to analyze the use of digital assets, the activities of specific users, and the technology resources consumed by a DAM application. Depending on the DAM application, reports can identify the assets that are most frequently viewed or downloaded, the number of assets uploaded in a specified time period, the number of uploaded assets by type, the number of assets shared with external parties, the number of assets that have been updated or superseded, the most active DAM users, the most frequent search terms, the amounts of storage and bandwidth

utilized in a specified time period, and other activity. Reports allow decision-makers to identify underutilized assets that may require modification, repurposing, or replacement. Reports can also track the lifecycle of specific assets, identifying those that remain useful as well as obsolete or dormant assets that can be deleted or transferred to an external archival repository.
- Some DAM applications provide an integral library of stock images or access to an external collection of images that organizations can incorporate into presentations, documents, web pages, blogs, and other content. Depending on the terms and conditions of the usage license, an organization may be allowed to resize, crop, change color schemes, overlay logos, or otherwise modify the stock images for inclusion in content that is not offered for sale.

IMPLEMENTATION ISSUES

A DAM implementation begins with selection of a product and vendor that can satisfy an organization's requirements. Digital asset management is a well-established technology. Highly functional DAM applications of proven effectiveness and reliability are widely available from many qualified suppliers. The earliest DAM applications were intended for on-premises installation. Those products remain popular with many organizations, but existing and prospective customers are increasingly attracted to cloud-based DAM providers. Each implementation approach has advantages and limitation that must be carefully evaluated.

Product Evaluation

Selection of a DAM application begins with the evaluation of proposals submitted by qualified suppliers. Depending on its purchasing policies and practices, an organization may request proposals from DAM suppliers that it has identified through prior sales contact, market research, attendance at a trade show where DAM applications are exhibited, or by other means. Alternatively, the organization may issue a public request for proposals or bid invitation to obtain competitive responses from multiple DAM suppliers. In either case, a DAM application and its vendor must satisfy the following general requirements:

- A DAM application must be actively marketed in a fully operational general-release version that can be delivered and installed within a reasonable period of time after an order is placed. Experimental, developmental, or near-release products are unacceptable. The com-

mercial availability requirement applies to all standard and optional DAM components, including add-on modules developed by a DAM vendor's business partners or other external parties.
- DAM applications are complex products. A successful DAM implementation requires a significant financial expenditure as well as a serious commitment of time and effort for planning, product configuration and customization, staff training, modification of work routines, migration of existing assets, and integration with external resources. An on-premises installation will also require IT staff involvement for product installation, testing, operation, and ongoing maintenance. To justify procurement of a given DAM application or cloud-based DAM service, an organization must have reasonable assurance that it will remain commercially viable for the foreseeable future as evidenced by recent sales of the application or service to new customers and a continuing history of functional upgrades.
- An organization's information technology unit is presumably capable of supporting its existing computing and networking environment, but it may be reluctant to or unwilling to introduce unfamiliar components that will require additional training or staff. A DAM application intended for on-premises installation must be fully compatible with a prospective customer's computing and networking infrastructure, including but not necessarily limited to computers, peripheral devices, operating systems, database management software, and network connections. Whether installed on premises or cloud-based, a DAM application must be compatible with an organization's information security and backup protection protocols and practices.
- A DAM implementation will likely expand as it is integrated into an organization's business processes. Consequently, it must be able to serve a progressively larger user population and store an increasing quantity and variety of digital assets. It must permit the future addition of user licenses, and it must not impose impractical limits on the number, size, or other characteristics of digital assets it can upload, store, or process.
- Some DAM products are easier to use than others. To warrant serious consideration, a DAM application must be easily learned and convenient to use for its intended purposes on a day-to-day basis by properly instructed nontechnical employees. DAM applications with many features typically target mid-level to advanced users, but a given product must be suitable for novice or occasional users who need to perform basic tasks. Advanced capabilities aside, an organization must determine whether the core features and functions of a given DAM application can be mastered by the majority of users.

- Vendor commitment is essential for a successful DAM implementation. A DAM vendor must provide clear evidence that it has the appropriate knowledge, experience, and resources to support an organization's requirements. To evaluate a vendor's qualifications, an organization will need information about the company's history, including information about the vendor's involvement with activities and technologies related to digital assets, the vendor's financial stability and likely continued viability as evidenced by the company's latest financial statement or other appropriate documentation, and the number of DAM installations the vendor has successfully completed and types of customers.
- A DAM application must have a proven history of reliable operation and effective maintenance support in multiple installations, including organizations with requirements that are similar to those of the prospective customer. As evidence of satisfactory performance, the vendor must provide contact information for reference accounts, but an organization should reserve the right to contact other installations.
- A DAM vendor must present a realistic implementation timetable and project management plan, including specific tasks and milestones associated with product delivery, installation, configuration, testing, training, and acceptance. The vendor must specify the qualifications of employees who will be assigned to a prospective customer's account as well as employees who will service the customer postinstallation. The DAM vendor must identify subcontractors, business partners, or other third parties who will be involved in the DAM implementation and their specific responsibilities.
- Some DAM vendors sell their products through business partners, dealers, or other authorized agents or representatives who are responsible for software installation and testing, database configuration, required customizations, customer training, and postinstallation support. The DAM vendor must identify subcontractors or other third parties who will be involved in the organization's DAM implementation and their specific responsibilities. Their qualifications must be evaluated.

On-Premises vs. Cloud Implementation

Most DAM applications are available for on-premises installation on an organization's own servers or as cloud-based services. The popularity of cloud-based DAM applications has increased steadily and continued growth is expected, particularly among small to medium-size organizations that lack the capital funds or in-house technical resources necessary for an on-premises installation. Reflecting this trend, DAM software developers have introduced cloud implementations of their long-established on-premises products, and some newer DAM applications are exclusively available in cloud implementations.

Subject to minor variations, the on-premises and cloud-based versions of a given DAM application provide equivalent functionality for capture and use of digital assets, but each approach has advantages and limitations:

- An on-premises implementation gives an organization direct control over installation, testing, customization, and operation of a DAM application and the security of digital assets it maintains. An organization that operates its own DAM application controls the allocation of resources that the software requires, the devices on which digital assets are stored, the timing of backup intervals, and the hours of availability, as well as scheduled downtime for software maintenance and upgrades.
- A well-managed on-premises installation may offer a performance advantage over a cloud-based DAM application. An organization can select servers, storage devices, and network infrastructure for efficient operation of a DAM application, and it can prioritize upgrading of these components as needed to maintain a desired level of responsiveness as user activity and the quantity of digital assets increase.
- Because an on-premises DAM implementation is connected to an organization's local area network, it typically supports faster data access and transfer rates than cloud-based DAM services, which are limited by internet bandwidth. This is an important consideration given the large file sizes associated with many visual assets, but this advantage does not apply to organizations with a geographically distributed workforce, external contractors and consultants who must access the DAM application, or other authorized users who are not connected to the local area network on which the DAM application operates. In such situations, latency delays associated with a virtual private network or other secure access methods can negate any performance advantage associated with an on-premises DAM installation.
- An organization may prefer an on-premises DAM implementation for customized integration with external applications that are also installed on-premises and operate within a closed network. This is particularly the case with legacy applications that may not be easily integrated with a cloud-based DAM application. Such integrations may require a high-level of in-house technical expertise or the ser-

vices of a consultant who is knowledgeable about both the DAM application and the legacy application. By contrast, some cloud-based DAM providers offer prebuilt integrations with popular applications hosted by other cloud-based services. Implementation of prebuilt integrations typically requires limited involvement by an organization's information technology staff.
- An on-premises DAM installation may be required in countries with data sovereignty laws that require the storage of business records within national boundaries or in other approved political jurisdictions. Such requirements are more likely to affect an organization's financial records than audio-visual content, but some DAM implementations may include photographs that depict recognizable individuals, which may be subject to regulations that restrict cross-border transfers of personal data. With some cloud services, customers have no control over the location where their data is maintained, but an organization that prefers a cloud-based DAM application may be able to find a provider that operates a local data center. The organization must determine, however, whether backup copies are also maintained locally.
- For many organizations, the start-up costs associated with an on-premises DAM implementation will offset whatever performance or control advantages a local installation might offer. An on-premises installation will require the up-front purchase of server and user licenses for DAM software. An organization may also need to purchase new servers and networking components or upgrade its existing ones. If an on-premises installation does not need to increase its data storage capacity when a DAM application is initially implemented, it will likely need to do so eventually to accommodate an increasing amount of digital content and metadata. Additional servers and networking components may likewise be needed to accommodate a growing user community.
- Over time, an on-premises DAM implementation will incur continuing charges for software upgrades and technical support, as well increased energy and staff costs to operate, maintain, and backup the servers on which digital assets are stored.
- Cloud-based DAM providers typically charge an initial fee for configuration services plus annual subscription charges that will vary with the number of licensed users and the amount of storage required for digital assets. Because this pricing model minimizes start-up costs it may be preferred by organizations that have limited access to capital funds but sufficient annual budgets to manage ongoing expenditures. Cloud-based pricing may also attract well-

funded organizations if a lengthy approval process for capital investment will delay a DAM implementation.
- Over a multiyear period, the accumulated annual charges for cloud-based services will exceed the start-up costs associated with an on-premises installation of a given DAM application, but an on-premises DAM implementation will incur annual charges for software updates, technical support, and in-house staff, as well as the cost to operate and maintain the server and storage devices components on which the DAM application and digital assets reside. These recurring charges must be factored into a cost comparison. They will affect the break-even point after which the cost of an on-premises DAM implementation will be lower than a cloud-based service.
- As noted in a preceding section, DAM implementations are storage-intensive. The quantity of digital assets will increase over time, often unpredictably. A sudden influx of high-resolution images, video recordings, and other large assets can create an urgent need for additional storage. In certain situations, the expanded storage requirement may be temporary; some assets being reviewed for a new product launch or marketing campaign, for example, may be deleted after the review is completed. As one their most important advantages, a cloud-based DAM service allows an organization to scale up or down quickly to address unanticipated changes in storage requirements or the number of authorized users. By contrast, expansion of storage capacity in an on-premises DAM implementation will require the time-consuming acquisition, installation, configuration, and testing of new storage devices.
- A cloud-based DAM implementation does not involve an irreversible commitment. If a given cloud provider proves unacceptable, an organization can discontinue the service, change to a different provider, or switch to an on-premises installation of the same or a different DAM application, although data migration, retraining, and the development of new integrations with external applications can be complicated and burdensome. This flexibility is not possible with an on-premises DAM implementation, which will be costly and time-consuming to replace, especially if voluminous digital asset or extensive customizations are involved. The capital expenditures to purchase DAM software and the technology infrastructure to operate it are sunk costs that cannot be recovered.
- On-premises and cloud-based DAM implementations are not mutually exclusive options. A hybrid DAM implementation combines the performance advantages of an on-premises DAM installation with flexibility of a cloud-based DAM service. The on-premises application is used for digital assets that require frequent and fast access

by local users, assets that contain confidential information requiring tight security controls, assets that will be processed by customized workflow, or assets that require integration with external applications. The cloud component offers scalable storage to meet changing capacity requirements as well as convenient access to digital assets by authorized users in geographically dispersed locations. Some DAM software developers offer an integrated combination of on-premises and cloud components. Authorized users access digital assets through a unified interface that supports simultaneous searching of on-premises and cloud repositories. As a more complicated alternative, an organization can assemble a hybrid implementation from on-premises components and cloud services offered by different vendors.

SUMMARY OF MAJOR POINTS

- Digital asset management applications are optimized for storage, cataloging, indexing, retrieval, distribution, and protection of photographs, video recordings, logos, illustrations, animation, and other visual and audio content. These digital assets are important and, in some cases, revenue-generating resources that must be safeguarded and tightly controlled.
- A DAM application creates and maintains a centralized repository as a single, authoritative resource for efficient storage, reliable retrieval, and systematic control of an organization's digital assets.
- DAM applications became commercially available in early 1990. At the outset, they were niche products intended for media-intensive enterprises like publishers, broadcast companies, film studios, and music producers. The market for DAM technology subsequently expanded in the early 2000s to include museums, libraries, archives, and historical societies with large collections of digital images as well as corporate communications departments, creative teams, product managers, sales teams, and marketing departments.
- Organizations use DAM applications to store, retrieve, control, and distribute an increasingly diverse array of digital content, including product designs and specifications, customer support materials, user manuals, training materials, survey results, and licensing agreements. Some organizations also use DAM applications for storage and retrieval of office documents, spreadsheets, source code files, and web and app development files, but other technologies are better suited to such digital content.

- DAM applications do not create digital assets; they collect, store, and manage content that is created by desktop publishing applications, graphic design software, video and audio production systems, three-dimensional modeling software, digital cameras, document scanners, and other applications or devices. Assets can be uploaded to a DAM application individually or in batches.
- DAM applications support customer-defined file plans consisting of a hierarchical framework of folders and subfolders nested to multiple levels. Digital assets might be organized by type, by the products or activities to which they relate, by the department that created them, by date, or in another way that will enable them to be located with needed.
- Most DAM implementations involve a combination of descriptive metadata, which supports retrieval of digital assets; administrative metadata, which supports a DAM application's control and management processes; technical metadata, which documents the structure and format of digital assets; and rights metadata, which documents the intellectual property rights and access restrictions that apply to digital assets.
- Digital assets can be retrieved by manually browsing through the folders and subfolders maintained in a DAM repository or by searching the metadata values associated with folders, subfolders, or individual assets. DAM applications support a full range of conventional retrieval operations plus functionality that is tailored to visual assets.
- Authorized users can display retrieved assets as thumbnail images or in larger sizes for preview and selection for full display or downloading. Selected digital assets can be downloaded for modification, annotation, enhancement, or other processing by external applications.
- Integrations allow a DAM application to receive assets and metadata from or transfer digital content to an external system. Some DAM vendors offer prebuilt integrations with popular business applications and online services.
- Access privileges can be controlled at the repository, sub-repository, folder, subfolder, or asset levels. Organizations can broaden, narrow, revoke, or otherwise redefine user privileges as circumstances warrant. DAM applications provide reliable mechanisms to authenticate users. An audit log provides a comprehensive historical record of user interactions with specific digital assets.
- Most DAM applications can track the various versions of a given asset to allow authorized users to compare them, determine which is the most recent, and rollback to a previous version where appropriate.

- Most DAM applications allow organizations to create automated workflows that facilitate and expedite the uploading and processing of digital assets. Depending on the complexity of asset management processes to be automated, a workflow script may be written by a trained employee, by the DAM vendor, or by a contractor or consultant who specializes in workflow implementations.
- Highly functional DAM applications of proven effectiveness and reliability are widely available from many qualified suppliers. The earliest DAM applications were intended for on-premises installation. Those products remain popular with many organizations, but existing and prospective customers are increasingly attracted to cloud-based DAM providers. Each implementation approach has advantages and limitation that must be carefully evaluated.

NOTES

1. *Oxford English Dictionary*, s.v. "asset (*n.*)," December 2023, accessed August 31, 2024, https://doi.org/10.1093/OED/2900381864. A subscription or library card is required to access to the online *OED*.

2. *Asset management—Vocabulary, overview, and principles,* ISO 55000:2024 (International Organization for Standardization, July 2024), https://www.iso.org/obp/ui/en/#iso:std:iso:55000:ed-2:v1:en.

3. *Information technology—IT asset management—Part 1: IT asset management systems—Requirements,* ISO 19770-1:2017, Edition 3 (International Organization for Standardization, December 2017), https://www.iso.org/standard/68531.html.

6

✢

Web and Social Media Archiving Applications

According to Internet Live Stats, which provides real-time statistics about technology-related activities, there are more than 1.5 billion registered websites (unique hostnames) globally, of which about 200 million are actively maintained and visited, however occasionally.[1] The World Wide Web hosts hundreds of social media sites, which are broadly defined to include major global providers and smaller social media platforms that focus on particular geographic regions, demographic groups, or special interests. According to Statista, a business intelligence provider that consolidates data from multiple sources, there are over 4.6 billion registered users of social media sites. Reflecting the global reach of social media for communication and information sharing by organizations and individuals, the number of registered users is projected to approach 6 billion in 2027.[2] The quantity of text, images, video recordings, and other digital content posted on web and social media sites cannot be reliably estimated, but it is thought to total in the exabytes and growing. An estimated 250,000 new websites are registered annually. Petabytes of content are added to social media platforms daily. Users of popular video-sharing sites alone contribute hundreds of hours of new content totaling more than a terabyte of data every minute.

Web and social media archiving applications create a historical record of this influential, expansive, and ephemeral category of digital content. Web archiving applications collect and preserve selected web pages or entire websites, including embedded documents, linked sites, and other associated elements. Social media archiving applications perform the same function for text, images, comments, and other information posted on social media platforms. Both applications are specialized tools that are designed to navigate web and social media sites, capture digital content at a specific moment in time, save it in a designated repository, and make it available to authorized users in its original form with all visual and functional attributes intact. While they are conceptually similar, web and social media archiving applications differ in the specific functionality they support and the technical and procedural challenges they must address. Some applications support both web and social media archiving. Others are optimized for either web or social media content.

Web and social media archiving applications address an important aspect of information governance that is not covered by other technologies discussed in this book. Web and social media archiving are most closely aligned with the digital preservation applications discussed in chapter 3, but these technologies differ in focus and functionality:

- From the outset, web and social media archiving have been viewed as aspects of digital preservation, which was defined in chapter 3 as managed activities to ensure continuing availability and usability of digital content. As discussed below, web and social media archiving initiatives in cultural heritage organizations emphasize the preservation of historically significant web content and social media posts. Digital preservation projects have a broader scope that encompasses all types of digital content. Digital preservation applications can upload and store data, documents, images, video recordings, and audio recordings that are created by a variety of applications, saved in different formats, and transferred from local or cloud-based repositories.
- Digital preservation applications can store web pages and social media posts, but they are not optimized for that purpose. They merely preserve snapshots of web and social media content rather than faithful replicas of websites and social media platforms. For their part, digital preservation applications will periodically inspect digital content for deterioration, format obsolescence, or other changes that may cause data loss or impact the content's usability over time. Most web and social media archiving applications do not provide equivalent capabilities.
- Digital preservation is concerned with digital content that is in the inactive phase of the information lifecycle. Content is typically transferred to a digital preservation repository when it no longer subject to change. By contrast, web and social media archiving applications capture digital content at a moment in time, but web pages and social media posts may be edited, expanded, deleted, or otherwise modified after they are archived.

- Digital preservation applications are intended for content with continuing value that merits indefinite retention. Permanent preservation is the objective of many web and social media archiving initiatives, but some organizations archive web pages and social media posts for legal, regulatory, or business reasons rather than for historical research. Such archived content may be deleted when its purpose is fulfilled.

The enterprise content management and records management applications discussed in previous chapters can store snapshots web and social media content of short-term value, but they cannot save working replicas of web pages with embedded hyperlinks, interactive elements, or complex structures. As discussed in the following, web and social media archiving applications are a distinct product group with unique capabilities.

HISTORY

Cultural heritage organizations have played a leading role in promoting and adopting web and social media archiving as they have for digital preservation generally. The Charter on the Preservation of Digital Heritage, adopted by the UNESCO General Conference in 2003, called for the preservation of the culturally significant digital content, including web pages, of all countries, regions, and communications for the benefit of present and future generations. The charter warned that failure to take urgent action will result in the rapid and inevitable loss of valuable knowledge resources. The International Internet Preservation Consortium (IIPC), a group of national and regional research institutions, was formed in the same year to identify and develop best practices for web archiving and preservation of internet content. The Internet Memory Foundation, which was established in 2004 as the European Archive Foundation, changed its name in 2010 to reflect its goal of preserving web content for heritage and cultural purposes.

Concerned about the ephemeral nature of web content and the loss of information that is unavailable elsewhere, a number of libraries and archives initiated web archiving projects in the late twentieth and early twenty-first centuries. Some of these projects had a national focus. Many national libraries, for example, are responsible for collecting works published in their countries. That responsibility extends to electronic publications, including web content. In 1996, the National Library of Australia in cooperation with other cultural heritage agencies began collecting web publications and websites that document significant political, social, and cultural developments related to Australia and Australians. The National

Library of Sweden began harvesting content from Swedish web domains in 1997. The Library of Congress began collecting and preserving websites of historical and cultural significance in 2000. The UK Web Archive Consortium was formed in 2004 by the British Library, the National Archives, and four other institutions concerned about the preservation of UK websites of cultural and scholarly importance. In the same year, the Bibliothèque Nationale initiated a project to collect French websites. The Royal Danish Library and National Library of Norway began collecting national websites in 2005 and 2006, respectively. By 2010, dozens of individual libraries and consortia had introduced programs to selectively preserve significant websites related to specific areas of research interest. Web archiving projects initiated by libraries, archives, and other cultural heritage organizations have increased since that time, but archived content accounts for a small percentage of the huge quantity of information available on web and social media sites.

The most ambitious and best-known web archiving initiative predates most of the library-based initiatives described above. The Internet Archive was founded in 1996 as a nonprofit entity dedicated to the preservation of web content at specific points in time. To accomplish this, the Internet Archive developed technology to collect websites, store them in a format that reliably preserves their content and appearance, and make them available through a browser-based interface, the Wayback Machine, which it introduced in 2001. Unlike the library-based programs, which focused on selected web content, the Internet Archive is not selective; its goal is to preserve as much of World Wide Web as possible. At the time this chapter was written, it had preserved over 860 million web pages. The Internet Archive subsequently broadened its digital preservation mission to include digitized textual, video, and audio content in addition to websites. In 2006, The Internet Archive introduced its Archive-It subscription service to enable cultural heritage institutions and other nonprofit organizations to create their own web archives, which are stored and preserved in data centers operated by the Internet Archive.

The Internet Archive began offering web archiving tools under a free software license in 2004. By the mid-2010s, open source and commercial web archiving applications were available from multiple software developers, but this is not a rapidly growing aspect of information governance technology. As with the digital preservation applications discussed in chapter 4, the number of web archiving applications is limited, surprisingly so given the many companies, government agencies, and nonprofit organizations that use their websites to publicize information about their products, services, activities, and accomplishments. Most software developers are relatively small independent companies that specialize in web archiving. As discussed in a later section, some web archiving vendors have broadened their markets by expanding their products to include social media archiving and related functionality, such as archiving content from collaboration sites and mobile message apps.

There are no statistics about the size or future growth of the market for commercial web and social media archiving applications. Market forecasts by computer industry analysts treat web and social media archiving as a component of enterprise information archiving, a broadly defined category that includes RMA applications, email archiving, digital preservation, digital asset management, and other on-premises products and cloud-based services for data collection, storage, retrieval, retention, and security services. A Google Trends analysis indicates that searches for the phrase "web archiving" peaked in the first decade of the twenty-first century and have stabilized at a low level since that time. At the time this chapter was written, searches for the phrase "social media archiving" had not generated enough data for trend analysis.

BUSINESS NEED

As discussed above, libraries, archives, and other cultural institutions preserve web and social media content as important scholarly resources that are needed for research and the expansion of knowledge. By contrast, the business case for web and social media archiving is based on legal and operational requirements:

- Web and social media archiving captures information about an organization's initiatives and accomplishments at specific points in time. Companies use their websites and social media posts to present information about their products and services, to publish media releases, to document important developments in the company's history, to issue announcements that promote the company's image and brand identity, and to support existing and prospective customers with knowledgebases and troubleshooting guides. Government agencies use websites and social media posts to promote transparency of government actions and to share information with the public. Nonprofit organizations use websites and social media posts to disseminate information about their activities, achievements, and the communities they serve. Organizations of all types use websites and social media posts to provide information about their history, mission, values, and leadership. Preservation of this information supports long-term strategic planning, decision making, reputation management, evaluation of customer engagement, and other business matters.

- Web and social media archiving captures information that is not available elsewhere. While much website and social media content is derived from documents and images that are stored on network servers or in other repositories, some web pages and social media posts contain information that is either unique or not otherwise accessible. Company websites often contain blogs, newsletters, and white papers that are only published on the internet. Government agencies use websites to publish the agendas and minutes of meetings of public bodies. Some agencies post video recordings of meetings on social media sites. Colleges and universities use websites to publish course catalogs, schedules, and other documents that were previously issued in printed form. The websites of museums, libraries, historical societies, and other cultural organizations assemble collections of visual materials from multiple repositories. Some websites include forums, comment sections, and other community-generated content that has no counterpart in an organization's files, databases, or other records. Many social media posts are composed in real-time and typed directly rather than uploaded from previously prepared content.
- Web and social media archiving may be required to comply with recordkeeping regulations. According to FINRA Rule 2210, for example, a financial services firm subject to the Financial Industry Regulatory Authority must retain retail communications made through its website or social media posts for a minimum of three years. Web archiving will also confirm compliance with FINRA's requirement that a regulated firm's website include a readily apparent reference and hyperlink to BrokerCheck, which provides information about broker-dealers and investment advisors. Pharmacovigilance regulations require manufacturers of drugs and medical devices to retain adverse event reports that are submitted via websites. In situations like these, web and social media archiving applications enable a regulated entity to provide government investigations and auditors with proof of compliance.
- Most government agencies are regulated by archival laws and regulations, which specify retention periods, storage locations, formats, and other requirements for public records. Archival laws and regulations may also require government agencies to preserve records of permanent value, either by maintaining them in a secure repository or by transferring them to an archival authority's custody. Those recordkeeping regulations apply to web pages and social media posts that contain evidence of official agency business or information about government policies, procedures, operations, and activities that is not available in other records.

- In many countries, freedom of information laws require government agencies to make their records available to the public when requested, subject to certain exceptions. These laws apply to public records in all formats, including web and social media content that government agencies are obligated to retain, even if the content has been removed from websites or social media platforms. Web and social media archiving is necessary to ensure public availability of such content.
- Some countries have legal deposit laws that require government agencies, private publishers and, in some cases, authors to deposit copies of their publications in a designated repository operated by a national library or similar agency. These laws apply to publications in all formats, including web and social media content that is considered a publication. As noted above, many websites and social media platforms contain information that is unavailable elsewhere, and some of that content could reasonably be considered a publication to which legal deposit laws apply. Interpreting their responsibilities broadly, some national libraries archive all or most websites that are created in or related to their countries. This may be accomplished by crawling relevant websites or by working with publishers and webmasters to obtain their agreement to submit their web content to the national library for archiving.
- Web and social media archiving may be required to preserve content that is considered relevant for ongoing or imminent litigation, government investigations, and other legal proceedings. Product descriptions and claims included in web pages and social media posts may be used as evidence in contract litigation, patent infringement disputes, product liability cases, and government investigations involving false advertising, misrepresentation of services, and antitrust violations.
- Social media posts by an organization's officials and employees may be relevant for government investigations and civil litigation related to sexual harassment, discriminatory hiring practices, wrongful termination, trade secret disclosure, and other workplace violations. In such situations, failure to preserve web and social media content exposes an organization to fines and other penalties for spoliation of evidence. As a preventive measure, an organization can use social media archiving applications to preemptively identify and block posts that may violate its code of conduct or other policies.

STANDARDS AND GUIDELINES

Some authorities cite the concepts and principles presented in ISO 14721:2012, *Space data and information transfer systems—Open archival information system (OAIS)—Reference model* and other digital preservation standards discussed in chapter 4 as relevant for web and social media archiving. They provide a framework for long-term preservation of any digital content. Several standards deal specifically with web and social media archiving:

- ISO 28500:2017—*Information and documentation—WARC file format* provides a standard way to structure and format content collected from websites, including HTML pages, images, video and audio files, JavaScript, and other components without any loss of information or functionality. WARC is a preservation format that is used by most web archiving projects. Developed by the International Internet Preservation Consortium, it is a more flexible and scalable extension of ARC, a web archiving format developed by the Internet Archive. Compared to ARC, the WARC format supports a broader range of data types and is better suited to streaming media and other complex digital objects. WARC has largely replaced its predecessor for new archiving initiatives, but some organizations maintain older web content that was archived in the ARC format. Open source software is available to convert ARC files to the WARC format.
- ISO/TR 14873:2013, *Information and documentation—Statistics and quality issues for web archiving* establishes a framework for collecting web archiving statistics, including the volume of data archived, the frequency of archiving, the types of web content archived, and the use of archived content. It discusses preservation methods and provides quality management guidance for librarians, archivists, engineers, and managerial staff who are directly involved in web archiving.
- The WACZ (Web Archive Collection Zipped) format was introduced by Webrecorder, an independent project that develops open source software for web archiving, in 2021. It bundles WARC files, indexes, page lists, metadata, and contextual information in a single file using ZIP compression. WACZ is not an international standard.

FEATURES AND CAPABILITIES

The International Internet Preservation Consortium defines four stages of web archiving: selection, harvesting, preservation, and access. The four stages, which may occur sequentially or concurrently, are equally applicable to social media archiving. Selection is the process of determining which web or social media content will be archived. As discussed in a later section, the selection of web and social media sites to be archived is based on an organization's mission and collection development policies rather than technological considerations.

Web and social media archiving applications support the other three stages. Harvesting is the stage in which content is collected from the selected web and social media sites. In the preservation stage, the collected content is stored and retained in its original form. The access stage makes the preserved content available for use. These stages are discussed in the following sections.

Content Capture

Web and social media archiving depend on systematic and accurate harvesting of content from web and social media sites. As a simple and inexpensive approach to web archiving, content can be harvested by saving snapshots of selected pages as PDF files, but that process does not create a fully operable replica that faithfully reproduces the appearance, content, and functionality of a web page. Because PDF snapshots are static representations of web content, they cannot capture dropdown menus, embedded videos, animation, or interactive page elements. A PDF snapshot of a given page may have truncated page borders, misaligned layouts, and distorted images. Embedded hyperlinks may lead to content that is no longer available.

- To create workable preservation copies, web archiving applications utilize web crawlers, specially designed software that visits websites to harvest content. Web crawlers, sometimes termed "web spiders," are also used for web indexing, search engine optimization, data mining, and other purposes unrelated to web archiving. Web crawlers intended for archiving applications are optimized for collection of content to be transferred to a designated preservation repository.
- In most web archiving implementations, web crawling is limited to publicly accessible websites, the so-called surface web, which is indexed by search engines. Most archiving initiatives exclude the deep web, which consists of membership sites, intranets, financial services sites, and corporate websites that include personal, medical, and other confidential data. The deep web is different from the dark web, which is often used for illegal activities.
- To initiate the capture process, an organization creates a seed list that defines the scope of a web archiving initiative based on the organization's selection policy and archiving objectives. The seed list specifies the URLs of websites to be visited, the pages to be visited within a given site, the frequency of visits to the same site, and the content to be captured.

- The seed lists for web archiving projects undertaken by libraries, archives, and other cultural heritage organizations may contain hundreds or thousands of URLs. By contrast, a company, government agency, or nonprofit organization that wants to preserve its own web content may need to visit a smaller but still significant number of sites. A university's web archiving program, for example, may visit all of its town op-level domains plus externally hosted sites that include faculty research and other related content. A multinational company may crawl its websites in all countries where it does business plus the websites of its competitors. Some archiving initiatives may encompass an organization's intranet as well as websites available on the public internet.
- A crawler navigates through the seed list automatically as instructed. Crawl frequency may vary be site. Important sites that change frequently may be crawled daily or several times per day. Other sites may be visited weekly, monthly, or at longer intervals. Some web and social archiving applications allow authorized users to request capture of content from a site that is not included in a seed list. Such requests may involve one-time capture of content needed for a project or business operation or recurring visits to the specified web or social media site.
- Web archiving projects undertaken by cultural heritage organizations have relied on open source crawlers, which are available at no charge for use and customization by any organization. The Heritrix crawler, the best-known example, was developed by the Internet Archive, which uses it for its web archiving operations and for the Archive-It service. Commercial web archiving applications may use proprietary crawlers that were developed in-house or customized versions of open source crawlers.
- Crawling a large website may take hours or even several days. Because crawling can degrade performance, some websites require a crawler to pause between requests, which can further slow the capture process. In small-scale archiving projects, a crawler may visit websites on the seed list sequentially, but that process can be time-consuming. To expedite content collection, multiple instances of a crawler might visit multiple websites concurrently. While concurrent crawling requires greater coordination and more computational resources than sequential visits, it is the preferred approach for large web archiving projects.
- Whether sequential or concurrent crawling is utilized, a crawler's ability to visit a given website may be limited by restrictions imposed by the site's owner. The restrictions are communicated in a robot exclusion protocol, which is specified in a robots.txt file that is placed in

a website's root directory. An exclusion protocol prohibits a crawler from capturing content from all or part of the website, although the prohibition may be intentionally or inadvertently ignored. Upon notification by a website owner, some organizations will remove content that was archived in violation of a robot exclusion protocol.
- As a matter of policy, some libraries, archives, and other cultural heritage organizations request explicit permission from website owners before initiating the crawling process, but such requests can delay web archiving. Some websites block visits from specific IP addresses, while others only allow visits from certain IP addresses. A crawler may also be blocked by password-protected sites, sign-in pages, paywalls, or sites that require membership. Unindexed websites are typically inaccessible to conventional web crawling.
- Web crawlers capture text, images, PDF files, video and audio recordings, and JavaScript files that enable interactive content, as well title tags, descriptions, timestamps, and other metadata. Compared to search engine crawlers, which typically focus on textual content and metadata needed to index a web page, the crawlers used for web archiving take a more comprehensive approach. In addition to content, they capture fonts, icons, cascading style sheets, forms, and other formatting elements that allow an archived site to be reproduced as fully and faithfully as possible. With some web crawlers, however, an organization can limit archiving to or exclude specific types of content—images, videos, or PDF documents, for example.
- Web crawlers can follow hyperlinks that are embedded within web pages. Capturing linked pages is necessary to ensure that a harvested web page will be a fully operational replica of the original at the time it was visited. If this is not done, a given link may refer to a page that was modified or removed from the internet after the initial web page was harvested. Capturing linked pages is essential for compliance with recordkeeping regulations that require preservation of all content from an archived website.
- Because the inclusion of linked pages can expand the scope of a given archiving initiative beyond the initial seed list and selection policy, an organization may limit the number or types of hyperlinks to be followed within a given page. The organization may also control the depth of content harvesting by limiting the crawler's visits to hyperlinks within a linked page.
- Certain website components can be difficult for web crawlers to capture. Examples include content that is generated dynamically from a database, interactive content that relies on JavaScript or other dynamic features, 3D models, forms that contain multiple pages,

content that loads continuously as a user scrolls, and content requiring a specific plug-in.
- Social media archiving applications can collect content from all major social media platforms and some lesser known ones. Capture of content from social media sites involves challenges that are not encountered in conventional web crawling. Social media sites store voluminous quantities of user-generated data, including textual and multimedia content that is subject to frequent and unpredictable additions, deletions, or other changes. A given site's layout may be subject to frequent changes as well. A social media post may have many comments. As an additional complication, a social media site may include spam and bot-generated posts, which the content collection method must distinguish from user-generated content.
- Some social media sites provide an application programming interface (API) that allows authorized parties to collect posts, comments, and other user-generated content. Alternatively, a web crawler may be customized for collection of content from a given social media site. In general, however, the use of web crawlers to capture social media content poses more technical complications than content collection via an application programming interface. API-based content capture is the method preferred by commercial social media archiving applications, although customized crawlers may be used for content that is not available through an application programming interface.
- An authentication token is usually required to access a given social media site via an application programming interface. An organization must establish a developer account and apply to the social media site to obtain the token. Given basic programming skills and an understanding of HTTP protocols, content archiving via an application programming interface can be a straightforward process, but each social media site has its own API with distinctive features and limitations. Even with knowledgeable technical support, voluminous content, varied media types, and other factors can complicate the archiving process.
- Content collection must adhere to a social media site's terms of service, which specify its data access and privacy policies. To avoid overloading a social media site and degrading its performance, an application programming interface may limit the number of requests that can be submitted in a given time frame. It may further restrict the amount and type of content that can be accessed. A customized crawler can access a broad range of publicly available content, but unrestrained access may violate a social media site's terms of service.
- Archiving captures a web page or social media site at a given point in time. Social media sites are subject to additions and deletions

throughout a given day. Website content may change at any time, particularly for sites that include comments, survey responses, or other user-contributed content or that cover news, weather, sports, or other topics that may be updated unpredictably when specific events occur. Frequent visits to a given site are necessary to keep up with these changes. Some commercially available archiving applications can monitor web and social media content in real-time to ensure that all changes, even intraday changes, are captured. Such real-time monitoring can pose technical challenges where continuous changes and voluminous content involved, and some web and social media sites may prevent it by limiting the number of daily visits from archiving applications.

- As an alternative to web crawling and API-based capture of social media posts, several software developers offer a browser extension that supports on-demand archiving of individual pages or poses This approach to content capture does not utilize a seed list. Instead, the user navigates to a desired page or post and initiates the archiving process by activating the extension, which captures the content and other elements necessary to reproduce the page or post.
- While the captured content might be saved as a PDF file, on-demand archiving is not a preservation-oriented technology; it is primarily intended for lawyers, investigators, journalists, and others who need faithful reproductions of selected web pages or social media posts for discovery, proof of compliance, competitive analysis, research, protection of intellectual property rights, or other purposes. Because the web pages or social media sites to be visited must be manually selected, on-demand archiving is not suitable for large-scale archiving projects that collect content by frequent visits to multiple sites.

The web and social media archiving applications discussed in this chapter differ from web and social media scraping applications, which extract specific data elements from within web pages or social media sites for immediate analysis. Web scraping applications use crawlers to visit websites. Social media scraping applications connect to a social media platform via an application programming interface. In either case, scraping is limited to certain parts of web pages and social media posts that contain relevant information. Web and social media scraping applications are used by retail businesses, marketing firms, real estate companies, the travel and hospitality industry, and other organizations for research, price comparison, brand and reputation monitoring, competitive intelligence, sentiment analysis, strategic planning, and other purposes. As with on-demand archiving, web and social media scraping applications are not intended for long-term preservation of digital content. The scraped information is often of short-term value. It may be exported into a database or spreadsheet for further processing and discarded when no longer needed.

Storage and Preservation

Content captured from web and social media sites will be transferred to a designated archival repository for storage, preservation, and access by authorized users. The preservation repository must also ensure the accessibility, integrity, security, and usability of web and social media content:

- The content capture methods discussed in the preceding section can generate unpredictable amounts of information. Web and social media archiving initiatives are typically storage-intensive. Capacity requirements will vary with the scope of a given archiving project, the number of web and social media sites to be visited, the frequency of content capture, the nature of the content to be archived, and the depth of crawling for embedded hyperlinks. The preservation repository must be scalable to provide increased capacity over time, particular if archiving projects will include high-resolution images, videos, and interactive elements.
- A preservation repository may be on-premises or cloud-based. Commercially available web and social media archiving applications are typically marketed as complete solutions that include a cloud-based preservation repository as an integral component. Some commercially available applications can be installed on-premises, but that implementation option is not actively promoted and may ultimately be discontinued by vendors who offer it. All commercially available applications allow authorized users to download web or social media content from their cloud repositories for local storage. With browser extensions for on-demand archiving products, users can save captured web pages and social media content in whatever storage repository is available to them.
- Some cultural heritage organizations use Archive-It, which—like commercially available web and social media archiving products—is a complete web archiving solution that stores customer content in a cloud-based preservation repository. Unlike commercially available web and social media archiving applications, however, Archive-It's customer base is limited to nonprofit organizations. Some web archiving projects initiated by national libraries, consortia, and other organizations operate their own preservation repositories, which reside on local servers or in data centers operated by cloud storage providers.

- The International Internet Preservation Consortium views web archiving as an aspect of digital preservation. It recommends that libraries, archives, and other organizations integrate their web and social media archiving initiatives with their digital preservation systems, which may be a digital preservation application of the type discussed in chapter 4. As with other types of digital information, web and social media content must be monitored to ensure its continued stability and migrated to new formats when necessary to maintain its usability. A digital preservation implementation provides the technological infrastructure and expertise to support this requirement.
- Where available, integration with a digital preservation application is the preferred approach for long-term stability and accessibility of archived web and social media content. Organizations that do not have a digital preservation application may store archived web and social media content in an enterprise content management system or a records management application. As discussed in preceding chapters, ECM and RMA products can accommodate a wide variety of digital file formats and provide excellent functionality for storage, retrieval, security, and protection of digital content. Some commercially available web and social media archiving applications provide preconfigured integration with specific ECM and RMA products. Alternatively, most ECM and RMA products provide application programming interfaces for customized integration with web and social media archiving applications.
- While some commercial applications store archived web content in proprietary formats, most web archiving applications use the WARC file format. As discussed above, WARC is an international standard for storage of web content and metadata. It is the preferred choice for most organizations because it can capture web pages in their entirety. PFA, TIF, or other file formats may be used if archiving is limited to selected web elements, such as documents or images. Social media applications offer users a choice of file formats, including XML, HTML, and JSON in addition to WARC. Applications intended for on-demand archiving can export web or social media content in WARC, PDF, MIME HTML, and other formats.
- As noted above, web and social media archiving are storage-intensive activities. If a website is crawled frequently, most of the content will be the same from one visit to the next, and some pages will not have changed at all. Similarly, most social media sites retain previous posts, including videos and images, unless they are deleted by the account owner or removed for violating the site's terms of service or community standards. Some web and social media archiving applications use duplicate detection algorithms to minimize redundancy

and reduce storage requirements. With duplicate detection, a web or social media archiving application stores a base version plus the incremental changes that are detected in subsequent visits to a given site. When a web page or social media content archived on a given date is displayed, the archiving application will reconstruct it by integrating the changes with the previously archived base version. Duplicate detection can be disabled if legal considerations, regulatory compliance, or research projects require a complete record of a website at specific points in time. Duplicate detection is ineffective in reducing storage requirements for news sites, e-commerce sites, weather forecasting sites, online forums, and other websites that change frequently.

- Web and social media archiving applications use time stamping to identify content that was archived on a specific date. Time stamps may be needed to verify archived content for regulatory compliance, to establish and enforce intellectual property rights, or to authenticate content for admissibility as evidence in legal proceedings. Timestamps prove that specific content was included in or removed from a given web or social media site at a particular point in time. Content curators and researchers can also use them to distinguish different versions of archived content, to establish a chronology of events, and to track in content changes over time.
- Like digital preservation technology, some web and social media archiving applications use digital signatures to verify the continued integrity of archived content. The digital signature functions as a secure seal that provides reliable evidence of data loss or tampering. It employs checksums to detect bit-level corruption or modification of content over time. As explained in chapter 3, a mathematical algorithm calculates a checksum value that represents the content's state when it is ingested. This calculation provides a baseline for future detection of corruption, data loss, or unauthorized alterations that may compromise the reliability and usefulness of archived content. When the content is reexamined, any change will result in a different checksum value.

Access and Retrieval

Archived web and social media content is accessed through a replay or playback module that can retrieve archived content for display in a compatible browser.

- Web and social media content archived by libraries and other cultural heritage organizations is often intended for public access, subject to

legal restrictions. To comply with open records laws, government agencies may also make archived content available to the general public. Companies and some nonprofit organizations typically limit access to employees or other authorized parties, although a public portal may provide access to selected content.
- As with other technologies, access privileges are determined by organizational policy and managed by the system administrator. Access privileges may be defined for individuals or groups. Access can be limited to specific content. Web and social media applications support password controls and other mechanisms to prevent unauthorized access to archived content. Some applications encrypt archived content in transit and in storage.
- Commercial web and social media applications include a playback module as an integral component. Several open source playback tools are available for viewing of archived web content in a compatible browser.
- Metadata facilitates access to archived web and social media content. A website's URL, language, date and time of capture, and date of last modification are collected automatically when the site is visited by a web crawler. Web pages often include a title, a brief description of page contents, author information, keywords, and other HTML tags that are collected during the crawling process. Additional metadata, such as the content type and creation date, is captured for PDF files, documents, videos, and other non-HTML content included in websites.
- Some web archiving applications allow authorized users to enter additional metadata for archived content, but—given the size and complexity of many websites—manual metadata entry is only practical for selected high value content.
- Web archiving applications use metadata to construct an index for retrieval of archived content. The URL, data and time of capture, and other index data is stored in a Capture Index (CDX) file, which is created as part of the web archiving process. Keeping index data in a separate file permits faster search and browsing than direct searches of WARC files.
- As one of the most common retrieval operations, authorized users can search for an archived website by its URL combined with a date or range of dates. Searches may also be based on a URL prefix. Emulating the Wayback Machine, some applications display a timeline or calendar that indicates the dates when a given site was archived. To locate desired content, a user may need to browse through archived web pages that were archived on multiple dates. Social media applications allow authorized users to search for posts by a specific author.

- Some web and social media applications support full-text searching of web pages or social media posts. Because web and social media sites contain voluminous amounts textual information, full-text indexing may be limited to selected archived content.
- Some web and social media archiving applications support a broad range of retrieval functionality, including Boolean operations, phrase searching, wildcard characters in search strings, and the ability to narrow searches based on content type, date, or other criteria. Some social media archiving applications can search for posts that contain specific emojis.
- Retrieved web pages and social media posts can be displayed on a browser or downloaded to a local repository for offline viewing. Some web and social media applications allow users to create folders of saved search results for later display. Additions and deletions can be made to a given folder. Retrieved content can be downloaded to a local system.
- Web and social media applications that utilize cloud-based repositories will retain archived content until it is removed by the customer. Some web and social media applications allow an organization to specify purge dates for content that does not to be retained indefinitely. When an account is closed, archived content will be returned to the customer or discarded as instructed by the customer.
- An archived site can be navigated in the same way as the original site. Authorized users can select desired pages from drop-down menus, scroll through a displayed page, view animations and videos, and click on embedded hyperlinks, assuming that the linked pages were archived.
- To facilitate identification of new content, some web and social media archiving applications allow a searcher to limit retrieval to web pages that have changed or social media posts that are new since a specified date. Some applications can display two web pages from different dates side-by-side for comparison with changes highlighted. Change reports can identify web and social media sites that have changed since a given date or range of dates. Some web and social media archiving applications monitor specific web and social media sites and issue alerts, based on keyword searches or other criteria, when changes are detected. Web monitoring software that notifies an organization about changes in specific websites is separately available from third-party suppliers.
- Some social media applications will monitor an organization's social media posts in real-time to identify sensitive information, profanity, or other inappropriate content that requires further investigation and corrective action. Some applications use artificial intelligence to

alert an organization when negative comments are included in social media posts.
- Search results can be exported for offline viewing by a compatible browser, either as a screenshot or as a folder with links to archived content in its full native format.

Other Capabilities

In keeping with its mission to provide universal access to all knowledge, the Internet Archive stores books, video recordings, music, and other content in addition to web pages. Its Archive-It subscription service can likewise capture and store a broad spectrum of digital content, but the open source software used by most web and social media archiving projects have a more limited purpose. By contrast, many commercial web and social media archiving applications offer enterprise archiving capabilities that overlap with technologies discussed in other chapters. Going beyond websites and social media platforms, they can capture digital content from various sources:

- Some organizations use text messaging, instant messaging, and chat applications as an alternative or supplement to email. Regulations require certain companies to retain these communications. Some web and social media archiving applications can also archive email messages and attachments, but the email archiving applications discussed in chapter 5 support a broader range of features and functions for capture and storage of messages.
- Recognizing the widespread use of videoconferencing for business meetings, some web and social media archiving applications can capture video recordings, audio content, and meeting transcriptions produced by videoconferencing platforms. They can also archive lists of participants, in-meeting and postmeeting chat logs, and files that are shared with participants.
- Some web and social media archiving applications can capture messages, blogs, discussion forums, to-do lists, assignments, schedules, and other content stored by collaboration platform that facilitate communication, coordination, and cooperation by teams, committees, and other groups that are working on a project or other initiative.
- Some web and social media archiving applications can capture documents, images, and other files that are stored in a variety of formats on shared drives, by cloud-based file-sharing services, or in other repositories. They can also capture metadata, access permissions, and comments associated with these files. While these content manage-

ment capabilities can be useful, the ECM applications discussed in chapter 2 provide a more comprehensive range of storage, retrieval, version control, and workflow processing functionality. Compared to web and social media archiving products, ECM applications can also be integrated more easily with external applications.

IMPLEMENTATION ISSUES

A web or social media archiving project must have a well-defined purpose and manageable scope that will guide the selection of content to be archived. Once the purpose and scope of the archiving initiative are determined, an organization must select an archiving application that meets its requirements. In particular, it must decide whether it will utilize open source software or a commercial archiving product based on affordability, functionality, and other criteria. Before archiving begins, the organization must identify and carefully consider legal and ethical issues that may be associated with collecting web or social media content that is owned by others.

Content Selection

As noted in a preceding section, the selection of content to be included is the first stage of a web or social media archiving project. The selection stage determines the types of content to be archived. Apart from the Internet Archive, unselective archiving of web and social media sites is not a manageable objective. To be sustainable, the scope of a web or social media archiving project must be aligned with an organization's mission, compatible with the interests of content creators and users, technically feasible, and implementable with available resources. For example:

- A university library's archiving initiatives may focus on web and social media content that supports the institution's research and educational mission, is compatible with the library's collection development policy, and complements other material in the library's holdings. A public library or local history society may limit web and social media archiving to content related to significant activities, important events, and noteworthy attractions in the community that it serves.
- An art museum may archive web and social media sites that contain information about works in its collection, websites and social media posts related to artists whose works it has acquired or would like to acquire, websites of other museums and galleries that collect similar

works, websites and social media posts related to art festivals or other cultural events, and websites that include exhibition catalogs, blogs, or educational resources.
- Charities, professional associations, and other nonprofit organizations may limit archiving projects to web content or social media posts related to their operations and programs or that document significant events and issues that impact their clients, donors, members, or other stakeholders.
- Companies typically limit web and social media archiving to content that directly impacts their business operations. Such sites include their own internet and intranet sites and the sites of their business partners and competitors, as well as news sites, blogs, market research sites, and other web and social media sites that may discuss or review their products, services, activities, and competitive positions.

Careful planning in the selection stage is essential for successful implementation of a web and social media archiving application. The scope of an archiving project must be based on clearly articulated objectives and a realistic assessment of the organization's technological capabilities and resources, staff expertise, and budgetary constraints. Selection of sites to be included must be defined based on cultural, scholarly, business, or other considerations. To determine the interests and needs of the intended audience for archived content, input must be obtained from all parts of the organization that will be affected by the project. If archived content will be available to researchers or other users outside the organization, as is common in cultural heritage projects, their requirements must be identified and evaluated.

The selection stage is a continuing process rather than a one-time event. Web and social media sites will change over time. The emergence of new sites, increased security measures and access restrictions, and updates to the content, format, and other characteristics of existing sites can affect an archiving initiative. After archiving begins, a project's scope must be reviewed regularly to determine whether it is working as planned and to identify technical challenges, resource limitations, usability problems, or other issues that require attention. The scope will need to be modified, as necessary, to address changes in the organization's objectives, priorities, computing environment, staffing, budget, and intended audience.

Open Source vs. Commercial Software

As noted in a preceding section, web and social media archiving applications are available as open source software developed by nonprofit organizations and as commercial products. Open source software is used in many web and social media archiving projects initiated by libraries and other cultural heritage organizations, while commercial software is typically preferred by business users. While they support similar features and functions , the two approaches differ in cost and the complexity of implementation.

- Most open source software is available free of charge. That is its principal attraction for web and social media archiving projects in organizations with limited budgets, although an open source implementation can incur significant expenditures for computing resources and staff support.
- The cost of commercial web and social media archiving software depends on the implementation method, the number of users, the quantity of content to be captured and stored, and other factors. Commercial web and social media archiving applications are available for on-premises installation, but most vendors emphasize cloud-based services that offer completely preconfigured solutions with relatively low start-up costs.
- Open source software can be time-consuming to implement and require considerable technical expertise to maintain. A fully operational implementation for web and social media archiving may require separate programs for content capture, creation and maintenance of an archival repository, and retrieval of archived content. These components may be offered by different suppliers that may not offer technical assistance for installation and troubleshooting. Considerable effort may be required to enable these components to work together in a given implementation. As an added complication, some open source archiving software utilizes specific third-party tools, which an organization must obtain and install separately.
- By contrast, commercial web and social archiving software is designed for rapid implementation and ease of use. While some technical expertise will be required for an on-premises installation, cloud-based web and social media archiving software is optimized for easy implementation by nontechnical users.
- Most open source licenses allow an organization to customize a web or social media archiving application to suit its requirements and preferences. Open source code is fully and transparently available to interested parties. The most popular open source licenses allow users to modify the software as they see fit. Customers cannot modify commercial software and do not have access to its source code, although they may be able to adjust certain operating parameters and preferences within limits permitted by the developer.

- Open source software is provided to users without warranties, guarantees, or claims about its capabilities, reliability, or fitness for a particular purpose. Technical support is provided by its community of users. Most open source projects have a group of core developers, but other individuals or groups may contribute to the software's continuing development by correcting errors in the program code, make changes that improve the software's performance, and add features and functionality that other organizations may find useful. The user community also provides discussion forums, program documentation, and other assistance to enable organizations to install and operate open source software.
- Commercial software developers offer customers software upgrades, technical support, and training resources, which may be free of charge for a specified period of time. On-premises web and social media archiving applications are supported by a limited-time warranty. When the warranty period elapses, an organization must purchase annual maintenance contracts for technical support and software upgrades. With cloud-based web and social media archiving applications, customers pay a monthly or annual subscription fee that includes technical support. As with other technologies discussed in this book, cloud-based implementations regularly incorporate software modifications and enhancements.

Legal and Ethical Concerns

Web and social media archiving selection policies and operations must comply fully with laws and regulations in the countries and subnational jurisdictions where web and social media content will be collected, stored, or used. Apart from legal deposit requirements, no laws or regulations expressly allow or prohibit web or social media archiving, but some laws have implications for archiving projects. The most widely publicized legal issues relate to copyright violations, but other laws and regulations may limit or prohibit archiving of certain web content and social media posts. Intersecting with legal issues, web and social media archiving also raises significant ethical concerns that must be considered.

- Web and social media archiving are typically limited to publicly accessible content, but many websites and social media platforms contain copyrighted material. Copyright law gives authors and artists exclusive rights over their original writings or artistic works. Copyright protection is automatic and absolute. It begins as soon as a written or artistic work is fixed in tangible form, as it would be

in a web page or social media post. Registration of the work is not required.
- Web and social media content that is protected by copyright cannot be lawfully reproduced, downloaded, or shared without the copyright holder's permission. These restrictions apply unless an exception applies or the content is excluded from copyright protection, as is the case with works in the public domain, works for which the creator has declined copyright protection, and most web pages and social media posts created by government agencies.
- To avoid copyright infringement, some organizations request permission from web and social media sites before archiving protected content. This adds a time-consuming work step to the archiving process, and it is impractical for websites with many hyperlinked sites, each of which must be contacted for permission. As a complicating factor, creators of web pages or social media posts may include copyright-protected material that they did not create themselves and for which they cannot give permission to archive. In some cases, this copyright material may be included in a web page or social media post on condition that further reproduction will be prohibited.
- In cultural heritage organizations and educational institutions, the legality of archiving copyright-protected web and social media content must be evaluated in the context of fair use exceptions or Creative Commons licenses, which allow limited use of copyrighted material for teaching, scholarly research, and some other purposes. Whether and to what extent a given archiving initiative complies with fair use requirement may be a matter of interpretation based on the purpose of archiving and the way in which the archived content will be used. It is unlikely that the fair use exception applies to archiving websites for competitive intelligence, market assessment, data analysis, or other uses that confer a business advantage. In some cases, a website's terms of use explicitly prohibits archiving copyrighted content regardless of intended use.
- Some web and social media archiving projects will comply with a copyright holder's request to remove content for which copyright protection is verified and permission has not been obtained. Upon notification, organizations will also remove archived content that violates intellectual property rights related to trademarks and trade secrets.
- The terms of service for some websites and social media platforms prohibit archiving of all or specified content without the permission of the website's owner or the creator of a social media post. This prohibition, which is typically based on copyright law, applies to archiving by any means, including crawling, an application program-

ming interface, scraping, or screen snapshots. Some sites ask users to check a box, click a button, or otherwise explicitly affirm agreement with the terms of service. In other cases, the terms of service includes an implicit opt-in provision, although an organization might argue that it was not aware of the opt-in provision.
- Some web and social media sites are protected by digital rights management technology that prevents or limits the reproduction, sharing, or use of copyright-protected content. Some countries have laws that prohibit organizations from using countermeasures to circumvent these controls. As discussed in a preceding section, some websites use robot exclusion protocols to prevent archiving of all or selected pages. Such protocols may be designed to restrict access to copyright-protected content or simply to limit archiving activity, which can have an adverse impact on a website's performance. A web crawler can be configured to ignore robot exclusion protocols, which are instructions rather than contractual obligations. Compliance is an ethical matter not a legal requirement, although repeated violations may lead a website's owner to implement stricter controls to protect its intellectual property.
- Web pages and social media posts may contain personal information that is not known and should not be available to the general public. Most social media platforms and some websites have privacy policies that prohibit reproduction, sharing, or use of such nonpublic personal information by third parties without the consent of the data subject. This restriction applies to web and social media archiving applications.
- Many countries have personal privacy and data protection laws that prohibit collection or use of nonpublic personal information without the consent of the data subject in most situations and mandate destruction of such information when it is no longer needed for its original purpose. Most of these laws are based on the widely publicized General Data Protection Regulations, which control the collection, storage, use, and retention of personal information in member states of the European Union. Violations are punishable by fines and other penalties. As an additional complication, data protection laws allow a data subject to rescind consent at any time, in which case the subject's personal information must be deleted from any archival repositories in which it is stored.
- National data protection laws prohibit the transfer of nonpublic personal information to countries that do not provide an equivalent level of privacy protection. Some countries have data residency laws that mandate the storage of certain information within the territorial boundaries of a country or, less commonly, a state, province, or

other subnational jurisdiction. These laws limit the locations where content collected by web and social media archiving applications can be stored.
- As a fundamental principle of systematic records management, an organization is the owner of recorded information that it creates and maintains in the course of its business. As such, the organization is solely empowered to make decisions about its continued retention provided that it does not violate legal, regulatory, and contractual mandates. Organizations regularly delete or discard information, including web and social media content, that it determines to be obsolete, incomplete, unclear, or erroneous. If such information is archived by others without permission before it is removed from a web or social media site, it may be retained longer than the originating organization intended. When this occurs, the archiving entity usurps the organization's control over disposition of its own property. While this may not be illegal, it is ethically questionable because continued availability of the archived content may ultimately harm the originating organization.

SUMMARY OF MAJOR POINTS

- Web archiving applications collect and preserve selected web pages or entire websites, including embedded documents, linked sites, and other associated elements. Social media archiving applications perform the same function for text, images, comments, and other information posted on social media platforms. These applications address an important aspect of information governance that is not covered by other technologies discussed in this book.
- Cultural heritage organizations have played a leading role in promoting and adopting web and social media archiving. Concerned about the ephemeral nature of web content and the loss of information that is unavailable elsewhere, a number of libraries and archives initiated web archiving projects in the late twentieth and early twenty-first centuries. Web archiving projects initiated cultural heritage organizations has increased since that time.
- The Internet Archive was founded in 1996 as a nonprofit entity dedicated to the preservation of web content at specific points in time. To accomplish this, the Internet Archive developed technology to collect websites, store them in a format that reliably preserves their content and appearance, and make them available through a browser-based interface.
- Web and social media archiving captures information about an organization's initiatives and accomplishments at specific points in

time. Much of this information is not available elsewhere. In some organizations, web and social media archiving is required to comply with recordkeeping regulations, freedom of information laws, and legal deposit laws. Web and social media archiving may also be required to preserve content that is considered relevant for ongoing or imminent litigation, government investigations, and other legal proceedings.
- Web and social media archiving depends on systematic and accurate harvesting of content from web and social media sites. To create workable preservation copies, web archiving applications utilize specially designed software that visits websites to harvest content. Web crawlers capture text, images, PDF files, video and audio recordings, and JavaScript files that enable interactive content, as well title tags, descriptions, timestamps, and other metadata.
- The capture process begins with a seed list that defines the scope of a web archiving initiative based on the organization's selection policy and archiving objectives. A crawler navigates through the seed list automatically as instructed. Web archiving projects undertaken by cultural heritage organizations have relied on open source crawlers, which are available at no charge for use and customization by any organization. Commercial web archiving applications may use proprietary crawlers that were developed in-house or customized versions of open source crawlers.
- Some social media sites provide an application programming interface (API) that allows authorized parties to collect posts, comments, and other user-generated content. Alternatively, a web crawler may be customized for collection of content from a given social media site.
- Archiving captures a web page or social media site at a given point in time, but that content is subject to change. Frequent visits to a given site are necessary to keep up with these changes.
- Content captured from web and social media sites will be transferred to a designed archival repository for storage, preservation, and access by authorized users. The preservation repository must be scalable to provide increased capacity over time, particular if archiving projects will include high resolution images, videos, and interactive elements.
- Where available, integration with a digital preservation application is the preferred approach for long-term stability and accessibility of archived web and social media content. Web and social media content must be monitored to ensure its continued stability and migrated to new formats when necessary to maintain its usability. A digital preservation implementation provides the technological infrastructure and expertise to support this requirement.

- Most web archiving applications use the WARC file format, an international standard for storage of web content and metadata. WARC is the preferred format for most organizations because it can capture web pages in their entirety.
- Access privileges for archived content are determined by organizational policy. Web and social media applications support password controls and other mechanisms to prevent unauthorized access to archived content. Some applications encrypt archived content in transit and in storage.
- Some web and social media archiving applications support a broad range of retrieval functionality, including Boolean operations, phrase searching, wildcard characters in search strings, and the ability to narrow searches based on content type, date, or other criteria. Some web and social media applications support full-text searching of web pages or social media posts.
- Going beyond websites and social media platforms, some web and social media archiving applications can capture electronic communications, videoconferencing content, information from collaboration sites, and documents, images, and other files that are stored on shared drives, by cloud-based file-sharing services, or in other repositories.
- To be sustainable, the scope of a web or social media archiving project's content selection policy must be aligned with an organization's mission, compatible with the interests of content creators and users, technically feasible, and implementable with available resources.
- Web and social media archiving applications are available as open source software developed by nonprofit organizations and as commercial products. Open source software is used in many web and social media archiving projects initiated by libraries and other cultural heritage organizations, while commercial software is typically preferred by business users.
- No laws or regulations expressly allow or prohibit web or social media archiving, but some laws have implications for archiving projects. The most widely publicized legal issues relate to copyright violations, but other laws and regulations may limit or prohibit archiving of certain web content and social media posts. Intersecting with legal issues, web and social media archiving also raises significant ethical concerns.

NOTES

1. See https://www.internetlivestats.com.
2. Statista.com, https://www.statista.com/markets/424/topic/540/social-media-user-generated-content/#overview.

7

✣

E-Discovery Software

In the context of legal proceedings, discovery is a formal pretrial process that allows the opposing parties to request information from each other to help them build their case or prepare their defense. This exchange of information ensures that both parties are aware of the arguments and evidence that the opposition intends to present at trial. While most often associated with lawsuits, discovery may be a component of other legal actions, including arbitration, mediation, regulatory investigations, administrative hearings, and family law matters. Depending on the circumstances, the scope, methods, and timeframe for discovery may be determined by negotiation and agreement of the parties involved in a legal matter or, if disputes arise, ordered by a court.

In the United States, discovery is governed by the Federal Rules of Civil Procedure (FRCP), which specify the types of information that opposing parties can request. US state courts follow their own discovery procedures, which are often based upon or similar to the FRCP. Some other common law countries have procedural guidelines that apply to pretrial disclosure of evidence. In Canada, for example, federal and provincial courts define rules of civil procedure. The Ministry of Justice defines the rules of civil and criminal procedures for courts in England and Wales. In Ireland, discovery is regulated by the Superior Courts Rules. In Australia, federal and state courts define discovery rules. In New Zealand, discovery rules are specified by the High Court. In South Africa, discovery rules are issued by the High Court and Magistrates' Courts. In India, discovery is governed by the Code of Civil Procedure.

Discovery rules in other countries may be less expansive than those that apply in the United States. According to FCRP Rule 26(b), discovery encompasses any nonprivileged information that is relevant to a party's claims or defenses, but a discovery request must be proportional to the needs of case, meaning that the value of the requested information must be balanced against the cost and burden of producing it. Unless limited by court order, a discovery request may include oral or written questioning of witnesses or subject experts, inspection of property or tangible items involved in a legal dispute, and medical examinations in personal injury litigation. A request for production of documents, a ubiquitous and crucial component of the discovery process, is a demand for recorded information relevant to the legal dispute. Such requests usually apply to information held by the opposing party, but document production requests are sometime submitted to third parties who may have recorded information that is relevant for a particular case.

FCRP Rule 34(a) interprets the term "document" broadly to include "writings, drawings, graphs, charts, photographs, sound recordings, images, and other data or data compilations" in any medium. The definition applies to paper documents, photographic records, and digital content, which the FCRP describes as electronically stored information (ESI). While Rule 34 does not define ESI, the Sedona Conference *Glossary*, a widely respected source discussed in a later section, interprets it to mean "information that is stored electronically, regardless of the media or whether it is in the original format in which it was created."[1] A discovery request may encompass ESI at any stage of the information lifecycle, although inactive data and documents can be difficult to locate. According to FCRP Rule 26(b), the requested ESI must be reasonably accessible and the discovery request must be proportional to the needs of the case, meaning that the value of the requested ESI must be weighed against the difficulty and cost of providing it. FCRP Rule 26(f) requires the opposing parties to confer as soon as practicable to develop a plan for discovery, preservation, and disclosure of ESI, including the form in which it should be produced.

E-discovery software, the subject of this chapter, is designed specifically for electronic discovery, which the Sedona Conference *Glossary* defines as the process of identifying, locating, preserving, collecting, preparing, reviewing, and producing ESI in response to discovery requests. The relationship between e-discovery and information governance is widely acknowledged in legal publication and professional presentations. An effective and efficient discovery process depends on ESI that is well organized, stored securely, protected from accidental or malicious destruction, and accessible by a discovery team when needed. The Sedona Conference's *Commentary on Information Governance*, which was cited in the introduction to this book, highlights the importance of information governance for compliance with an organization's e-discovery obligations.

HISTORY

E-discovery software was introduced in the late 1990s and early 2000s amid growing awareness of the importance and difficulties of responding to discovery requests for electronically stored information. Several widely cited legal cases highlighted these e-discovery issues. In particular, *Zubulake v. UBS Warburg LLC* resulted in a series of influential judicial decisions that addressed the duty to preserve digital evidence and penalties for failure to do so, the discoverability of active and inactive ESI, and cost allocation to reduce the finance burden of e-discovery. These decisions, issued in 2003 and 2004, were followed by the 2006 amendments to the Federal Rules of Civil Procedure, which formally recognized ESI as a category of discoverable information along with paper documents. The FRCP amendments were clarified and expanded in 2010 and 2015.

The earliest e-discovery applications offered basic search capabilities that enabled attorneys and paralegal support staff to identify and retrieve ESI that was potentially relevant for discovery requests. These products, which offered a more efficient alternative to printing of electronic records for review and submission to the requesting party, were developed by legal technology experts and digital forensics specialists who recognized the discovery challenges posed by increasing quantities of digital documents and data. Early adopters included large law firms, corporate legal departments in industries with significant litigation exposure, and legal services firms that specialized in litigation support and forensic investigations.

E-discovery software improved steadily and significantly through the mid-2000s. Customer interest, driven by the proliferation of digital content and the complexity of legal proceedings, increased as well; a Google Trends analysis indicates that searches related to electronic discovery peaked in 2006 and have remained steady since that time. As the market expanded, some e-discovery software pioneers attracted investors who provided funding for product research and development. Others were acquired by large computer companies with the technological, marketing, and economic resources to refine and promote e-discovery applications. By 2010, e-discovery software began offering advanced features and functions such as data visualization tools, integration with external applications, and technology-assisted review capabilities based on machine-learning algorithms. The earliest e-discovery software was intended for installation and operation on an organization's own computers. In recent years, cloud-based e-discovery platforms, which do not require large capital expenditures or in-house technical expertise, have broadened the market to include small-to-medium size law firms, companies, and government agencies that could not afford or manage an on-premises e-discovery system.

BUSINESS NEED

E-discovery software is a specialized product with broad applicability. Legal proceedings that require discovery are a common aspect of business operations. In any given year, there is a reasonable likelihood that a company, government agency, or nonprofit organization will be a plaintiff or defendant in civil litigation involving a contract dispute, employment matter, personal injury claim, property dispute, or intellectual property violation. In the United States, where the annual rate of civil lawsuits initiated per capita is several times greater than it is in most countries, over three hundred thousand civil cases are filed annually in US district courts. According to the Court Statistics Project, an initiative of the Conference of State Court Administrators and the National Center for State Courts, over 15 million cases are filed in state courts each year.

Given the widespread use of digital technology for creation and storage of business information, ESI dominates discovery for most legal proceedings. E-discovery is a time-consuming, labor-intensive process that must be performed by a team of attorneys and support personnel who are familiar with matter for which discovery is required, the legal issues involved, and the types of data and documents to be disclosed or withheld. The discovery team must identify and retrieve potentially relevant ESI, catalogue it and assign unique control numbers, review it for relevance, redact privileged and confidential content, and eliminate duplicate or nonresponsive material. ESI that comes within the scope of a discovery order must be copies in an agreed-upon format on appropriate media for delivery to the requesting party and preserved until the applicable legal proceedings are resolved. All of this must be done in a legally defensible manner, often on a tight schedule.

A 2022 analysis by the US Chamber of Commerce Institute for Legal Reform estimated that annual litigation costs for tort claims alone equal 2.1 percent of the US gross domestic product. Excessive litigation costs are not a new concern. A 2010 analysis by Lawyers for Civil Justice concluded that US companies litigation costs equaled 16 to 24 percent of annual profit. A 2010 survey of major companies by the Institute for Legal Reform found that US litigation costs, which are much higher than they are in other countries, greatly increase the cost of business operations. The survey cited inefficient and expensive discovery as one of the contributing factors.

Various studies have confirmed that discovery costs account for 15 to 50 percent or more of total litigation costs. Estimated e-discovery costs cited in legal publications range from several hundred to several thousand dollars per gigabyte; the greater the complexity of the litigation, the amount of ESI involved, and the number of ESI custodians and storage locations, the greater the discovery burden. Many discovery orders are framed so broadly that they encompass large quantities of ESI. A discovery request in an employment discrimination case, for example, may compel the production of every document, email message, or database record that mentions specific employees identified by name or job title or that contains certain words or phrases with pejorative or derogatory connotations. A request of this type will require examination of much ESI, the majority of which may be irrelevant.

The business justification for e-discovery software is based on its potential to reduce these costs. As discussed in subsequent sections, e-discovery software provides features and functionality to automate, streamline, and expedite the discovery process. In particular, it can reduce the time and professional labor required for review of ESI for relevance and privilege, which is the most expensive part of the discovery process in most legal proceedings. The information collection and retrieval capabilities supported by e-discovery software may also be useful for early case assessment, the process of reviewing and analyzing the scope, risks, and cost of a legal matter in order to formulate strategy and evaluate settlement options. Apart from specific legal actions, e-discovery software's de-duplication, annotation, and redaction functions might be applied to any collection of digital documents. In particular, it can support fulfillment of public records requests received by government agencies. Such requests involve the identification, retrieval, review, and disclosure of nonconfidential data and documents that come within the scope of freedom of information laws.

STANDARDS AND GUIDELINES

The Electronic Discovery Reference Model (EDRM), which was introduced in 2005 as a comprehensive framework for the electronic discovery process, has had a decisive influence on the development of e-discovery software. The reference model was initially established as a collaborative project supported by legal professionals, companies, and others involved with discovery of electronically stored information. In the ensuing years, EDRM transitioned to a nonprofit organization that was acquired in

2016 by the Center for Judicial Studies, now known as the Bolch Judicial Institute, a unit of Duke University's Law School. Several ISO standards address e-discovery, and widely publicized e-discovery guidelines have been developed by the Second Conference, a nonprofit think-tank dedicated to research and education related to legal and policy matters.

EDRM

The Electronic Discovery Reference Model defines a nine-stage process for discovery of ESI that is relevant for litigation, government investigations, and other legal proceedings:

- Information Governance is the EDRM's foundational phase. It emphasizes systematic control of an organization's electronically stored information to address stakeholders' requirements, ensure retrievability of data and documents when needed, prevent unauthorized access to confidential and sensitive information, manage the lifecycle of electronically stored information from creation through disposition, and comply with applicable laws, regulations, and industry standards, as well as alignment with the organization's goals and policies.
- In the identification stage, an organization establishes the scope of e-discovery by locating potentially relevant ESI. The organization must determine the business operations that the presumably relevant digital content supports, the content's technical characteristics, its custodians and principal users, the repositories or devices where the content is stored, the procedures to obtain access to it, and any problems or challenges that might complicate or impede the e-discovery process. Accurate and thorough identification of relevant data and documents is essential to ensure the efficiency and effectiveness of subsequent EDRM stages. Successful completion of the identification stage depends on the collaboration of an organization's legal professionals, information staff, records managers, and users who are knowledgeable about specific digital content.
- In the preservation stage, an organization must take proactive steps to secure potentially relevant ESI; to safeguard it from unauthorized access, loss, alteration, or corruption; and to restore or reconstruct it if it is damaged or destroyed. The preservation stage includes implementation of a legal hold process to ensure that digital content identified as potentially relevant remain accessible and usable until the legal proceedings to which they pertain are resolved. Failure to preserve evidence exposes a litigant to sanctions for spoliation—that is, the intentional or negligent destruction of evidence in pending or

reasonably foreseeable legal proceedings. Possible sanctions range from adverse inference instructions, which allow a jury to view the content of the missing evidence as unfavorable to the spoliating party, to monetary penalties and, in extreme cases, dismissal of the spoliating party's claims or defenses.
- In the collection stage, an organization systematically gathers ESI that was identified as potentially relevant in the identification stage. The content is collected from local and remote repositories in a manner that preserves its usability and integrity.
- The processing stage organizes collected ESI and modifies it, as necessary, for review and analysis in the stages that follow. To the extent possible, duplicate data and documents are removed to reduce the quantity of content that must be reviewed and analyzed.
- In the review stage, data and documents are examined and evaluated to determine whether they come within the scope of a discovery request and whether they contain privileged or confidential information.
- In the analysis stage, ESI is examined in depth, prioritized, and categorized by the legal issues, key concepts, or other aspects of the matter to which the ESI pertains.
- In the production stage, ESI that comes within the scope of discovery is prepared and formatted for delivery to the requesting party by an agreed-upon method. The production stage requires the cooperation and collaboration of legal professionals and an organization's information technology staff.
- In the presentation stage, ESI is assembled for display to intended audiences in depositions, trials, hearings, arbitrations, or other legal proceedings.

While the EDRM is specifically designed for e-discovery, the nine stages outlined above are equally applicable to discovery of paper documents and photographic records.

ISO/IEC 27050 Series

Electronic discovery is explained and discussed by four international standards in the ISO 27050 series:

- ISO/IEC 27050-1:2019, *Information technology—Electronic discovery—Part 1: Overview and concepts* defines e-discovery terminology and describes e-discovery concepts and processes, including collection, processing, review, analysis, and production of electronically stored information.

- ISO/IEC 27050-2:2018, *Information technology—Electronic discovery—Part 2: Guidance for governance and management of electronic discovery* discusses policies, practices, roles, and responsibilities that address the management of e-discovery processes, mitigation of risks posed by e-discovery challenges, and compliance with e-discovery requirements.
- ISO/IEC 27050-3:2020, *Information technology—Electronic discovery—Part 3: Code of practice for electronic discovery* specifies requirements and provides recommendations for identification, preservation, collection, processing, review, analysis, and production of electronically stored information.
- ISO/IEC 27050-4:2021, *Information technology—Electronic discovery—Part 4: Technical readiness* provides guidance related to planning, preparation, and implementation of e-discovery processes and technology.

While it deals specifically with electronic discovery, the ISO/IEC 27050 series is part of the ISO/IEC 27000 family of standards, which provide broad coverage of information security issues and concerns related to data protection, privacy, information classification, information exchange, risk management, and compliance with legal and regulatory requirements. Policies, guidelines, and practices specified in the ISO/IEC 27050 series are aligned with the security management framework presented in other ISO/IEC 27000 series standards.

While it is not part of the ISO/IEC 27000 series, ISO/IEC 30121:2015, *Information technology—Governance of digital forensic risk framework* deals with strategic processes and decisions related to investigations that involve disclosure of digital evidence.

The Sedona Conference

Commentaries, white papers, and other publications issued by The Sedona Conference have had a significant impact on the development laws and rules for e-discovery in the United States and elsewhere. Widely cited Sedona principles and guidelines include the following:

- *The Sedona Principles: Best Practices, Recommendations & Principles for Addressing Electronic Document Production* have been revised several times since their initial publication in 2002. They provide practical guidance for attorneys and judges regarding preservation and disclosure of digital content that is subject to discovery. While *The Sedona Principles* do not deal specifically with e-discovery software, they do advocate the use of technology to search for relevant digital

content in cases with large quantities of electronically stored information.
- *The Sedona Guidelines: Best Practice Guidelines & Commentary for Managing Information & Records in the Electronic Age* establishes the relationship between e-discovery and information governance. *The Sedona Guidelines* emphasize the importance of systematic lifecycle management for digital content and provides guidance for preparing for and responding to e-discovery requests. *The Sedona Guidelines* acknowledge the impact of technology on information governance policies and procedures, but they do not address e-discovery software requirements.
- *The Sedona Conference Glossary: eDiscovery & Digital information Management*, first published in 2005 and revised multiple times since, defines hundreds of terms related to various aspects of e-discovery, including some terms that are relevant for evaluation and selection of e-discovery software.

FEATURES AND CAPABILITIES

Most e-discovery software developers align their products with the Electronic Discovery Reference Model, which is a conceptual construct that standardizes the e-discovery process. As discussed above, the EDRM's information governance, identification, and preservation stages establish the model's foundational framework. As explained in the following sections, e-discovery applications provide practical tools to implement the tasks defined in the EDRM stages 4 through 9.

Collection

The identification stage of the EDRM locates electronically stored information that may be relevant for a given legal matter. Collection, variously termed "document collection" or "data collection," is the process of gathering the identified ESI for evaluation by attorneys, litigation support specialists, forensic experts, and others involved in a given legal proceeding. A comprehensive, well-managed collection process is essential for defensible completion of later stages of the reference model. If ESI is not collected, it cannot be processed, reviewed, analyzed, produced for the requester, or presented in legal proceedings:

- E-discovery applications can collect and import ESI from designated repositories, including shared drives, personal computers, mobile devices, and cloud-based servers, as well as from databases, email

and messaging systems, ECM applications, records management applications, websites, social media platforms, and other technologies discussed in this book. They can also collect and import ESI that is stored on USB drives, removable hard disks, magnetic tapes, or other offline storage media.
- E-discovery applications typically collect copies of ESI. The originals remain in the repositories where the e-discovery application encountered them. The original ESI may be subject to preservation orders that prohibit its modification or deletion until the legal matters to which it pertains are resolved. By contrast, the copies collected by an e-discovery application may be annotated, redacted, or even deleted during the processing, review, and analysis stages of the EDRM.
- ESI must be collected in a transparent and trustworthy manner that preserves its evidentiary integrity. The collection process must be fully documented to establish a chain of custody that will affirm the ESI's authenticity and ensure its admissibility in legal proceedings. The documentation must indicate the devices or repositories from which ESI was obtained, the collection method used, the names and titles of persons who were involved in any aspect of the collection process, and the location where the ESI was stored after collection. An e-discovery application will maintain detailed logs that record all handling of and interactions with the ESI during collection.
- An on-premises e-discovery implementation will typically save collected ESI on local hard drives. Cloud-based e-discovery application providers store collected ESI on their own servers. Some e-discovery implementations employ hybrid storage arrangements. ESI is stored on-premises after collection, then transferred to cloud-based storage when processing is completed. Alternatively, on-premises storage may be reserved for ESI that requires frequent, fast access with other ESI stored on cloud-based servers.
- Whether on-premises, cloud-based, or a combination of both, the storage arrangement must be conveniently accessible to enable authorized users to retrieve and process the collected ESI. It must also be appropriately scalable to accommodate unpredictable accumulations of ESI without compromising performance and sufficiently secure to protect the collected ESI from unauthorized access and prevent alteration, deletion, or damage that will render it unreadable or inadmissible as evidence.
- The collection process use forensic tools to create bit-for-bit copies—often characterized as forensic images—of ESI in its original state. Forensic tools can capture the entire contents of a given storage device or medium, including all hidden files, data fragments, and deleted files that have not been overwritten, as well as metadata that

indicates the dates and times that files were created, modified, or viewed. An e-discovery application typically incorporates forensic tools as a standard component, but some collection processes may require third-party tools with specialized forensic capabilities for recovery of damaged or deleted files or for collection of ESI from operating systems, file systems, or storage devices that are not supported by an e-discovery application's built-in forensic tools.
- Like the digital preservation applications discussed in chapter 4, forensic tools perform fixity checking of collected ESI at the bit level to ensure its continued integrity and authenticity. A mathematical algorithm calculates a checksum value that represents the ESI's state when it is ingested. These calculated checksums are used to confirm that collected ESI has remained unchanged since it was collected. Calculated checksums also provide a baseline for future detection of corruption, data loss, or unauthorized alterations that may compromise the ESI's reliability and admissibility.
- An e-discovery application must be able to collect and differentiate ESI that is compressed, encrypted, or corrupted. Some e-discovery applications will scan documents for malicious software at an early stage in the collection process. In other cases, malware detection is performed in the ESI's original storage location before collection begins. Regardless of how they are detected, Infected files will be quarantined and removed for later handling.
- The scope of ESI collection may range from broadly inclusive or narrowly targeted, depending on the legal matter at hand. E-discovery applications provide filtering mechanisms that allow an organization to minimize the collection of irrelevant ESI, thereby expediting the discovery process and reducing the cost of processing, review, and analysis. Date filtering can align collected documents with the timeline of a case, while keyword searches can limit collection to documents that are likely to be pertinent. Filtering by email addresses, employee names, or data custodians will focus collection on documents that are created or maintained by individuals or groups known to be involved with the legal matter to which discovery pertains. Filtering by file type can eliminate system files, program files, log files, or other files that are unlikely to be relevant.

Processing

The processing stage of the EDRM prepares collected ESI for review and analysis. Processing work steps may be complicated by the quantity and diverse characteristics of collected ESI:

- An e-discovery applications must be able to process ESI that was collected from a variety of originating applications in a wide range of file formats, including unusual, proprietary, or discontinued formats. The processing stage begins with accurate identification of collected ESI. An e-discovery application may determine file types by examining their extensions, header information, or other metadata. If these indicators are damaged or absent, the e-discovery application may analyze a file's contents for clues to its format.
- Some e-discovery applications utilize specialized tools, including libraries of file types and integration with third-party software, to recognize files that cannot be identified by other means. These specialized tools use pattern recognition, machine-learning, and other artificial intelligence algorithms to increase the likelihood of accurate identification.
- Collected ESI may include compressed files, also described as container files, which combine multiple files and folders in a single package. Compressed files are typically recognized by their extensions. E-discovery applications will unpack their contents and apply the proper decompression algorithms to render individual files and their associated metadata usable for further processing.
- One of the objectives of the processing stage is to manage the cost of e-discovery by reducing the volume of ESI that needs to be reviewed and analyzed. To accomplish this, e-discovery applications will identify and purge collected ESI that is irrelevant for the legal proceeding for which it was collected. This includes comparing a file's digital signatures to those listed in the National Software Reference Library (NSRL) prepared by the National Institute of Standards and Technology, a process sometimes described as "de-NISTing." The NSRL list, which is continually updated, includes operating system files, software development tools, utility software, device drivers, and application software that is unlikely to come within the scope of a discovery order.
- E-discovery applications will identify and remove duplicates from collected ESI to eliminate redundant review and analysis. Deduplication can be applied to all ESI regardless of source or custodian. Alternatively, duplicates can be removed from selected ESI to preserve one instance of a given document from a particular source or custodian. Duplicates may be retained following removal from an ESI data set in case questions are raised about the deduplication process.
- As a variant form of deduplication, some e-discovery applications use email threading to display the entire chain of replies and related email stemming from an initial message. Email threading simplifies the review process by assembling the messages in a single conversa-

tional sequence that captures the context in which the messages were exchanged. Reviewers can focus on the entire thread rather than have to retrieve individual messages.
- During the processing stage, an e-discovery application will identify problematic ESI and set it aside for further attention and, if possible, replacement or other corrective action. Problematic ESI may include unrecognizable files, files that cannot be opened by their native applications, files that were corrupted by recording or transmission errors during collection, files that are password-protected, encrypted files for which decryption algorithms are unavailable, and multilingual ESI containing characters that are difficult to identify and decode. As an additional complication, multilingual ESI often requires translation before it progresses to the review and analysis stages.
- Some e-discovery applications provide malware detection tools that will scan collected ESI for viruses or other harmful content. Malware detection is usually done early in the processing stage to prevent damage to collected ESI. Suspicious files will be quarantined for disinfection or deleted. Malware detection can increase the time required for processing, especially if large quantities of ESI involved. It may also incorrectly identify legitimate files as infected, which will exclude potentially relevant ESI from review and analysis. Malware detection tools can remove or neutralize harmful content, but some authorities caution that the disinfection process may inadvertently alter the content of files. To address concerns about the integrity of ESI processing, an e-discovery application may maintain audit logs that track malware detection and disinfection of specific ESI.
- To facilitate review and analysis, an e-discovery application can convert ESI from diverse sources to a normalized format, such as PDF, during the processing stage. Optical character recognition may be used to convert files of digital document images to searchable text.
- During the processing stage, an e-discovery application will extract creation dates, author's names, titles, and other metadata from collected ESI. Metadata that might be extracted from email messages includes the sender, recipient, date, and subject. The extracted metadata is converted to a structured format that can be used to create a searchable index to support review and analysis. Metadata extraction does not alter the original ESI.

Review

As discussed above, the processing stage prepares ESI for the review and analysis, the two most difficult and time-consuming EDRM stages. In the review stage, ESI is evaluated for relevance and importance for the legal matter for which it was collected. ESI that is considered relevant will be advanced to the analysis stage and ultimately delivered to requesting party. Irrelevant ESI is withheld from discovery, as are confidential communications between clients and their attorneys, private communications between a client and spouse, work product prepared by attorneys in connection with a case, documents related to a joint defense agreement, and other ESI protected from disclosure by legal privilege doctrine.

The review stage dominates many e-discovery initiatives. ESI review is performed by a team that is led by attorneys who are familiar with the legal proceeding for which discovery was ordered. Other team members may include paralegals and legal assistants who will organize documents and perform searches, litigation support consultants who specialize in e-discovery, information technology and cybersecurity experts who can address issues of data integrity and protection, and subject matter experts who can evaluate documents that require knowledge of specific industry, discipline, or business operation. A project manager may be responsible for coordinating and monitoring the review process, keeping it on schedule, and allocating budgetary and other resources as needed.

In addition to ESI, the review team will have access information about the litigants, ESI custodians, and the chronology of the legal matter for which discovery is ordered. E-discovery software provides capabilities that facilitate the review team's work:

- E-discovery applications typically save processed ESI in a centralized repository to which stringent security controls can be applied. Access to specific documents is determined by a project manager or system administrator based on each team member's role in the review process. Among its other advantages, a centralized ESI repository allows access by authorized team members, regardless of their geographic locations or time zones.
- Search functionality allows team members to retrieve ESI by the document type, the date, the creator or recipient, the custodian, the source from which it was collected, the subject terms assigned as metadata, and the words or phrases that specific documents contain. E-discovery applications offer the same range of search capabilities as other technologies discussed in this book. Boolean operators, relational expressions, proximity searching, wildcard characters in search terms, and similar retrieval functions are widely supported.
- Some e-discovery applications offer advanced search capabilities that use semantic analysis, syntactical analysis, natural language processing, and machine-learning algorithms to identify relevant ESI that might otherwise be overlooked. Concept searching retrieves ESI that deals with specified themes or topics that are not represented by

subject metadata or the words that a document contains. To accomplish this, a given search term or phrase is expanded to encompass synonyms, variant spellings, and related terms. Context searching expands search terms by using syntactical and semantic clues to identify potentially relevant passages within documents. With both concept and context searching, users can provide feedback to improve the algorithms for future searches.
- E-discovery applications allow team members to categorize ESI based on relevance, privilege status, confidentiality level, or legal issues or aspects of a case to which they relate. This categorization process, described as tagging or coding, groups document for further review and analysis. Before reviewing begins, the legal team defines the set of tags that will be used to categorize documents. Reviewers examine individual documents to determine the appropriate tags, which are selected from a toolbar. Some e-discovery applications support keyboard shortcuts for commonly used tags. A second-pass review may be used to verify the accuracy of assigned tags.
- E-discovery applications increasingly support predictive coding and other artificial intelligence algorithms to automatically categorize documents for relevance. With predictive coding, also known as technology-assisted review (TAR), an attorney or subject matter expert familiar with the legal matter at hand reviews and codes a selected group of documents manually. Predictive coding algorithms use the precoded documents as a training set to develop a model for automatic categorization of the remaining documents. Further training or other adjustments may be necessary based on a subsequent manual review of a sample of the algorithm's output.
- E-discovery applications can assemble batches of related documents to be assigned to specific team members for review. This approach allows managers to balance workloads or make effective use of reviewers with specialized expertise, subject knowledge, or prior experience with similar legal proceedings. Batching also increases the likelihood that documents related to a given facet of a case will be evaluated and tagged in a consistent manner.
- E-discovery applications provide tools to redact personally identifiable information, protected health information, trade secrets, or other sensitive or confidential information that must be excluded from disclosure to the requesting party.
- E-discovery applications support collaboration functions that allow team members to concurrently review, collectively tag, and share notes about specific documents. Collaboration allows tagging to be double-checked by team members. Some e-discovery applications

provide a messaging component that allows team members to communicate with each other without leaving the application.
- E-discovery applications can generate managerial and statistical reports about the progress of the review process, the productivity of individual team members, the distribution of documents across specific categories, the number of documents tagged as privileged or confidential, the number of pages with redactions, and the number of documents that require the attention of specialized reviewers. Reports can also track access to specific documents and changes made to tags by individual reviewers.

Analysis

The subset of collected ESI that is determined to be relevant in the review stage passes to the analysis stage for in-depth evaluation. The review and analysis stages are closely related. Accurate and thorough identification of relevant documents—and removal of irrelevant ESI—is essential for successful and manageable analysis. Both the review and analysis stages require a multidisciplinary team effort led by attorneys who are supported by e-discovery specialists, technology specialists, and subject matter experts. Depending on the quantity of ESI involved and complexity of the legal matter for which discovery is ordered, review and analysis may be performed by the same team or different teams.

In some respects, an analysis team extends the review team's examination of ESI, but the two stages address different aspects of the e-discovery process. As discussed in the preceding section, the review stage involves a granular assessment of individual documents for relevance and privilege. By contrast, the analysis stage is concerned with organizing and understanding ESI to identify and prioritize themes and patterns that will guide a litigant's strategy and decisions. While both stages rely on the retrieval capabilities discussed above, e-discovery software provides features and functions that are specifically intended for the analysis stage:

- An e-discovery application can generate data maps that provide an overview of an organization's information technology environment and digital information assets, including data, documents, and email. Data maps may be prepared for the collection, processing, and review stages of the EDRM. To support the analysis stage, a data map identifies the sources, formats, custodians, quantities, date ranges, and storage repositories for relevant ESI. It enables the legal team to allocate resources efficiently and schedule its work more effectively by identifying the most important documents and prioritizing them for analysis.

- An e-discovery application can generate social network maps that depict the connections and interactions between individuals, including plaintiffs, defendants, witnesses, and other stakeholders who are directly involved in a legal matter as well as data custodians, managers, and external parties whose roles, communications, and actions may be important. The individuals to be included in a social network may be derived from the text of documents, email metadata that identifies the names of senders and recipients, and input from attorneys, managers, or others who are familiar with the people involved and the legal matter for which discovery is ordered. An e-discovery application may also identify individuals whose frequent communications suggest a high level of involvement with the matter under investigation.
- Timeline graphs depict the sequence of events that are critical to a case. A timeline chronology may be based on information obtained from ESI or interviews with persons who are knowledgeable about key events in a case. An e-discovery application may also examine calendar entries for important persons and extract creation dates, revision dates, or timestamps from documents, email, instant messages, call logs, digital photographs, audio and video recordings, transaction records, web browsing histories, and social media posts.
- Word clouds and keyword heat maps depict the frequency and distribution of specific words or phrases in documents. E-discovery software extracts the words from specified ESI. The analysis team can use these visual depictions to obtain a preliminary overview of the main topics or issues covered in a document set, to formulate retrieval strategies for targeted searches, or to identify themes, concepts, patterns, or unexpected terms that warrant further investigation.
- As noted above, the analysis stage organizes ESI to identify and prioritize themes and patterns. An e-discovery application can use machine learning and natural language processing to group ESI based on conceptual or topical similarities in text or metadata. This allows related documents to be analyzed together in clusters, which can be labeled and annotated by authorized team members to indicate their importance, the legal issues to which they pertain, or to provide questions or instructions for further examination. Some e-discovery applications will suggest labels for specific clusters.

Production

Following analysis, the production stage of the EDRM prepares relevant, nonprivileged ESI—the so-called production set—for delivery to the requesting party. The production set is checked for relevance and privilege, finalized, and delivered in an agreed-upon or court-order format that will be usable by the requesting party and compatible with all applicable security requirements. In the United States, the opposing parties in a legal proceedings typically discuss the format and delivery method during an initial conference, which is required by Federal Rules of Civil Procedure their state counterparts, and in subsequent communications. E-discovery software provides features and functions to support the production effort:

- Continuing a practice that dates from the late nineteenth century, an e-discovery application will apply Bates numbering before ESI is delivered to the requesting party. Bates numbering assigns a unique, nonremovable identifier to each page or document in the production set. Bates numbers are used for reference and citation in discussions between parties, depositions, and court proceedings. An organization can specify the starting digit, prefixes, suffixes, length, and page position for Bates numbers.
- E-discovery software can convert ESI to common formats, such as TIF or PDF, which may be image-only files or searchable text. A requesting party may prefer to receive word-processing files, spreadsheets, email messages, and other digital documents in their native formats. Less common delivery include HTML files and plain text files. Some e-discovery applications can deliver load files, which contain metadata with links to the actual documents in the PDF or TIF format. Load files are intended for uploading into a requesting party's e-discovery review platform.
- E-discovery software preserves metadata during the collection and processing stages of the EDRM. Handling of metadata during the production stage will be determined by the provisions of a court order or agreement between the parties. A production set can include metadata selectively or in its entirety. Alternatively, an e-discovery application allows authorized users to modify, selectively redact, or exclude metadata from documents in the production set.
- E-discovery software may can generate production logs and reports that includes the Bates number range, title, date, and other information for each document in a production set. An e-discovery application can also generate a log of privileged documents withheld from a production set and a log of redactions, modifications, or other actions that involve the production set.
- An e-discovery application supports encryption of ESI in transit, secure file transfer protocols, or recording on removable hard drives, USB drives, or other physical media for delivery of the production

set to the requesting party. Documents can be watermarked to deter unauthorized sharing of documents in the production set.
- Privileged documents are tagged during the review and analysis to prevent their inclusion in the production set. If an agreement or court order requires the return of privileged documents that are inadvertently sent to the requesting party, e-discovery software will identify and remove them when a clawback request is received. An e-discovery application can generate reports that document compliance with clawback requirements.

Presentation

The final stage of the EDRM builds on the work of previous stages to incorporate ESI into presentations for use in depositions, hearings, trials, arbitrations, mediations, and other legal proceedings. Examples of such presentations include opening and closing statements, deposition summaries, mediation and arbitration briefs, expert reports, hearing exhibits, and summaries prepared for settlement conferences. The intended audience may be judges, hearing panels, arbitrators, juries, witnesses, and the opposing parties.

E-discovery software doesn't provide features and functions intended specifically and exclusively for the presentation stage, but those responsible for preparing presentations can draw on capabilities employed in other EDRM stages:

- A legal team can use an e-discovery application's search functions and data visualization tools to identify, view, and select ESI for formulation of legal arguments and pretrial collaboration.
- A legal team can use an e-discovery application's content organization capabilities to create and manage digital trial bundles and exhibits consisting of document, email messages, digital photographs, and other ESI. The contents of trial bundles and exhibits can be categorized, indexed, and hyperlinked for convenient reference and quick retrieval of evidence during trial preparation and legal proceedings. Digital trial bundles and exhibits can be shared with cocounsel and others.
- Review and analysis tools allow authorized users to highlight and annotate documents included in trial bundles. Redaction tools can be used to remove or conceal personal, medical, or confidential information that is protected by privacy legislation or trade secret laws.
- Bates numbers can be applied to individual documents and pages in a trial bundle to facilitate reference and citation during trial

preparation, depositions, hearings, and court proceedings. Bates numbers are also used to create lists that identify exhibits to be used at trial.
- E-discovery software can enable attorneys to prepare visuals, including timelines, charts, and graphs for presentation at trials and other legal proceedings. The visuals can incorporate documents, email messages, social media posts, and other digital evidence from the production set.
- Many courts accept digital submission of evidence. E-discovery software can export ESI for uploading to a court's e-filing system in PDF, TIF, or other formats that are compatible with the court's requirements. Annotations can be removed and personal or confidential information can be redacted prior to submission. Export settings can be customized for inclusion or omission of Bates numbers and metadata.

Integration with External Applications

E-discovery software is one of a group of applications that automate legal operations and activities in law firms, legal aid organizations, and in-house legal departments. Taken together, these applications complement rather than compete with one another. Some e-discovery applications provide prebuilt integrations that permit the exchange of ESI with selected legal software at various stages of the EDRM. Where prebuilt integration is unavailable or inadequate, application programming interfaces or other tools can be used to develop customized connections with external software for uploading or downloading of ESI.

- ESI that is collected and processed by an e-discovery application can be transferred into or uploaded from a legal case management system, which stores information about legal matters and tracks their progress from inception through resolution. Case management and e-discovery software have different purposes. Designed to streamline law office operations and improve client services, case management applications have a broad focus. They store client data, schedule court dates, track billable hours, generate invoices, and provide other capabilities that are unrelated to e-discovery. By contrast, e-discovery applications are designed specifically for identification, collection, processing, review, and production of ESI in response to court orders or other requests. Some vendors offer a comprehensive suite of legal automation applications that include case management and e-discovery components, which can be implemented in combination or separately.

- Legal hold software is designed to prevent the inadvertent or intentional destruction of data and documents that are deemed relevant for litigation or other legal proceedings. A legal hold application will issue notifications to individuals or departments informing them of their obligation to preserve specific data and documents until the legal matters to which they pertain are resolved. The application will track receipt of legal hold notifications and sent follow-up reminders. An effective legal hold process is a precondition for the collection phase of the EDRM. Some legal hold software will prevent the destruction or alteration of data and documents that are stored on an organization's servers. With appropriate integration, this ESI can be transferred into an e-discovery application for processing and review.
- Some e-discovery applications can be integrated with trial preparation software, which provides features and functions to support the organization and presentation of evidence in a courtroom setting. Documents, email messages, and other relevant ESI can be transferred directly into trial preparation software, eliminating the need for manual reentry. Metadata and annotations can be transferred as well. Categorization schemes and Bates numbering are preserved during transfer process. Compared to e-discovery software, trial preparation software provides a broader range of presentation capabilities. In particular, it can generate slide shows, multimedia displays, interactive timelines, animated models, and other demonstrative visuals for opening statements, presentation of evidence, testimony of expert witnesses, and closing arguments.
- As previously noted, e-discovery software can upload documents from repositories maintained by other information governance technologies discussed in this book, including electronic content management, records management, email archiving, and digital asset management applications. Some ECM vendors target law firms and in-house legal departments with products that combine document management and case management features and functions. Certain ECM applications offer built-in integration for direct transfer of relevant documents and metadata to selected e-discovery applications for processing and review. The ECM application's retrieval capabilities can identify the documents to be transferred.

IMPLEMENTATION ISSUES

An e-discovery software implementation begins with the selection of a product that can satisfy a legal team's functional requirements.

E-discovery applications are available for on-premises installation or hosted by a cloud service provider.

Product Evaluation

A thorough assessment of an organization's requirements and comprehensive market research are preconditions for evaluation and selection of e-discovery software. The assessment must be based on input from attorneys, paralegals, information technology specialists, and other stakeholders who will be involved in or affected by an e-discovery implementation. The assessment should review the organization's existing e-discovery processes, determine the types and complexity of ESI to be handled, estimate the quantity of ESI to be processed, and identify the sources from ESI will be collected. Sources for market research to identify e-discovery software vendors and products include legal technology publications, vendors' websites, professional forums, reports prepared by industry analysts, and demonstrations and educational sessions at conference and trade shows.

When the needs assessment and market research are completed, proposals should be requested from qualified suppliers. In some organizations, proposals must be solicited by a competitive procurement process. In other cases, an organization may simplify identify several qualified suppliers and ask them to submit proposals. Regardless of procurement procedures, the following considerations apply to the evaluation and selection of e-discovery software:

- An e-discovery application must address all stages of the EDRM. It must be able to collect and process ESI created by diverse applications in a variety of standard and propriety file formats. It must provide basic and advanced search capabilities, and offer a full range of features and functions to facilitate and simplify ESI review, analysis, production, and presentation. As with other technologies discussed in this book, industry-leading e-discovery products offer similar capabilities, but there may be significant differences in ease of implementation, learning, and use.
- Documents, email messages, and other ESI that is collected and processed by e-discovery software may contain confidential or sensitive information about individuals or organizations. An e-discovery application must incorporate rigorous security measures to prevent intrusion by malicious actors as well as unauthorized access to ESI by an organization's own employees at all stages of the EDRM. The security measures must be compatible with the organization's requirements and protocols for controlled access, prevention of data

leakage, encryption of sensitive information in storage and transit, and data recovery following an adverse event. The e-discovery application must provide effective audit mechanisms that monitor authorized use and detect unauthorized activity. It must also comply with applicable laws and regulations related to privacy of personal data, dissemination of protected health information, and protection of trade secrets.
- Litigation, investigations, and other matters for which e-discovery is required can involve large and unpredictable quantities of digital content. An e-discovery application must be able to accommodate the anticipated volume of ESI to be collected, processed, and reviewed, and it must be sufficiently scalable to accommodate future increases in the quantity of ESI without a degradation of performance or an unsustainable increase in cost.
- The evaluation of e-discovery software should be limited to commercially available products that are in use at customer sites at the time the software is evaluated. While it can be helpful to know the roadmap for a product's future direction, all advertised capabilities must be fully tested and reliably operational at the time an e-discovery application is considered for implementation. Near-release products or those with essential features and functions that are promised for future availability are not acceptable for mission-critical e-discovery initiatives.
- An e-discovery vendor's qualifications are as important as a product's features and functions. An e-discovery application developer may sell its software directly to customers or indirectly through a network of resellers, business partners, or other authorized representatives. In either case, the vendor must have proven experience in e-discovery implementations as documented by customer references. A prospective purchaser is responsible for due diligence to determine the vendor's market position, confirm its financial stability, and assess its long-term viability.
- An e-discovery software developer must have an active research and development program and a track record of continuing product improvement to repair defects, enhance performance, incorporate new features, adapt to changes in legal and regulatory requirements, and take advantage of the latest technological innovations, such as machine-learning algorithms and other approaches to artificial intelligence. A vendor's commitment to continuous improvement can be assessed by examining the product's release history.
- The most powerful e-discovery software offers supports a broader range of features and functions than an organization may need and that any given user can master. The e-discovery vendor must be able

to provide a level of customer training tailored to an organization's requirements and reliable, responsive technical support when problems arise. In-person or online training sessions covering basic and advanced capabilities should be supported by tutorials, user manuals, and other educational resources, which are updated promptly when significant enhancements or other changes are made to the e-discovery application.
- An e-discovery vendor must have a coherent, transparent pricing model, which may be based on the number of users, the quantity of ESI processed, the features utilized, or other factors. The cost of standard and optional capabilities must be clearly enumerated. Hidden fees are unacceptable. Costs must be competitive, predictable, aligned with an organization's budget, and sustainable as usage patterns, the quantity of ESI, or functional requirements change.
- Some organizations want e-discovery software to integrate with legal technology, content management, email systems, or other applications that are relevant for e-discovery initiatives. Such integration can simplify workflows and data transfers, eliminate manual intervention in e-discovery processes, and save time at all stages of the EDRM. Evaluation favors products that offer prebuilt integration with applications that an organization already owns. If integration will be accomplished through an application programming interface, the required level of effort, technical expertise, and cost must be determined.

On-Premises vs. Cloud Implementation

The earliest e-discovery applications, introduced in the late 1990s and early 2000s, were intended for on-premises installation and operation on an organization's own servers and computing infrastructure. Those products remain available and widely utilized, but their developers have since broadened their product lines to include cloud-based offerings with comparable capabilities. In recent years, these cloud-based e-discovery applications have attracted increased attention and customers. New companies have entered the e-discovery market with cloud-native applications that have no on-premises counterparts. Like other information governance technologies discussed in this book, cloud-based e-discovery applications have benefited from the growing adoption of cloud-first policies by companies, government agencies, and nonprofit organizations. Such policies prioritize cloud offerings for new applications or as replacements for software that is installed on internal servers.

Subject to minor variations, the on-premises and cloud-based versions of most e-discovery applications are functionally equivalent, but each approach has advantages and limitations that can impact the efficiency, effectiveness, and cost of e-discovery initiatives:

- An on-premises implementation gives an organization direct control over installation, testing, customization, and operation of an e-discovery application and the security of the ESI it collects, processes, and stores. An organization that operates its own e-discovery installation controls the allocation of resources that the application requires, the devices on which ESI is stored, the timing of backup intervals, and the hours of availability, as well as scheduled downtime for software maintenance and upgrades.
- Properly managed, an on-premises e-discovery implementation may offer a performance advantage over a cloud-based application. An organization can select servers, storage devices, and network infrastructure for efficient operation of an e-discovery application, and it can prioritize upgrading of these components as needed to maintain a desired level of responsiveness as the number of active users and the quantity of ESI increase.
- On the other hand, enhancing the performance of an on-premises installation will require time and effort, and any upscaling is generally irreversible. By contrast, cloud-based e-discovery implementations are immediately scalable at any stage of the EDRM. An organization can add or remove users and increase or decrease storage capacity to address changes in the size of its legal team or the quantity of ESI to be collected, processed, and reviewed. Cloud providers can allocate or reduce resources for a given customer on demand without disrupting e-discovery operations.
- Hardware and software upgrades, which may be difficult and costly in on-premises e-discovery installations, are handled by cloud services without customer involvement. Cloud providers monitor performance continuously and will upgrade their e-discovery platforms to increase processing power, expand storage capacity, fix software defects, and incorporate software enhancements. These improvements are implemented in the background or during off-peak hours to ensure that e-discovery services remain accessible. Customers are typically notified in advance if scheduled maintenance will disrupt service.
- For many organizations, the start-up costs associated with an on-premises e-discovery implementation will offset whatever performance or control advantages a local installation might offer. An on-premises installation will require the upfront purchase of e-discovery software licenses. An organization may also need to buy new servers and networking components or upgrade its existing ones.

Postinstallation, an organization must purchase service agreements for continuing technical support of e-discovery software. Charges for such agreements, which must be renewed annually, are typically based on the cost of the installed software.
- As one of its most important advantages, a cloud-based e-discovery implementation involves minimal start-up costs. Cloud customers pay a monthly or annual subscription fee based on the number of licensed users, the amount of storage needed, the specific e-discovery capabilities utilized, and the desired level of customer support. Capital expenditures for new or upgraded servers, storage devices, network components, and other information technology infrastructure are eliminated. An organization does not need to purchase e-discovery software licenses, but a cloud provider may charge a one-time setup fee for new customers. Over time, accumulated subscription fees charged by a cloud provider will exceed the start-up cost of an on-premises e-discovery installation, but that point may not be reached for five years or longer.
- A cloud-based application is preferable for an organization with a short-term or intermittent need for e-discovery capabilities—to deal with occasional litigation, regulatory investigations, or other nonrecurring legal matters of defined scope and limited duration, for example. Cloud-based services can be temporarily suspended or permanently terminated when they are no longer needed. In such situations, an on-premises e-discovery implementation will be underutilized, but its start-up costs cannot be recaptured and certain operating costs will continue.
- Compared to an on-premises installation, a cloud-based e-discovery application can be deployed more rapidly with less involvement by information technology staff or consultants. This is an important consideration for small organizations or those with limited in-house technical expertise or limited access to consultants. Servers, storage devices, and network components do not need to be expanded or upgraded for the e-discovery implementation. E-discovery software does not need to installed, configured, and tested. The e-discovery application is pretested, fully operational, and ready for use on the provider's cloud servers.
- Cloud-based e-discovery services can be accessed from any location with a reliable internet connection. The global reach of cloud-based archiving is well suited to geographically dispersed legal teams or to multinational organizations that want a uniform e-discovery platform for all locations where it does business. On the other hand, internet connections have bandwidth limitations that will affect data

access and transfer rates, which may pose problems where large quantities of ESI are involved.
- As previously discussed, cloud-based e-discovery providers offer prebuilt integrations with popular applications hosted by other cloud-based services. Implementation of these prebuilt integrations typically requires limited involvement by an organization's information technology staff. An organization may prefer an on-premises e-discovery implementation for customized integration with a case management system, content management system, or other external applications that are also installed on-premises. This is particularly the case with legacy applications that may not be easily integrated with a cloud-based e-discovery application. Such integrations may require a high-level of in-house technical expertise or the services of a consultant who is knowledgeable about both the e-discovery application and the legacy application.

SUMMARY OF MAJOR POINTS

- E-discovery software is designed to identify, locate, preserve, collect, process, review, and produce electronically stored information (ESI) in response to discovery requests. Given the widespread use of digital technology for creation and storage of business information, ESI dominates discovery for most legal proceedings.
- The relationship between e-discovery and information governance is widely acknowledged in legal publication and professional presentations. An effective and efficient discovery process depends on ESI that is well organized, stored securely, protected from accidental or malicious destruction, and accessible by a discovery team when needed.
- E-discovery applications were introduced in the late 1990s and early 2000s amid growing awareness of the importance and difficulties of responding to discovery requests for electronically stored information. E-discovery products have improved steadily and significantly since that time.
- E-discovery is a time-consuming, labor-intensive process that must be performed by a team of attorneys and support personnel who are familiar with matter for which discovery is required, the legal issues involved, and the types of data and documents to be disclosed or withheld. Discovery costs account for a significant percentage of total litigation costs. The business justification for e-discovery software is based on its potential to reduce litigation

costs by automating, streamlining, and expediting the discovery process.
- The Electronic Discovery Reference Model (EDRM), which was introduced in 2005 as a multistage framework for the electronic discovery process, has had a decisive influence on the development of e-discovery software. Most e-discovery software developers align their products with the EDRM.
- The identification stage of the EDRM locates electronically stored information that may be relevant for a given legal matter. A comprehensive, well-managed collection process is essential for defensible completion of later stages of the reference model.
- The processing stage of the EDRM prepares collected ESI for review and analysis. It prepares ESI for the review and analysis, the two most difficult and time-consuming EDRM stages.
- In the review stage, ESI is evaluated for relevance and importance for the legal matter for which it was collected. ESI that is considered relevant will be advanced to the analysis stage and ultimately delivered to requesting party.
- The review stage involves a granular assessment of individual documents for relevance and privilege. By contrast, the analysis stage is concerned with organizing and understanding ESI to identify and prioritize themes and patterns that will guide a litigant's strategy and decisions.
- The production stage of the EDRM prepares relevant, nonprivileged ESI for delivery to the requesting party. The production set is checked for relevance and privilege, finalized, and delivered in an agreed-upon or court-order format that will be usable by the requesting party and compatible with all applicable security requirements.
- The final stage of the EDRM builds upon the work of previous stages to incorporate ESI into presentations for use in depositions, hearings, trials, arbitrations, mediations, and other legal proceedings.
- E-discovery software can be integrated with other legal technology applications, including case management software, legal hold software, and trial preparation software. Depending on the product, integration may be built-in or implemented via an application programming interface.
- E-discovery software is available from a number of qualified suppliers. Leading e-discovery products offer similar capabilities, but there may be significant differences in ease of implementation, learning, and use.

- The e-discovery market is increasingly dominated by cloud-based applications, which require minimal start-up costs and in-house technical expertise. Cloud-based applications have broadened the e-discovery market to include small organizations and those with occasional or intermittent e-discovery requirements.

NOTE

1. The Sedona Conference Glossary: eDiscovery & Digital Information Management, Fifth Edition," *Sedona Conference Journal* 21, 263-392-178 (2020), accessed September 1, 2024, https://thesedonaconference.org/publication/The_Sedona _Conference_Glossary.

8

✢

GRC Software

GRC is an abbreviation for governance, risk, and compliance, a triad that encompasses a broad range of operations and activities in for-profit companies, government agencies, educational and cultural institutions, scientific and technical research organizations, professional associations, philanthropic foundations, community-based organizations, religious groups, and other nonprofit entities. International standards and other sources define each GRC component. According to ISO 37000:2021, *Governance of organizations—Guidance*, governance is a "human-based system by which an organization is directed, overseen, and held accountable for achieving its defined purpose."[1] ISO 31073:2022, *Risk Management—Vocabulary* defines risk as "the effect of uncertainty on objectives," where uncertainty is a "deficiency of information" related to a particular matter and the effect is a "deviation from the expected."[2] The definition notes that risk is often expressed as a combination of the consequences of a potential event and the likelihood of its occurrence. Other sources define risk as the probability of an adverse outcome if defined threat is able to exploit a specific vulnerability. ISO 37301:2021, *Compliance management systems—Requirements with guidance for use* defines compliance as the act of meeting mandatory or voluntary obligations.[3] Dictionary definitions similarly equate compliance with adherence and obedience.

GRC software provides an integrated suite of application modules that address an organization's governance, risk, and compliance requirements and initiatives.

- All GRC software provides strong risk management and compliance modules as core components. Risk management and compliance are closely related concerns, noncompliance with regulatory mandates and internal policies being a significant source of risk for many organizations. As discussed later in this chapter, the GRC risk management and compliance modules provide features and functions to support the work of risk officers and compliance managers. Given the pervasiveness of risk concerns and compliance requirements, they have an enterprise-wide impact.
- To support governance functions, most GRC software provides modules for policy management, which provides a framework for organizational governance; board management, which supports the meetings, activities, and records of an organization's board of directors or other governing bodies; and audit management, which is a concern for an organization's governing body and its management.
- Other GRC modules vary from product to product. Possibilities, which are discussed later in this chapter, include business continuity, which is an aspect of risk management; cybersecurity management, which identifies and assesses threats to an organization's information technology infrastructure; privacy management, which tracks compliance with data protection laws and regulations; performance management, which supports strategic planning and decision-making; and ESG management, which addresses environmental and social concerns related to organizational governance.
- Some GRC software suites include other modules that are tangentially related to governance, risk, and compliance. Examples include health and safety management, complaints management, quality management, and change management.

Features and capabilities supported by these GRC modules and their importance for information governance are described in the following sections. As discussed later in this chapter, various software developers offer single-purpose governance, risk management, and compliance applications, but an integrated GRC framework provides a unified view and coordinated control of these interrelated functions.

HISTORY

The concept of enhancing organizational effectiveness by integrating governance, risk management, and compliance initiatives dates from the early 2000s. The GRC abbreviation was reportedly introduced in 2002 by OCEG, a nonprofit organization originally founded as the Open

Compliance and Ethics Group. OCEG equates the GRC triad with principled performance, which it defines as the ability achieve objectives (governance) while addressing uncertainty (risk management) and acting with integrity (compliance). The consulting firm PricewaterhouseCoopers similarly discussed the GRC concept in a 2004 white paper that advocated a performance strategy that emphasizes business integrity, ethics, and values to meet the accountability and transparency demands and expectations of an organization's investors, regulators, customers, employees, and other stakeholders.

Introduction of the GRC concept coincided with legislative developments that forced organizations to examine their existing governance structures, risk management processes, and compliance programs. In the United States, the Sarbanes-Oxley Act of 2002 addressed a series of corporate accounting scandals by requiring public companies to strengthen their governance structures and internal controls to address financial risks and ensure compliance with regulatory reporting mandates. Despite complaints about the costs and challenges involved, companies took steps to align their strategic and operational objectives with risk management and compliance programs. Governing boards and audit committees gave greater attention to financial and operational risks. Internal controls were documented and tested. Employees received training about their compliance responsibilities. While Sarbanes-Oxley requirements were limited to public companies, many nonprofit organizations voluntarily adopted measures to improve their governance, risk, and compliance initiatives. By the end of the decade, the importance of the GRC triad was widely acknowledged by business executives and academic researchers. A Google Scholar search for "GRC" in combination with the terms "governance," "risk," and "compliance" retrieved about 115 citations to business and scholarly publications for the period from 2002 to 2004 and almost ten times that number for the period from 2005 to 2010.

Software that supports an integrated framework of governance, risk management, and compliance capabilities was introduced in the mid-2000s. By 2010, GRC products were offered by more than two dozen vendors. Functionality and customer acceptance improved steadily and significantly in the years that followed. The earliest GRC software was intended for on-premises installation, typically in large companies with sufficient budgetary resources and appropriate technical expertise, but the introduction of cloud-based configurations offered a simpler, more affordable solution that attracted medium-size and smaller organizations. As with other information governance technologies discussed in this book, some of the earliest GRC software developers remain in business as independent entities; others were acquired by larger computer companies interested in expanding their product lines. A Google Trends search for the phrase "GRC software" suggests sporadic initial interest until 2015 but the number of searches has increased steadily since that time. Various industry research reports expect the global market for GRC software to continue to expand through the early 2030s.

BUSINESS NEED

Early adopters of GRC software included large organizations with significant risk exposures and heavily regulated companies with burdensome compliance requirements, but the features and capabilities described in this chapter are broadly useful. Every organization needs governance mechanisms that ensure accountability, transparent business practices, and ethical decision making. Every organization must identify threats, assess vulnerabilities, and mitigate risks that can disrupt essential operations. Every organization has compliance obligations imposed by legal and regulatory authorities as well as by internal policies, standards, and industry best practices.

GRC software does not offer unique functionality to address these requirements. Dozens of software developers market standalone applications for risk management, compliance, and specific governance functions, but—as discussed later in this chapter—GRC software provides a comprehensive, integrated approach that can simplify procurement, deployment, user training, and information sharing. The GRC framework is relevant for all business processes, operations, and activities, including those related to information governance, risk, and compliance.

- Effective governance mechanisms ensure that an organization will act diligently and prudently when making decisions about the acquisition, maintenance, use, and disposition of assets. As a focused aspect of organizational governance, information governance is responsible for stewardship of information assets. To accomplish this, information governance establishes polices, processes, and controls that apply to information assets within the broader context of an organization's mission, strategy, and objectives. GRC software include board management, policy management, and other components to support information governance responsibilities.
- Risk oversight is widely recognized as the responsibility of an organization's governing body. Information risk is a focused aspect of general business risk. A risk management program must identify, assess, prioritize, monitor, and respond to threats and vulnerabilities related to creation, collection, loss, retention, usability, disclosure, and ownership of information. Such threats and vulnerabilities

may be associated with internal factors, such as an organization's information-related policies and practices, or external events, such as financial, regulatory, technological, geopolitical, or environmental developments that can affect an organization's information-related objectives or operations. As previously noted, risk management is a core GRC component.
- Compliance's mission is to provide reasonable assurance that an organization conforms to applicable obligations. As a focused aspect of general business compliance, information compliance seeks to align an organization's policies and practices with applicable requirements for creation and collection, retention and disposition, storage and preservation, accessibility and disclosure, security and protection, and ownership of information. Information compliance encompasses legal and regulatory requirements, contractual obligations, standards and industry norms, internal mandates, and broader societal expectations related to ethical behavior and sustainability. Like risk management, with which it is closely related, compliance management is a core GRC component.

GRC software's integrated framework facilitates information sharing and collaboration among information governance, risk management, and compliance. It also allows these functions to communicate and cooperate with organizational units that have managerial responsibility for specific information-related processes, activities, and operations discussed in other chapters. Such units include information technology, information security, records management, and archival administration.

STANDARDS AND GUIDELINES

OCEG, a nonprofit organization that helps organizations attain principled performance through the integration of governance, risk management, and compliance, has issued several publications that it characterizes as GRC standards. There are no national, international, or industry standards that deal specifically with the GRC framework or GRC software, but various security and risk-related standards and guidance documents are relevant for GRC implementations.

OCEG Resources

OCEG, as mentioned earlier in this chapter, has been involved with GRC concepts since their inception. It has issued the following resources to support planning and implementation of GRC capabilities:

- The GRC Capability Model, also known as the OCEG Red Book, provides a framework for understanding, implementing, and evaluating GRC capabilities. It includes a GRC glossary and a five-level maturity model to help organizations assess the degree to which their GRC processes are integrated and aligned with business objectives.
- GRC Assessment Tools, also known as the OCEG Burgundy Book, provides a set of procedures for assessment of GRC capabilities by audit and assurance professionals. The procedures can be used for an enterprise-wide assessment or a review of a specific business unit or program. They can also be used for self-assessment by employees, consultants, and others involved in GRC implementations.
- The OECG Policy Management Capability Model supports the development, review, communication, monitoring, and enforcement of policies. It supports alignment of policies with an organization's objectives, regulatory requirements, and ethical practices. The Capability Model views policy management as a foundational aspect of principled performance based on the integration of governance, risk, and compliance.
- The OECG Integrated Data Privacy Capability Model establishes a framework for governance, management, and assurance of data privacy aligned with the GRC Capability Model.

ISO Standards

The following international standards deal with governance, risk management, and compliance management. Additional standards were in development at the time this chapter was written:

- ISO 37000:2021, *Governance of organizations—Guidance* presents principles that enable boards of directors and other governing bodies to perform their duties effectively, exercise responsible stewardship, behave ethically, and generate value for an organization and its stakeholders.
- ISO 37004:2023, *Governance of organizations—Governance maturity model—Guidance* enables an organization to assess the efficiency and effectiveness of its governance structure and highlight areas for improvement.
- ISO 24143:2022, *Information and documentation—Information Governance—Concept and principles* recognizes information governance as a strategic framework for managing an organization's information assets and an integral component of organizational governance. It provides guidance for governing bodies regarding the effective, efficient, and accountable creation, use, preservation, and disposition of information.

- ISO/IEC 38500:2024, *Information technology—Governance of IT for the organization* presents principles for responsible and strategic use of information technology, including a model that shows the main tasks for IT governance and a framework for the operation of IT governance arrangements. The standard aligns IT governance, as an aspect of organizational governance, with the principles presented in ISO 37000. Other standards in the ISO/IEC 38000 series deal with specific aspects of IT governance that are outside the scope of this chapter.
- ISO 31000:2018, *Risk management—Guidelines* presents generic principles, a framework, and processes that are broadly applicable to any type of risk.
- ISO/IEC 31010:2019, *Risk management—Risk assessment techniques* discusses and categorizes risk assessment methods.
- ISO 31073:2022, *Risk management—Vocabulary* defines terms related to risk and risk management.
- Other international standards discuss the application of ISO 31000 to specific types of risks. Examples include ISO 31022:2020, *Risk management—Guidelines for the management of legal risk* and ISO/TS 31050:2023, *Risk management—Guidelines for managing an emerging risk to enhance resilience*.
- ISO/IEC 27001:2022, *Information security, cybersecurity and privacy protection—Information security management systems—Requirements* is the most widely cited standard for information security, including assessment and treatment of risks related to an organization's information-related operations and information assets. Key terms and fundamental concepts are defined and discussed in ISO/IEC 27000:2018, *Information technology—Security techniques—Information security management systems—Overview and vocabulary*.
- ISO 18128:2024, *Information and documentation—Record risks—Risk assessment for records management* discusses identification, analysis, and evaluation of risks related to records, records management processes, and recordkeeping systems.
- ISO 37301:2021, *Compliance management systems—Requirements with guidance for use* discusses the development, implementation, operation, and improvement of a system to enable an organization to promote a culture of compliance and meet its compliance obligations.

COSO Guidance

COSO, the Committee of Sponsoring Organizations of the Treadway Commission, is a private-sector initiative jointly sponsored by the American Accounting Association, the American Institute of Certified

Public Accountants, Financial Executives International, the Institute of Management Accountants, and the Institute of Internal Auditors. COSO has issued thought papers that deal with issues that are relevant for GRC initiatives:

- The COSO Enterprise Risk Management (ERM) Framework discusses the role of governing bodies and management in managing risks to protect and enhance stakeholder value in a wide range of organizations and industries.
- The CPSO Internal Control-Integrated Framework (ICIF) defines the requirements and components of an effective system of internal controls and emphasizes their importance for organizational governance. Other COSO thought papers deal with specific aspects of internal control, including monitoring internal control systems, blockchain and internal controls, and internal controls for sustainability reporting.
- COSO guidance on Enhancing Board Oversight discusses a good judgment process for a governing body's oversight of management decisions and actions.
- COSO guidance on Improving Organizational Performance and Governance discusses the importance of COSO's internal control and risk management frameworks for organizational governance and management.

NIST Special Publications

The NIST Risk Management Framework developed by the National Institute of Standards and Technology provides comprehensive guidance for managing security and privacy risks in public and private sector organizations. The NIST framework, which is explained and discussed in the following publications, aligns with GRC principles and objectives:

- NIST Special Publication 800-39, *Managing Information Security Risk: Organization, Mission, and Information System View* provides guidance for an enterprise-wide program to manage threats to an organization's mission, functions, and reputation. In addition to risk management professionals, the guidance is intended for governing bodies and executive management with oversight responsibilities for risk-related initiatives.
- NIST Special Publication 800-37, *Risk Management Framework for Information Systems and Organizations: A System Lifecycle Approach for Security and Privacy* explains the risk management framework. In addition to addressing risk and compliance issues, it emphasizes

a close linkage between risk management processes and organizational governance.
- NIST Special Publication 800-53, *Security and Privacy Controls for Information Systems and Organizations* provides a catalog of measures to protect organizational operations and assets from threats to security and individual privacy, including measures that strengthen governance and accountability for control of risks and compliance with risk management safeguards.
- NIST Special Publication 800-30, *Guide for Conducting Risk Assessments* discusses assessment as an integral component of an organization's risk governance initiatives and risk management processes.

FEATURES AND CAPABILITIES

Unlike the information governance technologies discussed in preceding chapters, GRC software is not designed to store, retrieve, preserve, or otherwise manage data or documents. Instead, it deals with the broader organizational context and structure in which data and documents are created, collected, and used. GRC software supports an organization's strategic framework. Rather than enhancing the efficiency and effective of specific business operations and activities, it focuses on alignment of business functions and processes with organizational goals and objectives. As described in the following sections, GRC software provides interrelated application modules that oversee and coordinate an organization's governance, risk management, and compliance obligations, operations, and issues.

Risk Management

ISO 37301:2021, which was cited at the beginning of this chapter, defines risk management as coordinated activities that direct and control an organization with regard to risk. Risk management is the most fully developed component of GRC software. Designed to complete with standalone risk management applications and dispersed risk management initiatives, GRC software provides a coordinated, enterprise-wide platform that integrates risk management with an organization's compliance requirements and governance framework. GRC risk management provides features and functions that allow organizations to proactively and systematically assess, monitor, and respond to threats and address vulnerabilities:

- As a core component, GRC software creates and maintains a centralized register or catalog that identifies, describes, categorizes,

prioritizes, and tracks risks that threaten an organization's mission, operations, or assets. Risk managers, department managers, and authorized employees can add risks to the register. GRC software maintains an audit trail that tracks register entries and changes.
- Register entries for each risk may include an identifying number and title; a description, including threats and consequences; the source of the risk; the likelihood of occurrence, ranging from remote to highly likely; the business operation or process that may be impacted by the risk; the organizational unit that is responsible for managing the risk; and the current threat level, indicating whether it is increasing, decreasing, or stable. A GRC application may provide basic list of these data elements, which can be expanded or edited to satisfy an organization's requirements.
- To enable risk managers and other stakeholders to focus their resources, GRC software provides a risk assessment tool that analyzes and prioritizes specific risks. The assessment tool assigns an impact rating to a given risk based on predefined criteria, including an organization's risk tolerance, the threats to which the organization is subject, the consequences of the threat, the likelihood of occurrence of the threat, vulnerabilities that the threat can exploit, and factors that adversely impact an organization's ability to control or recover should the threat materialize.
- To facilitate risk identification, some GRC applications have preformulated libraries of common and unusual risks from which an organization can select those that are relevant to its operations and activities. Tailored lists may be available for specific industries, such as financial services, healthcare, pharmaceuticals, energy, and manufacturing. Some GRC software incorporates lists of risks identified by specific regulatory authorities.
- The register may indicate the mitigation plan for a given risk. The possibilities include risk acceptance based on an informed decision about the likelihood of specific threat and the impact of the consequences; risk avoidance, which eliminates or restructures a vulnerable business operation or process to eliminate an unacceptable threat; risk transfer, in which the risk is accepted by an insurance company or willing third-party in return for an agreed-upon payment; and risk limitation through the implementation of safeguards that reduce vulnerabilities.
- Entries in the risk register must be reviewed and revalidated periodically by the employees who are responsible for specific risks as part of an organization's ongoing risk management process. Reviewers may add new information to register entries, reevaluate threats and vulnerabilities, modify risk mitigation plans, and raise or lower

risk priority levels to reflect changes in the organization's strategic objectives, business environment, and operating requirements. GRC software can establish a schedule for reviews by specific stakeholders and record their findings in the register.
- An incident management component maintains information about adverse events that require investigation or other action. It allows authorized stakeholders to report incidents, track the progress of investigations from inception through resolution, and estimate the financial and nonfinancial impact. Some GRC applications have prebuilt templates that standardize the types of information maintained about specific incidents, such as data breaches that expose confidential business plans, trade secrets, or sensitive personal information, and destructive weather, equipment failures, or software malfunctions that disrupt mission-critical operations. Incidents that pose compliance risks can be linked to applicable regulations.
- Authorized stakeholders can assign tasks that instruct employees to review entries in the risk register, obtain information about threats and vulnerabilities, evaluate risk ratings and priorities, implement or monitor the effectiveness of specific risk mitigation measures, respond to or investigate risk-related incidents, or participate in internal or external audits of risk management processes.
- GRC software can send notifications and alerts to stakeholders when a risk-related incident occurs or is imminent or when a risk review is assigned or overdue. GRC software can also notify an organization's employees about changes to risk management policies, procedures, and initiatives. Workflow functions can automate notifications, monitor task assignments, and track the progress of investigations related to specific risks.
- A documentation component stores, updates, and manages the review and approval process for risk management policies, mitigation plans, and recovery procedures, as well as audit reports, incident reports, investigation reports, and other risk-related documents. Some GRC applications have a library of prewritten risk management policies, procedures, plans, and guidelines that can be edited and customized for specific situations. Some GRC applications can link to insurance documentation or other content stored in external repositories.
- Some GRC software addresses third-party risks posed by an organization's relationships and interactions with suppliers, contractors, business partners, service providers, and other external entities. Information obtained from questionnaires completed by third parties or documentation collected from other sources is cataloged and categorized in a centralized register. The software supports due

diligence processes to assess a third party's reputation, integrity, and reliability. Background checks can be conducted when a third-party relationship is initially established and monitored on an ongoing basis to identify emerging issues. A risk rating can be assigned to third parties and increased or decreased based on predefined performance metrics, such as frequency of risk events, changes in credit ratings, adverse publicity, supply chain disruptions, and audit findings. Some GRC software offers access to rating services or other resources that provide up-to-date risk scores for continuous monitoring of third parties.
- Some GRC software includes modules for specific risk situations. An IT risk module, for example, is designed to manage cybersecurity incidents and data breaches. A business continuity management module helps organizations plan strategies for maintaining business operations and recovery from adverse events. An environmental management module focuses on risks associated with an organization's environmental impact and social responsibilities.
- GRC software can generate a variety of risk-related reports and visual aids. Examples include lists of risks ranked by severity of impact or likelihood of occurrence, reports of changes in risk ratings, incident reports, audit trail reports for changes to the risk register, and heat maps that identify high-priority risks. Most GRC applications also provide a customizable dashboard that uses text and charts to highlight important key risk indicators and display the current status of specific risks. The dashboard can also provide real-time access to incident reports, alerts and notifications, and other information that supports risk management.
- Like other technologies discussed in this book, GRC software increasingly utilizes artificial intelligence to support proactive risk management strategies and enable decision-makers to anticipate and respond effectively to risk-related events. Artificial intelligence algorithms can identify and assess overlooked threats and vulnerabilities, monitor and analyze trends and patterns to detect emerging risks that may not be recognized by human analysts, and predict the impact of specific risk scenarios. GRC software developers can be expected to enhance and expand these capabilities in future product releases.

Compliance Management

According to ISO 37301:2021, which was cited at the beginning of this chapter, compliance management affirms an organization's acceptance of and commitment to legal and regulatory requirements, industry standards, generally accepted best practices, internal policies, and community expectations. Compliance and risk management are closely related GRC components. Noncompliance with laws, regulations, and internal mandates is a major source of risk, and an organization's risk and compliance teams may have overlapping membership and responsibilities.

Just as risk management features and functions enable an organization to understand and address threats and vulnerabilities, GRC software allows organizations to identify, assess, adhere to, and monitor their compliance obligations. The GRC compliance and risk components share certain information and support similar capabilities. The two components can be used in combination to obtain a holistic view that will enhance decision making, optimize the allocation of resources, and eliminate redundant data storage and analysis.

- GRC software can maintain an enterprise-wide register that catalogs and categorizes an organization's compliance obligations. Risk managers, in-house legal counsel, department managers, and authorized employees can add compliance obligations to the register. GRC software maintains an audit trail that tracks register entries and changes. With some GRC applications, organizations can link entries in the compliance register to their counterparts in the risk register.
- Register entries for each compliance obligation may include an identifying number and title; a description, including the applicable law, regulation, standard, or other source of the obligation; the organizational unit that is responsible for compliance and the name or title of the responsible employee within the organizational unit; the risk of noncompliance; the fines, legal penalties, or other consequences for compliance violations; and notes that relate to the compliance obligation. A GRC application may provide a basic list of these data elements, which can be expanded or edited to satisfy an organization's requirements.
- GRC software can maintain a centralized repository of laws, regulations, regulatory advisories, interpretations and clarifications, standards, industry guidance, and other compliance mandates. Some GRC applications have preformulated libraries of widely applicable and industry-specific laws and regulations that specify compliance obligations. These legal and regulatory compliance obligations are subject to change over time. They must be reviewed periodically and updated as warranted. Some GRC software will monitor compliance-related developments and notify an organization when new laws and regulations are passed or when existing compliance obligations are revised or rescinded.

- In addition to laws, regulations, and other internal mandates, the centralized register of compliance obligations may include codes of conduct and other policies, procedures, and directives that specify internal rules and requirements that regulate the behavior of an organization's employees. Violation of these internal compliance mandates may be punishable by a warning, an adverse performance evaluation, or, for serious infractions, demotion or termination of employment.
- Authorized stakeholders can assign tasks that instruct employees to review entries in the compliance register; obtain information about previous or suspected compliance violations; evaluate, implement, or monitor the effectiveness of specific compliance measures; respond to or investigate compliance-related incidents; or participate in internal or external audits of compliance management processes.
- A compliance attestation is a formal declaration that an employee or organizational unit adheres to applicable compliance mandates. Many organizations require written attestations from managers and other employees for compliance obligations related to their duties. GRC software enables organizations to manage and document these written attestations. Some GRC applications provide predefined attestation templates, which can be customized to satisfy an organization's requirements. Workflow automation can route attestation templates to individual employees, schedule due dates for submission, monitor the receipt of attestations, and send reminders for overdue attestations. Some GRC software will alert compliance officers, managers, or other interested parties when completed attestations are below an expected level. Attestations stored by the GRC software are available for management review and compliance audits.
- Some GRC software provides checklist, scoring systems, and other mechanisms to support the periodic assessments that identify compliance lapses and issues. Most GRC applications support customizable dashboards that provide a real-time overview of compliance incidents, pending and overdue compliance tasks, compliance audits, and the status of compliance training.
- To manage compliance-related incidents, GRC software maintains information about compliance lapses and issues that require investigation or other action. Authorized employees stakeholders to report incidents. Some GRC applications provide customizable templates that solicit information about suspected compliance violations, including the date and time, details about the incident, and the business processes or organizational units affected. Documentation to support an incident report can be attached to a template. Compliance officers, attorneys, or other stakeholders can track the progress

of investigations from inception through resolution and estimate an incident's financial or nonfinancial impact.
- GRC software allow compliance officers and other authorized stakeholders to schedule periodic or special compliance audits, allocate personnel or other resources to specific audits, issue notifications and reminders to the involved parties, store audit reports, and track audit responses and corrective actions.
- GRC software can generate a variety of compliance-related reports and visual aids. Examples include compliance status reports and graphs by department, business process, or geographic location; reports that assess the effectiveness of internal controls; lists of completed, ongoing, and overdue tasks; summary reports and charts of audit findings; reports of changes in laws and regulations that specify compliance requirements; compliance risk rating maps; compliance-related incident reports; and training status report and graphs.

Policy Management

Policies are an essential component of an organization's governance framework. As defined in ISO 37000: 2021, which was cited at the beginning of this chapter, governance policies establish an organization's intentions and directions. They specify standards and expectations for decisions, operations, activities, and actions. Policies provide guidance and direction for the organization's stakeholders, including members of governing bodies, executive management, and employees. They also have an impact on an organization's investors, customers, suppliers, business partners, and, in the case of government agencies, the public.

GRC software supports the development, dissemination, monitoring, and updating of policies, procedures, directives, protocols, approved practices, codes of conduct, and related documents.

- GRC software's policy management component maintains a centralized online repository of the latest versions of approved policies. Authorized employees can access specific policies on a need-to-know basis. Policies can be retrieved by titles, topics, or other criteria.
- Centralization minimizes the likelihood that a superseded policy will be mistaken for the official version or that a withdrawn policy will continue to be enforced. These problems can occur when departments or other business units maintain their own policy files.
- The centralized repository may also store previous versions of a given policy as well as policies that have been withdrawn without a replacement. These obsolete policies provide a historical record of

policies in effect at specific points in time. To avoid confusion, they are clearly identified as superseded or no longer in effect.
- Some GRC software will distribute selected policies, or links to copies stored in the centralized repository, to individuals or groups based on their roles and responsibilities. Recipients are required to confirm receipt of policies distributed to them. GRC software will track acknowledgments that affirm that employees have read, understood, and are in compliance with the policies. Employees will receive notifications for policies that require periodic reaffirmation.
- GRC software provides templates to simplify the creation of policy documents and standardize their format across an enterprise. To support collaborative review and editing, annotation tools allow stakeholders to include comments or questions without altering the text of a policy. The software will maintain an audit trail that tracks changes made by specific stakeholders. Some GRC applications also incorporate chat functions and other communication tools to facilitate discussion among stakeholders working on a given policy.
- Some GRC applications include a library of preformulated templates that are a useful starting point for policies related to commonly encountered business matters, including ethical conduct, conflict of interest, employee behavior, workplace safety, remote working, business continuity, data privacy, and acceptable use of technology. These preformulated policies can be customized for compatibility with an organization's culture and business operations. GRC software may also provide preformulated policy templates for industry-specific topics, such as anti-money laundering, patient privacy, academic integrity, product quality, and supply chain management.
- Automated workflow can route newly drafted policies for review, comment, and approval by designated stakeholders. Policies under consideration for updating can be routed as well. A workflow script will monitor and expedite the review and approval process. Stakeholders will be notified when policy review is required by a specified date. An alert will be issued when a stakeholder's comments or approval are overdue. The workflow function can also maintain a review schedule of notifications for policies that require periodic updating. It will monitor the update process to ensure completion of reviews and approvals by a specified date.
- Like the compliance management component discussed in a preceding section, a GRC policy management module can require employees or other affected parties to submit written attestations that they understand and are complying with a given policy. The policy management module will track the receipt of attestations and send reminders for overdue attestations. Some policy management mod-

ules allow employees to request a temporary or permanent exemption from compliance with a specific policy. The policy management module will store information about the request, including the reason for the exemption, the evidence provided, reviewers' comments, and the decision to approve or reject the exemption.
- GRC software can generate a variety of reports and dashboard visuals. Examples include lists of policies that are in effect, undergoing review, superseded, or withdrawn; reports of policies acknowledgments submitted by employees; version history reports for selected policies; and lists of policies to be reviewed on specified future dates.

Audit Management

The GRC audit management module helps an organization execute and monitor audit engagements from inception through completion. Primarily intended for audit teams, the audit management module also supports the oversight responsibilities of audit committees as well as the work of financial officers and other senior executives whose decisions may be affected by audit findings and recommendations. The GRC audit management module's features and functions are closely aligned with the risk management and compliance management capabilities described in preceding sections:

- The GRC audit management module supports planning, scheduling, and resource allocation for audit engagements involving an organization's business processes, projects, contractors, suppliers, or other internal or external entities or activities. Audit managers, team leaders, and other authorized users can define an audit's scope, objectives, frequency, methodology, milestones, and budget.
- An organization can prioritize audits based on risk and compliance assessments performed by other GRC modules. Many audits are driven by risk identification or compliance failures. An organization may choose to focus its audit resources to mitigate threats, minimize vulnerabilities, or avoid penalties for noncompliance.
- The GRC audit management module allows audit teams to upload and store audit documentation, including work papers, evidence collected from an audited entity or other sources, checklists, notes, interim and final reports, recommendations, and remediation plans. Audit documentation can be viewed, edited, and annotated by team members or other authorized persons.
- Audit supervisors can use the GRC audit management module to track the status of audits, obtain an overview of a particular audit engagement, evaluate audit workloads, and monitor the progress of

specific tasks assigned to individual auditors, who can use the GRC application to log the time spent on specific tasks. The audit management module can generate various reports for open and completed audits, including audit schedules, audit status reports, audit findings, audit recommendations, and follow-up reports of corrective actions implemented or to be completed.
- Notifications can be issued to remind auditors of upcoming deadlines and to alert managers about audit tasks that are incomplete or appear to be behind schedule. A GRC audit management module can also track travel expense and other costs incurred by auditors. Notifications will be issued when these expenses exceed budgeted amounts. An audit management module can issue invoices for internal audits that are charged back to the business units being audited.
- Many audit engagements require fieldwork to inspect physical assets, conduct interviews, observe business processes, examine documents, test computer applications, or perform other tasks that involve site visits to the entity being audited. A GRC audit management module supports these onsite activities via a mobile app, which allows auditors to access and update audit workpapers, checklists, and other documentation from a smartphone or tablet. Auditors can also upload photographs or documents collected in the field.

Board Management

The oversight responsibilities of boards of directors and other governing bodies benefit from the risk and compliance management capabilities included with GRC software. Some GRC vendors also provide a dedicated module that is specifically intended for board management. These modules, which compete with standalone board management applications and services, support the following features and functions:

- A centralized repository stores board-related records, including minutes for meetings of the board and board committees, board policies and meeting rules, records of board decisions made outside of meetings, reports submitted to the board, and documents distributed to board members for information or action.
- The centralized repository can include a directory of active and prior board members, including a member's profile, contact information, leadership responsibilities, committee memberships, and the member's geographic location and time zone. The directory may also indicate a board member's tenure, including appointment date and length, terms of appointment, and the end date where applicable.

Some GRC board management modules can store conflict of interest declarations for individual board members.
- Search functions enable board members, support staff, and other authorized users to locate information in the member directory, meeting minutes, or supporting documentation. Access privileges are tightly controlled to prevent unauthorized disclosure of confidential or sensitive content in board records. Audit trails track the files that are retrieved, viewed, downloaded, edited, or annotated by specific members or support staff on specific dates.
- GRC board management modules provide tools to schedule board meetings, taking member's individual schedules into account. Board management modules also support the preparation and distribution of meeting announcements, agendas, and handouts, which can be combined to create members' board books, which can be printed or distributed digitally. With some GRC software, board books can be preloaded into tablets, which are made available in meeting rooms for use by members.
- GRC board management modules incorporate collaboration capabilities that allow board members to interact with one another. A real-time chat function allows members to send instant messages to other members to comment on agenda items or raise questions about specific matters during a meeting. As an alternative to conventional email, secure messaging capabilities allow members to communicate about board matters outside of a formal meeting. The secure messaging feature can also be used to share documents. Chats and messages can be saved as a record of member interactions, but members can choose to keep their chats and message private.
- GRC board management modules can record and track action items that arise at board meetings. Follow-up tasks can be assigned to specific members or board staff, and the expected completion date will be entered into their calendars. Reminders will be issued as the completion date approaches. Board members can monitor the progress of action items.
- Using a GRC board management module, support staff can set up votes or polls to obtain members' approval or opinions relating to specific matters. Voting and polling can occur during a board meeting or at another time. In the latter case, board members will be notified when a vote or poll is open and the time frame for response. The module will track the progress of a vote or poll, issue reminders as the response deadline approaches, tabulate the results, report the outcome, and keep records for future reference. A board management module can be configured for anonymous voting or polling where appropriate.

- Digital signature capabilities simplify members' approval of meeting minutes, resolutions, and other documents. The board management module will send signature requests to board members who can review and sign the documents online. Security features ensure the integrity of the signature process. The board management module stores the signed document and records the date of the signature and the IP address of the device used by the signer. Board members will be notified when the signature process is completed.

Other Components

Beyond the core capabilities described above, some GRC software supports additional application modules that deal with specific business operations and issues. Depending on the product, these additional modules may be standard features or extra-cost options. They may be integrated with other GRC components, such as risk management, compliance management, and audit management, to enhance their effectiveness:

- Several GRC applications include a business continuity module that is integrated with the software's risk management framework. Emphasizing continuity of IT operations, the business continuity module supports impact analysis and disaster recovery planning. An organization can use the module to identify its mission-critical business processes and IT assets; assess the financial, operational, and reputational impact of business disruption; and develop a prioritized disaster recovery plan that specifies recovery roles, procedures, and required resources. Disaster-planning objectives can be based on the maximum permissible recovery time for critical IT operations or the maximum permissible loss of IT assets from an adverse event. The organization can also schedule and document tests and exercises to validate the disaster recovery plan.
- A GRC business continuity module may be aligned with a cybersecurity management component that an organization can use to identify, assess, and monitor cybersecurity risks. The cybersecurity module maintains a centralized repository of cyber threats, vulnerabilities, and controls, all of which can be rated and prioritized. Some GRC applications can be integrated with threat intelligence sources, vulnerability scanning software, and other security tools. The monetary impact of data breaches, identity theft, infrastructure damage, and other cybersecurity events can be estimated to provide an informed justification for cybersecurity investments. Cybersecurity controls can be tested using widely accepted methods and the results documented in reports and visual displays. Some applications allow

an organization to map controls to cybersecurity standards and regulatory requirements. Cybersecurity deficiencies can be investigated and corrective actions planned.
- GRC privacy management modules help organizations fulfill their obligations to protect personal data in their custody and comply with privacy laws and regulations in all political jurisdictions where an organization operates. A privacy management module can collect user consent documentation related to disclosure and use of personal data. The module will record details about when, how, and from whom consent was obtained, as well as postconsent withdrawal or changes to a user's permissions and preferences. Customizable templates support privacy impact assessments that identify security vulnerabilities and other data protection concerns associated with specific business processes. Such assessments may be initiated when new projects, new technologies, or new business processes could affect the privacy of personal data. The General Data Protection Regulation and some other privacy laws mandates impact assessments for certain data processing operations.
- GRC performance management modules help organizations track and evaluate their governance, risk, and compliance initiatives. An organizations can define key performance indicators that are the basis for evaluation. Examples of performance indicators include timeliness of policy reviews to incorporate regulatory changes, stakeholder feedback about governance practices, the number of compliance violations, compliance training completion rates, incident response times, and time to resolve audit findings. Detailed performance reports can be generated for strategic planning, compliance audits, board presentations, continuous improvement programs, trend analysis, and other purposes. The performance management module can also issue alerts and notifications when key indicators indicate that attention or action is needed.
- Reflecting growing awareness of the importance of sustainability and ethical business practices, some GRC applications support an ESG management module that addresses an organization's environmental, social, and governance commitments and risks. The module provides a centralized repository for ESG data from internal and external sources. It allows an organization to define and track key ESG performance indicators such as energy consumption, greenhouse gas emissions, recycling practices, employee diversity, human rights practices, community engagement, board composition, and compliance and ethics programs. The ESG module can generate reports and graphics that monitor an organization's progress, identify ESG risks, and guide improvement initiatives.

IMPLEMENTATION ISSUES

An organization planning a GRC software implementation must consider the relative advantages and limitations of a cloud-based service vs. on-premises software installation. It must also determine whether an integrated GRC product from a single provider is preferable to separate procurement of standalone risk management, compliance, and governance applications from multiple suppliers.

Cloud vs. On-Premises

Predating the widespread acceptance of cloud-based computing, the earliest GRC software was intended for installation and operation on an organization's own computer network. As with other technologies discussed in this book, all GRC software developers have introduced cloud-based offerings, which now dominate the market. While some GRC products remain available for on-premises implementation, there is little interest in them. Most newer GRC applications are exclusively available as cloud offerings, and vendors have scaled back or discontinued active marketing of their on-premises software, which are increasingly viewed as legacy products.

As discussed in other chapters, some organizations have adopted a cloud-first policy that prioritizes cloud services over on-premises implementation when planning information technology initiatives. Cloud-based GRC software offers the significant technical and administrative advantages of other cloud-based applications:

- Compared to an on-premises implementation, cloud-based GRC software can be deployed more rapidly with fewer complications and less involvement by an organization's information technology staff or consultants. Cloud-based GRC software is fully installed, pretested, and reliably operational on the cloud provider's servers. Customer accounts can be initialized and serviced remotely. Vendor representatives do not need to visit the implementation site or have access to the customer's computer network.
- A cloud-based GRC implementation has minimal start-up costs. Customers pay a monthly or annual subscription fee based on the number of licensed users, the quantity of storage required, the specific capabilities required, and the desired level of customer support. Cloud-based services are compatible with widely installed web browsers. Capital expenditures for new or upgraded computing equipment, network components, and other information technology infrastructure are eliminated, but most organizations will incur one-

time charges for account setup and vendor-supplied training. Some cloud customers will also incur additional costs for customization, data migration, integration with external applications, and other services, which may be supplied by the cloud provider or a knowledgeable third party.
- As discussed in preceding sections, GRC software provides various modules for specific tasks. Cloud-based customers pay only for the modules they need. New capabilities can be added to a subscription plan as circumstances warrant. GRC modules can be phased in over time to simplify the implementation process and training requirements.
- Cloud-based GRC applications are immediately scalable. An organization can add or remove user licenses, storage capacity, and application modules to address changing requirements. Because customers only pay for the resources they use, operating costs can be aligned with need. Cloud providers can allocate or reduce resources for a given customer on demand without disrupting service.
- Hardware and software maintenance, which may be difficult and costly in on-premises implementations, are handled by cloud services without customer involvement. Cloud providers are responsible for maintaining their hardware infrastructure and replacing or upgrading servers, storage devices, and networking components to maintain responsiveness as customers are added and processing workloads increase. Cloud providers also upgrade their GRC software platforms regularly to optimize performance, improve user interfaces, fix defects, and incorporate new features. Capacity planning initiatives enable cloud providers to anticipate future needs and make the necessary modifications to avoid problems.
- Cloud-based GRC software is accessible from any location with a reliable internet connection. This is an important consideration for organizations with a geographically dispersed workforce or employees that work remotely or on a hybrid schedule.
- Cloud providers are responsible for backup protection and disaster recovery to prevent loss of a customer's information. Backup copies are produced on a regular schedule and stored in secure offsite repositories. Many providers have multiple, geographically dispersed data centers to maintain service when local disruptions occur. Data centers are protected by round-the-clock security personnel and surveillance. Customers' information is protected by encryption, multifactor authentication, regular security audits, malware detection, and other electronic safeguards. Cloud providers monitor their systems continuously for early detection of problems.

GRC Software vs. Standalone Applications

Single-function software is available for on-premises installation or from cloud providers for most of the GRC components discussed in this chapter. Designed for self-contained operation, these standalone applications are specifically and exclusively intended for risk management, compliance management, and governance functions, including board management, audit management, policy management, performance management, and cybersecurity management. The best standalone products provide features and capabilities that compare favorably with their GRC counterparts, but a cohesive suite of interrelated governance, risk and compliance applications offers significant advantages:

- GRC software provides an integrated framework of features and functions for governance, risk management, and compliance management. This consolidated approach gives organizations a unified view and coordinated control of these related functions. Governance establishes an organization's objectives, risk management identifies and mitigates threats to those objectives, and compliance ensures that the objectives are realized in accordance with legal requirements and an organization's internal standards.
- GRC software is easier and faster to deploy than multiple standalone applications with comparable functionality. Whether on-premises installation or a cloud provider is involved, all GRC components are acquired from a single supplier. Vendor selection, management approvals, contract negotiations, and other aspects of the procurement process will be simplified and streamlined. With more vendors and products to evaluate, the selection of standalone applications will take longer to complete, management approvals must be obtained for each procurement, multiple contracts will take longer to negotiate, and management of multiple vendor relationships will require greater administrative effort.
- GRC software's integrated approach offers logistical advantages. A single vendor is responsible for implementation, which simplifies on-premises installation or initial configuration of a cloud service. Standalone applications intended for on-premises implementation must be separately installed, configured, and tested on an organization's servers, often with significant assistance from the organization's information technology staff. With standalone cloud-based applications, an organization must work through an initial set-up process with multiple providers. While a cloud service requires less internal IT oversight than an on-premises installation, IT staff

assistance is often needed to address security, customization, and integration issues.
- Compared to multiple single-function applications acquired from different vendors, GRC software can be easier to learn and use. While they support different functions and have unique capabilities, individual GRC modules share some screen formats, menus, commands, user preferences, and operating procedures. This simplifies training, shortens the time required to attain a reasonable level of proficiency, and provides a more consistent experience for employees who need to use multiple modules.
- GRC modules support closely related functions and are designed to work together. Cross-functional information sharing is a standard feature. A centralized database stores information that can be accessed by all GRC components, assuming that users have the requisite permissions. A centralized database also minimizes data redundancy and enhances data consistency. By contrast, standalone applications maintain their own databases, which are not necessarily available to other software. Data maintained in siloed repositories may not be updated consistently. The resulting discrepancies can lead to errors in transaction processing and decision making.
- GRC modules can produce consolidated reports and support cross-functional workflows, incident investigations, and audits. Threats and vulnerabilities identified by the risk management module can trigger an audit by a governance component. Compliance reports prepared for board meetings can include information from risk assessments and auditors' recommendations for corrective action. Information from compliance investigations and risk assessments can influence the development or revision of governance policies. Unless prebuilt integration is provided, customized programming will be necessary to get standalone governance, risk management, and compliance applications to support such interactions.
- As noted above, GRC software simplifies procurement compared to separate acquisition of multiple standalone applications. GRC software may also be more economical for organizations that want cross-functional coverage, but a standalone application will be less expensive for organizations that are primarily interested in one GRC component. With some cloud-based services, however, customers pay only for the GRC modules they actually utilize.
- Proponents of standalone applications contend that they are more flexible and customizable than their GRC counterparts and offer advanced capabilities that are not generally supported by GRC software. A standalone risk management application, for example, may support several different simulation scenarios or risk models

tailored to particular business issues, such as environmental health or occupational safety, or specific industries, such as construction, transportation, or manufacturing. A standalone compliance application may incorporate specialized libraries of regulatory requirements for specific business activities or political jurisdictions. A standalone audit management application may offer an extensive selection of scheduling capabilities, staff allocation tools, and preformulated audit templates. A standalone board management application may provide a public portal to satisfy the open meeting requirements of government agencies. It should be noted, however, that GRC software developers are continuously working to improve and enhance their individual modules to make them more competitive with the best standalone applications.

SUMMARY OF MAJOR POINTS

- GRC software provides an integrated suite of application modules that address an organization's governance, risk, and compliance requirements and initiatives. The earliest GRC products were introduced in the mid-2000s. Functionality and customer acceptance have improved steadily and significantly since that time.
- Early adopters of GRC software included large organizations with significant risk exposures and heavily regulated companies with burdensome compliance requirements, but the GRC framework is relevant for all business processes, operations, and activities.
- Risk management, a core GRC component, provides features and functions that allow organizations to proactively and systematically assess and monitor threats and vulnerabilities. A centralized register identifies, describes, categorizes, prioritizes, and tracks risks that threaten an organization's mission, operations, or assets. A risk assessment tool analyzes and prioritizes specific risks. The assessment tool assigns an impact rating to a given risk based on predefined criteria.
- GRC software allows organizations to identify, assess, adhere to, and monitor their compliance obligations. Compliance and risk management are closely related GRC components. Noncompliance with laws, regulations, and internal mandates is a major source of risk.

    An organization's risk and compliance teams may have overlapping membership and responsibilities. The GRC compliance and risk

components share certain information and support similar capabilities. They can be used in combination to obtain a holistic view that will enhance decision making, optimize the allocation of resources, and eliminate redundant data storage and analysis.
- GRC software supports the development, dissemination, monitoring, and updating of policies, procedures, directives, protocols, approved practices, codes of conduct, and related document. GRC software's policy management component maintains a centralized online repository of the latest versions of approved policies. Authorized employees can access specific policies on a need-to-know basis.
- The GRC audit management module helps an organization execute and monitor audit engagements from inception through completion. Primarily intended for audit teams, the audit management module also supports the oversight responsibilities of audit committees as well as the work of financial officers and other senior executives whose decisions may be affected by audit findings and recommendations. The audit management module's features and functions are closely aligned with risk management and compliance management capabilities.
- Some GRC software supports additional application modules that deal with specific business operations and issues. Depending on the product, these additional modules may be standard features or extra-cost options. Examples include business continuity, cybersecurity management, privacy management, performance management, and ESG management.
- All GRC software developers have introduced cloud-based offerings, which now dominate the market. While some GRC products remain available for on-premises implementation, there is little interest in them. Cloud-based GRC software offers the significant technical, administrative, and economic advantages of other cloud-based applications.
- Standalone applications are widely available for risk management, compliance management, and governance functions, including board management, audit management, policy management, performance management, and cybersecurity management. The best standalone products provide features and capabilities that compare favorably with their GRC counterparts, but a cohesive suite of interrelated governance, risk, and compliance applications offers administrative and economic advantages.

NOTES

1. *Governance of organizations—Guidance*, ISO 37000:2021 (International Organization for Standardization, September 2021), https://www.iso.org/standard/65036.html.
2. *Risk Management—Vocabulary*, ISO 31073:2022 (International Organization for Standardization, February 2022), https://www.iso.org/standard/79637.html.
3. *Compliance management systems—Requirements with guidance for use*, ISO 37301:2021 (International Organization for Standardization, April 2021), https://www.iso.org/standard/75080.html.

9

Database Archiving Software

The preceding chapters have discussed technologies that manage digital documents, audio and video recordings, photographs, web pages, social media posts, and other types of unstructured records—so-called because they do not conform to a predefined model or predictable format. This chapter discusses software for archiving databases, which contain structured information. Databases are considered structured because they organize information according to a predefined schema that provides a formal description of a database's architecture, arrangement, and components. Database schema vary in complexity. Flat files, which are appropriate for straightforward tasks, have a simple database structure with a single table composed of individual records arranged in rows and data elements in columns. With relational databases, which are widely used for transaction processing, enterprise resource planning, customer relationship management, and other purposes, the schema consists of interrelated tables, data elements, and their associated indexes. NoSQL (Not Only SQL) databases often feature a flexible schema design that is well suited to analysis of very large data sets and other complex tasks. Data warehouses, which consolidate data from multiple sources, use specialized schema that are optimized for analytical processing and reporting.

Citing usage from the seventeenth century, the *Oxford English Dictionary* defines archiving as the act of transferring infrequently used files to a storage repository intended for that purpose.[1] The definition implies that the transferred files have value that warrants their continued retention. In keeping with that definition, database archiving is the process of moving inactive data from a source database to an archive database, where it will be retained for a period of time defined by organizational policy. The source database, sometimes termed a production database, is typically in active use for transaction processing, financial management, customer service, or other purposes. In some cases, however, the source database is inactive, having been created by an application that has been retired, replaced, or otherwise taken out of service.

Some database management applications support data archiving within the application itself. Inactive data is transferred to an archive file where it can be accessed when needed. No additional software is required. Database administrators can manage the archive file using the same interface and tools supported by the active database. This integrated approach is economical and simplifies the archiving process, but it has a significant drawback: it is limited to a particular database management application, which must be available to access the archive file. By contrast, the database archiving software discussed in this chapter can archive data from multiple database management applications. The archived data is accessible and usable independent of its originating application, which may no longer be in service.

In the spectrum of information governance technologies, database archiving occupies a position near the end of the information lifecycle. As such, it is nominally aligned with the records management applications discussed in chapter 2 and the digital preservation applications discussed in chapter 3, but database archiving serves a different purpose than either of those technologies. Database archiving applications replicate some of the retention functionality supported by RMA software, but those products are intended for unstructured records rather than structured data. Digital preservation applications manage historically significant paper documents, photographic media, or digital content that are transferred to a trustworthy repository for permanent retention. Database archiving applications deal principally with nonpermanent information that needs to be kept for a predetermined period of time. In most cases, the archived data will eventually be discarded, although some data may be retained for extended periods or indefinitely.

Database archiving is sometimes confused with database backup, which creates copies of data to support continuity of information-dependent operations following an adverse event, such as a system failure or data corruption. Backup copies of an active database are created at regular intervals, usually daily, to minimize data loss. Backup copies of archived data are typically created less frequently but they are nonetheless necessary for disaster recovery.

HISTORY

Offloading older data from active computer systems is a long-established practice. In the 1960s and 1970s, when mainframe computers had limited online storage capacity, inactive data was routinely transferred to offline media. By the 1980s, online storage capacities had increased, but so did the quantity of data to be managed. This was particularly the case in financial services, retail, telecommunications, energy, and other industries with high-volume transaction processing and recordkeeping regulations that mandated the retention of data after the transactions were completed. In response, database administrators began using custom-developed programs to move older data from active databases to separate files within the same application. By the late 1980s, offloading of inactive data to separate files was widespread, and most database applications supported it as a standard capability.

The transfer of older data to separate files was a limited-function precursor of database archiving software, which was introduced in the late 1990s and early 2000s. As noted above, database archiving software is not limited to offloading inactive data from a single application. It can import, process, and store inactive data from multiple database applications. Following a pattern discussed in other chapters, the earliest products were developed by small innovative companies, most of which were subsequently acquired by large computer manufacturers and software providers with greater research and development capabilities. The initial archiving products offered basic capabilities for data extraction, storage, retrieval, and purging to address the management of growing databases. These basic functions were enhanced and new features added from the mid-2000s onward.

According to Google Trends, searches for the phrase "database archiving" have demonstrated strong interest since 2010. A Google Scholar search indicates that database archiving has been discussed in a growing number of books, periodicals, technical reports, conference papers, and other popular and scholarly publications over that same period. Industry analysts predict significant market growth for data archiving products and services, but they do not differentiate database archiving applications from archiving products intended for digital documents, email, or other unstructured data.

BUSINESS NEED

Like the records management applications discussed in chapter 2, database archiving software addresses a commonplace and significant information governance issue: database lifecycle management:

- For companies, government agencies, and nonprofit entities, databases are an important category of recorded information. As such, they are subject to an organization's retention rules, which specify how long records related to specific matters must be kept to satisfy legal, operational, and historical requirements. In many organizations, however, those retention rules are not applied to production databases because there is no reliable way to do so. Some database management systems have no record retention functionality. Others provide limited retention capabilities that are difficult to implement without affecting other database operations. With relational databases, in particular, deleting older data or transferring it to a history file can disrupt the connections between tables, which can lead to processing errors or corrupted data.

- To avoid these technical challenges, some organizations retain older data in production databases indefinitely, but that practice is inconsistent with retention requirements for other records related to the same operations or activities. As an example, an organization's retention policy may mandate disposal of personnel files ten years after termination of employment, but a human resources database may contain information about employees who resigned or retired decades ago. Similarly, invoices, payment vouchers, and other payables documentation may be destroyed six years after payment, but information about individual transactions may remain in an accounts payable database for many years longer.
- Transfer of inactive data to an archive database is the first step toward lifecycle management. Database archiving applications provide retention capabilities that are similar to those associated with records management applications. As discussed later in this chapter, an organization can specify customized retention rules for archived data based on legal considerations, operational needs, or historical value. The rules can be applied manually or automatically to identify and purge data with elapsed retention periods. Database archive applications allow an organization to implement these retention actions without disrupting the operation of production databases.
- Aside from its role in record retention, a systematic approach to database archiving has a beneficial impact on an organization's computer operations. Reducing the size of a production database by moving inactive data to an archive database will correspondingly reduce storage requirements and costs for active data. The archive database will require more storage with each archiving operation, but it will not expand indefinitely. Because much archived data will be deleted when its retention period elapses, the size of an archived database can usually be kept within manageable limits. As explained later in this chapter, many database archiving applications support tiered storage options, which allow an organization to reduce storage costs by accepting a lower level of retrieval responsiveness for

archived data. In addition, many database archiving applications store archived data in a compressed format, which further reduces storage requirements.
- Reducing the size of a production database can also enhance database performance. Smaller databases can be searched more quickly than larger ones. Smaller databases also require less time for indexing, backup, updating, and maintenance operations, and they can be restored faster in the event of a system malfunction or other adverse event. Inactive records are transferred to an archive database, which will grow with each archiving operation; but because inactive data is retrieved infrequently, archive databases are not subject to the same performance demands as active databases.
- No computer application remains in service indefinitely. When a database management system is replaced, a database archiving application supports the extraction and orderly migration of data to the new system. Inactive data can be archived to reduce the completion time and cost of the migration effort. When a database application is retired without a replacement, database archiving software will provide continued access to inactive data until its retention period elapses, thereby eliminating the widespread and problematic practice of keeping a legacy application in operation until all data is purged.

STANDARDS AND GUIDELINES

No international standards deal specifically and exclusively with database archiving, but several standards discussed in chapter 4 provide a conceptual framework that is broadly applicable to long-term preservation of digital data of any type. In particular, ISO 14721:2012, *Space data and information transfer systems—Open archival information system (OAIS)—Reference model* defines a reference model for an archival system to preserve and provide access to digital content. Similarly, ISO 13008:2022, *Information and documentation—Digital records conversion and migration process* deals with planning issues, methods, and procedures for conversion of digital records from one file format to another and migration of digital records from one hardware or software platform to another.

While it not an international standard, Software Independent Archival of Relational Databases (SIARD) provides specifications for a vendor-neutral, platform-independent file format for database preservation. The SIARD format preserves the future readability and usability of relational databases, even if the software that created a given database is no longer availability. Developed by the Swiss Federal Archives in the early 2000s,

SIARD has since been issued as a Swiss e-Government standard. The Swiss Federal Archives offers a suite of open-source software tools to support SIARD implementations. The SIARD specification was promoted and further developed by the European Archival Records and Knowledge Preservation (E-ARK) project, a pan-European initiative for digital archiving based on the OAIS reference model. Various European archives have integrated SIARD into their digital preservation strategies.

FEATURES AND CAPABILITIES

Data archiving software is compatible with a variety of applications and repositories that maintain structured data, including relational database management systems, NoSQL database applications, big data file systems, data warehouses, and enterprise resource planning systems. It provides features and functions for selection of data to be archived, transfer of data from a source database to an archive database, retrieval of archived data by authorized users when needed, and return of archived data to the production database to support ongoing operations.

Data Selection

Database archiving begins with the selection of data to be transferred from a designated source to an archival repository. The source may be a production database used by an active application to support ongoing operations or a legacy database associated with a discontinued business operation or an application that has been decommissioned.

- Data selection is guided by a policy that specifies the types of data to be archived, how archiving will be accomplished, when archiving will occur, and how long the archived data is to be retained. An organization may have an enterprise-wide policy that applies to all databases that warrant archiving. Alternatively, tailored archiving policies may be developed for individual databases.
- Among its advantages, an enterprise-wide selection policy may be easier to implement and will ensure consistent archiving across a variety of databases, but it may be poorly suited to structured data with distinctive characteristics, access patterns, and retention requirements. Exceptions to an enterprise-wide policy may be necessary to address regulatory or operational requirements associated with specific business functions.
- A selection policy may exclude certain data from archiving. Examples include data that will soon be eligible for destruction; transitory

data that is not needed after a transaction, calculation, or report is completed; older data that is known to be obsolete; duplicate data; data that is subject to a legal hold for imminent or ongoing litigation or government investigations; and data that must be immediately accessible for any reason.
- Selection of data to be archived from a production database may be based on age, the level of reference activity as determined the date of last access or modification, the data's usefulness for ongoing business operations, the database size in relation to available capacity and system performance, or other factors. As an example, information from a customer order database may be archived after a sufficient period of time to allow for any problems with the order to be addressed. Similarly, information about registered card holders may be archived from a public library's database based on the date of last borrowing activity, the presumption being that some portion of inactive card holders have moved away, died, or are otherwise unlikely to use the library.
- In some cases, archiving may be limited to selected data elements. An automotive parts supplier may retain names, addresses, account numbers, and other basic information in its customer database indefinitely, but detailed information about individual orders will be archived five years after payment is received. A university may retain data about courses taken and grades received in its student information system indefinitely, but data about a student's campus address, tuition payments, financial aid, emergency contracts, and other matters will be archived after the student graduates.
- A database maintained by a decommissioned application may be archived in its entirety when the application is taken out of service. Alternatively, selected legacy data may be migrated into a replacement application and the remainder archived. When a human resources information system is replaced, for example, data for active employees is typically transferred to the new application. Data about former employees will be archived for a defined period of time to satisfy legal requirements, to simplify rehiring, or to respond to requests for confirmation of prior employment. When an electronic medical recordkeeping system is replaced, database records for patient under care will be transferred to the new system, while data for inactive patients will be archived.
- As discussed in a preceding section, many organizations, including those with well-developed retention policies for digital documents and paper records, allow structured data to accumulate indefinitely. In the absence of retention rules and purging procedures, many production and legacy databases contain information that has no

continuing legal, operational, or historical value. Such obsolete data can be selectively purged from a production or legacy database prior to archiving. The selection process, sometimes described as "carving out," may be based on age, anticipated future need, historical value, storage cost, or other predefined criteria. Information about inactive members may be purged from a professional association's database after a specified number of years, for example. Information about students is typically purged from a university library's database following graduation when borrowing privileges are revoked.

Archiving Process

Once the desired data is selected, data archiving software copies it to an archive database, along with supplemental information that documents the archiving process and enables an organization to access or restore the data when needed.

- This supplemental information might include metadata about the source database, the date and time when archiving was performed, access and usage restrictions, and details about the structure of the archived data and any format conversions, data compression, encryption, or other changes made during the archiving process.
- The archiving process can be activated manually or initiated automatically at prescribed intervals. In either case, an archiving request, usually formulated in the structured query language, instructs the archiving application to search a designated source database to select the data to be archived. The archiving application analyzes the source database to check dates, examine usage patterns, or otherwise identify data that satisfies the criteria specified in archiving request.
- The archiving request also specifies the database that will store the archived data. The archiving application will connect to the source database and make a copy of the data to be imported into the archive database, which may be implemented on-premises or by a cloud provider. The archive database may have the same structure as the source database or a different structure that is better suited to the storage and retrieval requirements of inactive data.
- Data is added to the archive database each time the archiving process is executed. Metadata about the archiving process is updated to document the additions.
- An archiving application may convert source data to a different format for long-term preservation, data exchange, compatibility with a data warehouse, or other reasons, but such format conversions may

affect the functionality of the archived data. A relational database may be converted to a CSV file, for example, but some data may be altered or lost in the process. Information about the database structure, data relationships, security restrictions, and other metadata may be omitted.

- Data archiving applications validate the usability and integrity of archived data. Validation is performed before, during, and upon completion of the archiving process. The tables, data types, and other characteristics of archived data are checked for conformity with expected database structure. Data elements are checked for values that are missing, out of range, or inappropriate. Checksum values, previously discussed in chapter 4, are verified to detect corrupted data. Periodic checksum validation is performed to confirm the integrity of archived data throughout its retention period.
- Depending on organizational policy, the archived data will be deleted from the source database when the process is completed and verified. This is done to make storage space available for new information and improve the performance of updates, indexing, and other operations that are affected by database size. Some organizations retain selected data in the source database for redundancy and immediate access when needed. If an archive database is located in a different political jurisdiction, retention in the source database may be necessary to satisfy regulations that mandate in-country retention of specific information.
- Backup copies may be created at several stages of the archiving process. The source database is typically backed up in its entirety before archiving begins to allow recovery of data that may be lost or damaged during the archiving process. The subset of data to be archived may be backed up before it is moved into the archiving database in case the archiving operation fails or data is corrupted during archiving. When the archiving process is completed, a backup copy is created of the archive database. The source database may be backed up again after the archived data is removed.
- Archiving can be resource-intensive and time-consuming, especially if large quantities of data or complex data structures are involved. It is usually advisable to run the archiving process during off-peak hours to avoid degrading system performance. To further minimize any adverse impact, a large database may be archived in increments to conserve system resources and minimize disruption of ongoing operations. Incremental archiving allows archived data to be validated in manageable segments. Problems can be detected and addressed at an early stage in the archiving process.

Storage and Retention

As explained above, a data archiving application transfers specified data from a source database into an archive database where it will remain in the archive until its retention period elapses, it is moved to another repository, or it is returned to the source database. The archive database may reside on a server operated by an organization's own data center or by a cloud provider.

- Some cloud providers offer hierarchical storage tiers the allow organizations to balance cost and retrieval responsiveness. The most expensive tier, sometimes described as hot storage, uses solid-state storage and high-performance hard drives for immediate and near-immediate retrieval, which is rarely needed for archived data. A lower tier, which may be described as cool storage, uses moderate performance hard drives. It is suitable for archived data that will be accessed infrequently but without undue delay.
- The lowest storage tiers, which may be characterized as cold or frozen, are the least expensive. They are intended for large quantities of archived data that will rarely be accessed but must be retained for legal reason or for future business reference, which becomes less likely as time passes. The lowest tiers store archived data on low-performance hard drives and offline media, such as magnetic tapes.
- Archived data can be moved from tier to tier based on its age and access activity to optimize storage performance and cost. This may be done manually by a system administrator or automatically by software that monitors data access patterns. Based on the information lifecycle concept discussed in previous chapters, the age of archived data is the principal predictor of future reference activity. Older data can be saved in lower and slower storage levels, then moved back up to faster levels when requested.
- Source databases with high transaction rates or large data types can overwhelm an archive database. To address this concern, some database archiving applications use data compression to reduce storage requirements and costs for archived data without any loss of information. Deduplication processes may also be used to detect and eliminate unnecessary copies of archived data.
- Archiving is intended for data that is in the inactive portion of the information lifecycle. The data's retention rules are determined by organizational policy. Data archiving applications store retention periods and disposition instructions for specific data in metadata fields. Nonpermanent data with elapsed retention periods will be flagged for deletion, which can be performed manually following a review and approval process or automatically.

- Some organizations use a combination of both approaches. Automatic deletion is the more practical method for large quantities of archived data. Manual review is time-consuming but may be necessary where retention rules must be overridden for regulatory compliance, legal discovery, or future reference need. Manual deletion is also suitable for ad hoc deletion requests for data for which retention rules have not been defined. Whether manual or automatic deletion is used, regular purging of obsolete data is necessary to control the size of the archive database and reduce storage costs.
- Archived data designated for permanent retention may remain in the archival repository indefinitely or be transferred to a digital preservation application. While they were developed for unstructured content, some preservation applications discussed in chapter 4 can store structured data.
- An archiving application can return archived data to its source database. This process, sometimes described as data restoration or data reactivation, may be needed if archived data is required for ongoing transactions, for business analysis involving historical data, for use in legal proceedings or investigations, or when older data is subject to audit. Data restoration may also be necessary if the source database and backup copies are corrupted or if an organization's archiving policy is changed. The restoration process is the reverse of data archiving. The data to be restored must be identified, extracted from archive database, validated for integrity and usability, and converted to the format required by the source database.

Searching and Retrieval

Archived data is inactive, but it must be retrievable when needed. Archived data is indexed for that purpose. As with other technologies discussed in the book, the quality of indexing has a direct effect on the retrievability of archived data. Most database archiving applications provide search functionality that is comparable to that supported by other information governance technologies.

- Indexes may be based on designated fields within archived data or on metadata. Indexing may conform to the source database's indexing patterns, but users of archived data may have different search requirements that must be analyzed to determine how the data will be indexed. As part of the planning process, an organization will determine retrieval requirements and specify the data fields to be used for indexing. Retrieval requirements are determined by analyzing search queries to identify the most frequently searched fields. Data

types and anticipated access patterns, including the types of searches that will be performed most frequently and acceptable retrieval times for archived data, must be considered.
- Searchable metadata may identify the source database by name or number, the source's database's location, and the archived data's characteristics, including its creator, type, format, date created or last modified, and date archived. Metadata may also contain keywords that identify subjects or concepts associated with the archived data. Keywords may also indicate the business operation, project, event, or other matters to which the archived data relates.
- Indexing archived data is a time-consuming and resource-intensive process. To minimize the impact on system performance, indexing may be performed in increments or during off-peak hours. With large archive databases, indexing may be limited to fields that are likely to be searched. Indexes consume storage space and are likely to grow over time. An archiving application must be scalable to support this growth.
- Indexing is typically performed before archived data is stored, although it may be performed poststorage if large quantities of data need to be archived quickly to free space in the source database. Indexes must be updated as new data is added to an archive database, and they may be modified to accommodate changes in search requirements. Some applications will monitor search activity and recommend index changes to support efficient retrieval.
- Changes to an existing index can introduce inefficiencies that can degrade retrieval responsiveness. Periodic re-indexing may be necessary to optimize the performance of indexes that are updated frequently.
- Authorized users can perform straightforward searches based on field values, dates, or other attributes of archived data. When needed, relational expressions, Boolean operators nested to multiple levels, proximity searches, wildcard characters in search strings, and other capabilities allow users to construct complex search statement. Some applications support search operations that span multiple archive databases.
- Some data archiving applications support full-text indexing. While it is more often associated with digital documents and other unstructured content, some structured databases include fields that contain descriptions, comments, notes, or other lengthy text entries. Full-text indexing allows users to search for archived data that contains specific words or phrases. It permits more detailed retrieval operations than are possible with metadata searches, which are limited to a rela-

tively small number of keywords that represent important subject or concepts.
- Search results are usually displayed in a tabular format with rows that represent database records and columns that represents individual fields. Some archiving applications allow a searcher to focus on relevant data by limiting the number of visible columns or selecting the columns to be displayed. Users can navigate through the results, which may span multiple screens. Search results can be sorted or narrowed by field values. Some applications allow system administrators to restrict the display of columns that contain confidential or sensitive data.
- All or selected search results can be downloaded for use in management reports or inclusion in presentations. Search results can be returned to the source database or transferred into other databases for use by employees, contractors, collaborators, or others who do not have access to the source database. Search results can also be exported to external software for statistical analysis, data manipulation, or other processing. Export formats might include CSV, PDF, XML, or native formats of popular applications.

Access and Security

Database archiving applications provide reliable mechanisms for preventing unauthorized access to archived data. Access and security measures must equal or exceed those that apply to the source database.

- Most organizations designate a system administrator who is authorized to set up user accounts, define privileges, and otherwise configure a database archiving application based on organization's access policies. Database archiving software uses the customary combination of usernames and passwords to verify identity. Some applications support multifactor authentication, biometrics, and other access controls for greater security. Access privileges can be integrated with an organization's existing user authentication mechanisms.
- Access privileges are typically based on a given user's need-to-know, as determined by a department head, a team leader, a project manager, or another person who is knowledgeable about the nature of the archived data to be accessed and the user's assigned duties. Authorized users can have full or partial access privileges for importing, retrieving, viewing, downloading, exporting, restoring, or deleting archived data and its associated metadata.
- An organization can broaden, narrow, revoke, or otherwise redefine access privileges as circumstances warrant. Access restrictions for

archived data may be increased or decreased when specific events occur. Some users may be given temporary access to archived data until a particular project or task is completed.
- Database archiving software can track authorized and unauthorized actions involving archived data, maintain event histories with dates and times, and generate audit logs and reports that provide a comprehensive record of user interactions with archived data. Audit logs and reports allow system administrators or other authorized individuals to review, reconstruct, and investigate suspicious searches, edits, deletions, unauthorized access attempts, or other events involving specific users, archived data, or metadata.
- Most data archiving applications support encryption in storage and transit for confidential business information, to maintain the privacy of personal data and protected health information, to prevent data breaches, and to satisfy regulations or industry standards that required encryption of stored data.
- Like source databases, archived data is at risk of loss or damage from system malfunctions, inadvertent deletion, natural disasters, malicious actions, or other adverse events. To mitigate risk, archived data is backed up during the archiving process, as previously described, and at regular intervals thereafter.
- Some database archiving applications will carry over any protective measures for personally identifiable information, such as data masking or redaction, from the source database. If this is not done automatically, these protective measures can be manually implemented within the data archiving environment.
- As previously discussed, archived data is eligible for deletion when its retention period elapses, assuming that the data is not subject to a continuing legal hold. To prevent unauthorized recovery of confidential data, some database archiving applications will overwrite obsolete data multiple times with random characters.

IMPLEMENTATION ISSUES

A database archiving initiative begins with development of a retention policy that will guide the storage and disposition of archived data. As part of the planning process, an organization decides whether it will implement database archiving on-premises or via a cloud provider. It must also select an appropriate product from a qualified vendor.

Retention Policy

The archiving applications discussed in this chapter support the lifecycle management of database content. They are not intended for indefinite retention of inactive data offloaded from production databases. Archived data will be deleted when its retention period elapses. Formalized retention rules are a precondition for a successful database archiving implementation:

- Information governance recognizes lifecycle management as a critical activity that must be based on formalized operating procedures. A data retention policy is an essential component of the database archiving policy discussed in a preceding section. Retention rules are necessary to prevent the accumulation of archived data that has no continuing value. Without retention rules, archive databases will grow to an unmanageable size. Retention rules also identify data that that should be deleted from production databases rather than archived.
- As with other types of recorded information, retention rules for archived data must be based on legal, operational, and historical criteria. At a minimum, an organization must retain archived data for the minimum time period specified in applicable laws and regulations or until time limits for civil litigation or other legal proceedings for which the data may be relevant have expired. Archived data should kept until it is no longer needed for business reference. Archived data with historical value should be retained permanently.
- Comprehensive research is required to identify legal and regulatory retention requirements. Operational retention guidance is typically prepared by records managers in consultation with key stakeholders in the business units that create and use recorded information. A subset of archived data may warrant permanent preservation for its historical significance or research value as determined by archivists, historians, or other knowledgeable persons. Some archived data may have potential for reuse for statistical analysis.
- Some organizations have media-neutral policies that specify how long recorded information pertaining to specific business operations, activities, or events are to be kept. To the extent possible such policies should be applied to archived data to ensure consistent retention of documents and data.
- A retention policy should consider archived data's relationship to other information that an organization maintains. In some cases, retention requirements for information contained in archived data may be satisfied by other records. As an example, data archived from

a human resources information system may be entirely replicated in inactive personnel files, which constitute a more complete record of a former's employee's work history. In such situations, the inactive personnel files, which may be stored in an electronic content management system or in paper form, will be retained for the period of time mandated by organizational policy. The archived data is considered a duplicate record, which can be discarded when no longer needed.
- To the extent possible, a retention policy should specify unambiguous retention rules based on elapsed time from the date that data was created or archived. Such rules permit the automatic identification and deletion of archived data with elapsed retention periods, the only practical approach where large quantities of data are involved. Retention rules that require time-consuming manual review of archived data prior to deletion should be avoided to the extent possible

Cloud vs. On-Premises Implementation

Database archiving applications were originally developed for on-premises deployment and onsite retention of archive databases. Most database archiving vendors have since added cloud versions to their product lines, and some new archiving applications are available as cloud-only offerings. Subject to minor variations, the on-premises and cloud-based versions of a database archiving application provide equivalent functionality. Each approach has advantages and limitations that must be evaluated in the context of an organization's information technology strategy:

- As noted in other chapters, some organizations have adopted a cloud-first strategy that prioritizes cloud services over on-premises implementation when planning new information technology initiatives or replacing existing applications. In particular, a cloud-based archiving services may be the preferred option where source databases are cloud-based, although on-premises archiving will work in those situations.
- Compared to an on-premises implementation, cloud-based database archiving software can be deployed more rapidly with fewer complications and less involvement by an organization's information technology staff or consultants. This is an important consideration for organizations where technical expertise is limited or fully occupied with other projects. Database archiving software is fully installed, pretested, and reliably operational on the cloud provider's servers. Customer accounts can be initialized and serviced remotely. Vendor

representatives do not need to visit the installation site or have access to the customer's computer network to support implementation.
- For many organizations, minimal start-up costs are a strong selling point for cloud-based database archiving. This is an important consideration where capital funding is unavailable or requires a lengthy review and approval process. Cloud customers pay a monthly or annual subscription fee based on the number of licensed users, the quantity of archived data to be stored, the specific standard and optional capabilities required, and the desired level of customer support. Capital expenditures for new or upgraded computing equipment, network components, and other information technology infrastructure are eliminated, but most organizations will incur one-time charges for account setup and vendor-supplied training. Some cloud customers will also incur additional costs for customization, integration with external applications, and other services, which may be supplied by the cloud provider or a knowledgeable third party.
- Hardware and software maintenance, which may be difficult and costly in on-premises implementations, are built into the subscription charges. Cloud providers are responsible for maintaining their hardware infrastructure and replacing or upgrading servers, storage devices, and networking components to maintain responsiveness as customers are added and processing workloads increase. Cloud providers also upgrade their database archiving software regularly to optimize performance, improve user interfaces, fix defects, and incorporate new features.
- Cloud-based database archiving applications are immediately scalable. An organization can add or remove user licenses, storage capacity, and application modules to address changing requirements. Because customers only pay for the resources they use, operating costs can be aligned with need. Cloud providers can allocate or reduce resources for a given customer on demand without disrupting service.
- Many cloud-based providers offer tiered storage options that may not be available in on-premises data centers. As discussed in a preceding section, tiered storage allows an organization to accept slower retrieval of archived data to achieve lower storage costs. The trade-off is usually favorable where large quantities of inactive data are involved.
- Cloud-based database archiving services are accessible from any location with a reliable internet connection. This is an important consideration where the databases to be archived are geographically dispersed.

- Cloud providers are responsible for backup protection and disaster recovery to prevent loss of archived data. Backup copies are produced on a regular schedule and stored in secure offsite repositories.
- Many cloud providers operate data centers in multiple locations to maintain service when local disruptions occur. Data centers are protected by round-the-clock security personnel and surveillance.
- As one of its most widely cited advantages, an on-premises database archiving implementation gives an organization direct control over installation, testing, customization, and operational management of the software and archived data. An organization that operates its own database archiving application controls the allocation of required resources, the devices on which archived data is stored, and the timing of archiving operations, as well as the hours of availability and scheduled downtime for software maintenance and upgrades.
- An on-premises installation also offers security features that some organizations require or prefer. Confidential archived data is stored on an organization's own server rather than on servers shared with other cloud customers. The organization has direct control of the network infrastructure that connects a database archiving application to active database management systems. It can implement customized firewalls, encryption protocols, incident response procedures, and other security measures to protect data during the archiving process and in storage. The organization determines the physical location where archived data is kept, which is essential for compliance with national laws and regulations that mandate in-country retention, and the level of security in place at that location.
- Assuming that the source database and archiving application are connected to an organization's local area network, an on-premises implementation typically supports faster data access and transfer rates than cloud-based archiving services, which are limited by internet bandwidth. This is an important advantage where large quantities of data will be archived frequently, but it does not apply to organizations where source databases are geographically distributed. In such situations, latency delays associated with a virtual private network or other secure communication methods can negate any performance advantage associated with an on-premises archiving installation.
- On-premises and cloud-based database archiving are not mutually exclusive implementation options. A hybrid archiving configuration is possible. An organization may store recently archived data on-premises then transfer to a cloud service after a predetermined period of time. Alternatively, on-premises archiving may be reserved for data with special security requirements or that must be available

quickly when needed, and a cloud service used for everything else. An organization transitioning from on-premises archiving to a cloud service can use a hybrid configuration to gradually phase out its on-premises installation.

Product Evaluation

Database archiving is a competitive segment of the market for information technology products and services. Database archiving applications with the features and functionality described in this chapter are available from large computer companies with broad product lines as well as from smaller software developers that specialize in data management. A comprehensive evaluation process with input from key stakeholders and other interested parties is necessary to identify a product that will satisfy an organization's technical requirements and operational needs at an affordable cost.

- As a fundamental requirement, a database archiving application must be compatible with an organization's information technology infrastructure and database environment. An on-premises archiving implementation must be able to run on the organization's physical or virtual servers and preferred operating system, and it must comply with the organization's testing and staging environment, network protocols, and security and backup protection standards and practices. A database archiving application must not disrupt the operation of an enterprise resource management system, customer relationship management system, or other software that interacts with the databases to be archived.
- A database archiving application must be able to accommodate the data types and formats associated with the organization's database management systems, including older DBMS versions and legacy applications where applicable. Most archiving applications are intended for use with relational databases, the product group for which they were originally developed. A subset of available products can operate with nonrelational databases that lack standardized data structures. Organizations with a mix of relational and nonrelational databases may need to limit archiving to relational databases, implement multiple archiving applications, or seek a comprehensive product that supports both database types.
- To warrant serious consideration, a database application must be commercially available in a fully operational general-release version. It must have a proven history of reliable operation and effective maintenance support in multiple installations, including organiza-

tions with requirements that are similar to those of a prospective customer Experimental, developmental, or near-release products, which may have reliability issues, are unacceptable for archived data that warrants management and retrieval.
- The commercial availability requirement applies to all standard and optional archiving components that a customer has ordered, including add-on modules developed by a vendor's business partners or other external parties. The vendor must be able to deliver and install the database archiving application within a reasonable period of time after an order is placed.
- In addition to commercial availability, a database archiving application must be actively marketed, fully supported, and subject to ongoing development and enhancement by its vendor. Some vendors offer multiple archiving solutions, some of which were acquired from other companies. Such acquisitions are common as a product group matures and vendors try to expand their product portfolios and customer bases. An organization needs to consider the continued viability of an acquired application and its relationship to the vendor's other products. When a vendor acquires a competing database archiving application, it may do so with the intention of phasing out its own presumably inferior product. Alternatively, the vendor may plan to phase out the acquired product and offer its own archiving software to the existing customers as a replacement.
- A database archiving application must have a proven history of reliable operation and effective maintenance support in multiple installations, including organizations with requirements that are similar to those of the prospective customer.
- Rapid deployment is a priority in many database archiving implementations. A database archiving application must offer out-of-the-box functionality that can be fully operational in a reasonable period of time without extensive and costly customization. While minor customization may be necessary, applications with prebuilt archiving capabilities are likely to be more stable, easier to use, and less expensive to maintain than heavily customized product configurations.
- In most implementations, the quantity and variety of archived data will increase over time. As inactive data is transferred from production databases it must be processed, stored, and indexed for retrieval when needed. The archiving application must be sufficiently scalable accommodate this growth cost-effectively and without performance degradation.
- Major technology companies and software developers typically sell their database archiving applications directly to large organizations.

Indirect marketing through authorized representatives and value-added resellers is common for small- to medium-size customers. Technology companies and software developers also rely on authorized representatives and value-added resellers in countries or regions where they do not have a local presence. Direct and indirect sales channels are not mutually exclusive, however. A technology company or software developer may partner with an authorized representative or value-added reseller to offer industry-specific archiving solutions or archiving implementations with extensive customization.
- Whether a direct or indirect sales channel is involved, a database archiving vendor must provide clear evidence that it has appropriate knowledge, experience, and resources to support a prospective customer's requirements. To evaluate a vendor's qualifications, an organization will need information about the company's history, including the vendor's involvement with database management technology, its financial stability and likely continued viability as evidenced by an up-to-date financial statement or other appropriate documentation, and the number of database archiving installations the vendor has successfully completed and types of customers. As evidence of satisfactory performance, the vendor must provide contact information for reference accounts, but a prospective customer should reserve the right to contact other installations.

SUMMARY OF MAJOR POINTS

- Database archiving is the process of moving inactive data from a source database to an archive database, where it will be retained for a period of time defined by organizational policy. The source database may be a production database used by an active application to support ongoing operations or a legacy database associated with a discontinued operation or an application that has been decommissioned.
- Database archiving software can archive data from multiple database management systems. The archived data is accessible and usable independent of its originating application, which may no longer be available. Most products are designed to work with relational database management systems, but other data sources may be supported as well.
- Database archiving software was introduced in the late 1990s and early 2000s. The initial products offered basic capabilities for data extraction, storage, retrieval, and purging to address the management

of growing databases. These basic functions were enhanced and new ones added from the mid-2000s onward.
- Database archiving has a beneficial impact on computer operations. Reducing the size of a production database by moving inactive data to an archive database will correspondingly reduce storage requirements and costs for active data. Reducing the size of a production database can also enhance database performance.
- When a database management system is replaced, a database archiving application supports the extraction and orderly migration of data to the new system. Inactive data can be archived to reduce the completion time and cost of the migration effort. When a database application is decommissioned without a replacement, database archiving software will provide continued access to legacy data.
- Database archiving begins with the selection of data to be transferred from a designated source to an archival repository. The selection may be based on age, the level of reference activity as determined the date of last access or modification, the data's usefulness for ongoing business operations, the database size in relation to available capacity and system performance, or other factors.
- Once the desired data is selected, data archiving software transfers it to an archive database, along with supplemental information that documents the archiving process and enables an organization to access or restore the data when needed. The archiving process can be activated manually or initiated automatically at prescribed intervals.
- The archive database may reside on a server operated by an organization's own data center or by a cloud provider. Some cloud providers offer hierarchical storage tiers that allow an organization to balance cost and retrieval responsiveness. Archived data can be moved from tier to tier, manually or automatically, based on its age and access activity to optimize storage performance and cost.
- Archived data is inactive, but it is indexed for retrieval when needed. Database archiving applications support a broad range of basic and advanced search functionality. Retrieved data can be viewed, printed, downloaded, exported, or returned to its original source.
- A data retention policy is an essential component of a database archiving initiative. Retention rules are necessary to prevent the accumulation of archived data that has no continuing value. Without retention rules, archive databases will grow to an unmanageable size. Retention rules also identify data that that should be deleted from production databases rather than archived.
- Database archiving applications were originally developed for on-premises deployment and onsite retention of archive databases. Most database archiving vendors have since added cloud versions

to their product lines, and some new archiving applications are available as cloud-only offerings. Subject to minor variations, the on-premises and cloud-based versions of a database archiving application provide equivalent functionality.
- Compared to an on-premises implementation, cloud-based database archiving software can be deployed more rapidly with fewer complications, lower start-up costs, and less involvement by an organization's information technology staff or consultants. Proponents of on-premises database archiving implementation claim that it gives an organization direct control over installation, testing, customization, and operational management of the software and archived data.
- Database archiving applications are available from large computer companies with broad product lines as well as from smaller software developers that specialize in data management. A comprehensive evaluation process with input from key stakeholders and other interested parties is necessary to identify a product that will satisfy an organization's technical requirements and operational needs at an affordable cost.

NOTE

1. *Oxford English Dictionary*, s.v. "archive (v.)," July 2023, accessed September 2, 2024, https://doi.org/10.1093/OED/7938598471.

Finding More Information

As noted in the introduction, this book explains the purpose and capabilities of nine technologies that support information governance and its constituent disciplines. As such, it is a foundational guide and starting point for information technology managers, records managers, and others who are responsible for planning and implementing information governance initiatives. The following sections indicate useful sources for additional information that will enable readers to deepen their understanding of specific topics and keep up to date with new developments and emerging trends.

VENDOR WEBSITES AND SOCIAL MEDIA POSTS

Product-specific information created by software developers and vendors are indispensable resources for anyone interested in information governance technologies. Vendor websites and social media posts provide convenient online access to a variety of product-related content, including:

- High-level overviews that emphasize a product's purpose, main benefits, and target markets.
- Technical specifications and datasheets that specify system requirements and file formats supported.
- Lists and explanations of core functionality and special capabilities, including add-on modules and customization options.

- Implementation guidance, including timelines, deployment requirements, and best practices for product installation and performance optimization.
- Case studies and reports of user experience that describe successful implementations and benefits achieved.
- Webinars and videos that demonstrate products and discuss specific features and benefits.
- Information about new and forthcoming products, as well as enhancements to existing products.

Some vendor websites include user manuals, training materials, reference guides, and knowledge bases that contain detailed information about their products and services, but some of these items may be limited to a vendor's existing customers.

INDUSTRY ANALYSIS

The websites and publications of industry analysts and market advisory firms provide estimates of adoption rates and projected growth for specific technologies. Content includes:

- Statistics about technology installations in specific industries and geographic locations.
- Identification and evaluation of customer needs and expectations.
- Analysis of emerging trends.
- Discussion of developments that may impact a given technology's continued viability.
- Comparisons and competitive assessments of leading vendors and products.

Examples of well-known industry analysts and market advisory firms include Gartner, Forrester, International Data Corporation, Omdia, and Nucleus Research. Their websites often contain summaries of or excerpts from market research and competitive intelligence reports that deal with specific topics, but access to the full reports requires a subscription.

PROFESSIONAL ASSOCIATIONS

The websites and social media posts of professional associations and groups contain information about industry standards, guidelines, and best practices for evaluating, selecting, and implementing information governance technologies. Available resources include:

- Webinars, online courses, tutorials, and other educational content for novice and experienced learners.
- Video recordings and podcasts that feature presentations by industry experts and experienced practitioners.
- Newsletters, blogs, and other publications that provide technology updates.
- Case studies of successful implementations.
- Expert opinions about vendors, products, and emerging trends.
- Reports about legal and regulatory developments that affect the selection, implementation, and use of information governance technologies.

Examples of professional associations and groups that are concerned with information governance include ARMA International, AIIM, The Sedona Conference, AHIMA, and the International Legal Technology Association.

TECHNOLOGY NEWS

Technology news websites provide information about emerging technologies, new information governance products and services, and user experiences with specific technologies. They also feature opinions and commentary from industry analysts, reports of regulatory changes that are relevant for information governance, and news of mergers, acquisitions, and other industry developments. Examples websites that specialize in technology news include eWeek, InfoWorld, ITPro Today, Computerworld, CIO, CMS Wire, and ZDNet.

SOFTWARE REVIEW SITES

Software review websites evaluate specific information technology applications. Typical reviews provide the following information about specific products:

- System requirements and technical specifications.
- Standard and optional features and functions.
- User interface characteristics.
- Compliance with relevant standards.
- Strengths and weaknesses compared to competing products.

- Comments and criticisms from organizations that have implemented the product.
- Performance and reliability issues.
- Quality and usefulness of available documentation.
- Vendor responsiveness and customer support.

Some software review websites assign numeric ratings to a given application based on aggregate scores from multiple users. Examples of websites that review the information governance applications discussed in this book include Gartner Peer Insights, G2, TrustRadius, Capterra, and SourceForge.

PUBLICATIONS

Bibliographic databases catalog and index publications in business, computer science, information science, and other fields related to information governance:

- WorldCat is the most comprehensive source for information about books, monographs, technical reports, and other publications in cataloged by libraries throughout the world. It is publicly available at www.worldcat.org. In addition to bibliographic information, the WorldCat database identifies libraries that have a particular publication in its collection.
- Various databases index business periodicals, academic journals, conference proceedings, technical reports, and other publications about the information technologies discussed in this book. Indexed items include market surveys and forecasts, industry reports, product announcements and reviews, vendor profiles, case studies of specific installations, and research and development projects related to technologies discussed in this book. Databases offered by ProQuest, EBSCO, Gale, and other suppliers are widely available in academic and public libraries. In addition to bibliographic citations and abstracts, many databases provide online access to the full text of indexed publications. Most databases can be accessed remotely through library websites and mobile apps, but a library card may be required.
- Google Scholar, which does not require a library card and is free of charge, indexes a wide range of publications, including technical reports, academic theses, preprints, and other materials that are not covered by other bibliographic databases. Google Scholar, which uses the same retrieval procedures as Google web searches, provides links to the indexed items where available.

STANDARDS

The international standards cited in this book are available from the International Standardization Organization (www.ISO.org). ISO standards are also sold by Techstreet, IHS Markit, Intertek Inform, and other providers. The American National Standards Institute sells international standards as well as standards from individual countries, professional associations, and other issuers. Standards and guidance issued by professional associations and other groups are online at the issuers' websites.

ISO standards are reviewed on a regular schedule for correctness and completeness. Obsolete standards are replaced or withdrawn. This book cites the latest version approved as of late 2024. The ISO website is the authoritative source for the latest revision of a given standard.

Index

access control/privileges: in DAM, 174–75; in database archiving, 287–88; with digital preservation, 112–15; with ECM, 33–35; with email archiving, 139–40, 142–44; in GRC, 265; with RMA, 63, 80; in web and social media archiving, 204–7
access copies, in digital preservation, 107, 114
active phase of information lifecycle: DAM in, 160; ECM in, 14–15, 25; RMA in, 60
advisory committee, for digital preservation, 117–19
AHIMA. *See* American Health Information Management Association
AI. *See* artificial intelligence
AIIM, 301. *See also* ANSI/AIIM
AIP. *See* Archival Information Package
American Health Information Management Association (AHIMA), 3, 301
The American Library Association, 94

ANSI (American National Standards Institute), 2, 303
ANSI/AIIM TR15-1997, *Planning considerations, addressing preparation of documents for image capture*, 22
ANSI/AIIM TR27-1996, *Electronic imaging request for proposals (RFP) guidelines*, 21
ANSI/AIIM TR33-1998, *Selecting an appropriate image compression method to match user requirements*, 22
ANSI/AIIM TR34-1996, *Sampling procedures for inspection by attributes of images in Electronic Image Management (EIM) and micrographic systems*, 22
ANSI/AIIM TR35-1995, *Human and organization issues for successful EIM system implementation*, 21
ANSI/AIIM TR40-1995, *Suggested index fields for documents in Electronic Image Management (EIM) environments*, 23

ANSI/ARMA 19-2012, *Policy Design for Managing Electronic Messages*, 133
ANSI/ARMA TR02-2007, *Procedures and Issues for Managing Electronic Messages as Records*, 133
application programming interface (API): for DAM, 174; for ECM, 37; for email archiving, 148, 149; for web and social media archiving, 200–201, 212–13
ARC, 196
Archival Administration, 5
Archival Information Package (AIP), 103, 109–12
Archive-It, 202
ARMA International, 2, 81, 301; on email archiving, 133
artificial intelligence (AI): in DAM, 170–72; ECM and, 29–30; in e-discovery, 228, 231; in GRC, 258; in web and social media archiving, 206–7
Association of Corporate Counsel, 3
audit logs: in DAM, 178–79; in digital preservation, 114; in ECM, 34; in email archiving, 145; in RMA, 80
audits: CoreTrust Seal and, 99; for digital preservation, 119; in e-discovery, 239; in GRC, 248, 261, 263–64
audit trails: of ECM, 26, 36, 91; in email archiving, 145; in GRC, 256, 259, 262, 265; shared drives and, 18
authorized users: of DAM, 163, 164, 173–75; of database archiving, 286; of ECM, 25–28, 30, 36, 49; of RMA, 70, 80–81, 85–86, 90; for web and social media archiving, 206
automatic classification/categorization, in email archiving, 142

backup copies, 4; in database archiving, 283, 292; in digital preservation, 102, 111, 121, 123; in ECM, 51; in email archiving, 150

biometrics: with database archiving, 287; with ECM, 34, 36; with RMA, 80
blockchain, 166
Boolean operators: in database archiving, 286; in digital preservation, 113; in ECM, 31, 32; in e-discovery, 230; in email archiving, 143; in RMA, 79; in web and social media archiving, 206
BrokerCheck, 194
business continuity module, in GRC, 266–67

Capstone, of NARA, 75
Capterra, 302
Capture Index (CDX), 205
Categories for the Description of Works of Art (CDWA), 165
CCSDS. *See* Consultative Committee for Space Data Systems
CDN. *See* content delivery network
CDWA. *See* Categories for the Description of Works of Art
CDX. *See* Capture Index
centralized repository: with DAM, 163–64; with e-discovery, 230; with GRC, 259, 261–62, 264–65; with RMA, 70, 72–73, 80
Charter on the Preservation of Digital Heritage, 191
check-out assets, in DAM, 176
checksums: in DAM, 168; in database archiving, 283; in digital preservation, 106, 110–11; in ECM, 26; ESI and, 227; in web and social media archiving, 204
CIO, 301
cloud services: for DAM, 167, 181–85; for database archiving, 282, 290–93; for digital preservation, 110, 111–12, 117, 120–21, 123, 190; for ECM, 39–40, 44, 51–53; for e-discovery, 220, 226, 240–43; for email archiving, 130, 150–51, 153–55; for GRC, 268–69; for web and social media archiving, 206, 211

CMS Wire, 301
cold storage tier: for digital preservation, 110; for email archiving, 137
Commentary on Information Governance, of Sedona Conference, 218–19
Committee of Sponsoring Organizations of the Treadway Commission (COSO), 253–54
compliance, 2–3, 5; with digital preservation, 119; with ECM, 42, 54; with email archiving, 128, 150; in GRC, 258–61; with RMA, 65–68, 87–88, 90; with web and social media archiving, 204
Computerworld, 301
concept searching, in e-discovery, 230–31
confidentiality, 3–4, 7; in database archiving, 287, 292; with digital preservation, 118; with ECM, 33–35; in e-discovery, 231; in GRC, 257
Consultative Committee for Space Data Systems (CCSDS), 94, 98
content capture: in digital preservation, 104–7; in ECM, 25–27; in web and social media archiving, 197–202
content delivery network (CDN), 177
content locking, in ECM, 35
content screening, in email archiving, 146–47
contingency plan, for digital preservation, 118
copyright: DAM and, 168, 173; digital preservation and, 113; RMA and, 86; web and social media archiving and, 211–13
CoreTrust Seal, 99
COSO. *See* Committee of Sponsoring Organizations of the Treadway Commission
cost overrun, with ECM, 54–55
Court Statistics Project, 220
CSV: in database archiving, 283, 287; in ECM, 25
cybersecurity: in e-discovery, 230; in GRC, 248, 258, 266–67

DAM. *See* digital asset management
DAM Foundation, 165
database archiving, 8, 275–97; access control in, 287–88; archiving process in, 282–83; backup copies in, 283, 292; business need for, 277–79; cloud services for, 282, 290–93; confidentiality in, 287, 292; data compression in, 279, 282; data selection in, 280–81; de-duplication in, 284; defined, 275–76; encryption in, 282, 288; features and capabilities of, 280–88; file formats in, 282, 287; history of, 276–77; implementation of, 288–95; indexing in, 285–87; in information lifecycle, 276, 284; legal affairs with, 285; metadata in, 282–83, 286, 288; on-premises, 282, 290–93; product evaluation for, 293–94; retention in, 278, 280, 281–85, 289–90; retention period with, 278; RMA and, 276; search and retrieval with, 285–87; security in, 287–88; standards and guidelines for, 279–80
data compression: in database archiving, 279, 282; in e-discovery, 228; in email archiving, 139; in ESI, 227; in RMA, 85; in web and social media archiving, 196
data escrow, in digital preservation, 112
Data Science, 5
de-duplication (duplicate detection): in DAM, 168, 177; in database archiving, 284; in e-discovery, 228–29; in email archiving, 131, 139; in web and social media archiving, 203–4
descriptive metadata, 26
Dictionary of Archives Terminology, 93–94
digital asset management (DAM), 8, 159–87; access control in, 174–75; in active phase of information lifecycle, 160; AI in, 170–72; for asset capture, 167–68; audit logs in, 178–79; authorized users of,

163, 164, 173–75; business need for, 162–64; CDN and, 177; centralized repository with, 163–64; check-out assets in, 176; checksums in, 168; cloud services for, 167, 181–85; de-duplication in, 168, 177; disaster recovery in, 163; ECM and, 159, 166–67, 174, 177, 178; encryption in, 175; features and capabilities of, 166–79; file plans for, 168–71; folder taxonomy in, 163; history of, 161–62; image recognition in, 172; implementation of, 179–85; inactive phase of information lifecycle and, 160; for indexing, 160; information technology and, 183; legal affairs with, 163; lightbox function in, 176–77; malware detection in, 168; maturity model for, 165; metadata in, 165, 166, 168–71, 177; on-premises, 181–85; password protection in, 175; product evaluation for, 179–81; retention period with, 161; retrieval with, 160, 162; for rights metadata, 169, 170, 186; RMA and, 159; search and retrieval with, 171–74; security in, 174–75; standards and guidelines for, 164–66; timestamps in, 178; workflows in, 177–78

Digital Asset Management News, 164

Digital Asset Management System Open Specification, 164

digital preservation, 8, 93–125; access control with, 112–15; access copies in, 107, 114; advisory committee for, 117–19; audit logs in, 114; audits for, 119; backup copies in, 102, 111, 121, 123; Boolean operators in, 113; business need for, 96–97; checksums in, 106, 110–11; cloud services for, 110, 111–12, 117, 120–21, 123, 190; confidentiality with, 118; content capture in, 104–7; contingency plan for, 118; cost of, 119–21; data escrow in, 112; defined, 93–94; ECM and, 97, 108, 114; emulation software for, 96, 98; encapsulation for, 96; encryption and, 105; features and capabilities of, 103–14; file plans for, 108–9; fixity in, 106, 110–11, 123; history of, 95–96; implementation of, 114–23; inactive phase of information lifecycle for, 94; legal affairs with, 103, 111, 118; malware detection in, 105; mature models for, 102–3; metadata in, 100, 103, 104, 106, 108–9, 113–14, 120; microfilm and, 95, 123; on-premises, 116–17, 120–21; open-source applications for, 115–16, 120–21; paper records and, 97, 105, 123; password protection in, 105, 113; peer-to-peer, 111; preservation copies in, 107, 114; preservation repository for, 98, 99, 105, 106; privacy with, 118; product evaluation for, 115–17; project manager for, 117–18; replication in, 111–12; retention in, 191; retrieval with, 112–15; RMA and, 97, 108, 114; scalability of, 121; standards and guidelines for, 97–103; sustainability in, 121–23; system administrator for, 113; technology for, 119; for web and social media archiving, 190–91, 202–4; wildcards in, 113–14

Digital Preservation Capability Maturity Model (DPCMM), 102

Digital Preservation Coalition (DPC), 93

Digital Preservation Coalition Rapid Assessment Model (DPC RAM), 102–3

Digital Preservation Handbook, by DPC, 93

digital signature: in e-discovery, 228; in GRC, 266; in web and social media archiving, 204

DIP. *See* Dissemination Information Package

disaster recovery: in DAM, 163; in email archiving, 131, 154–55; in GRC, 266, 269

discovery. *See* e-discovery

disposition, with RMA, 77–78, 85
Dissemination Information Package (DIP), 103, 112–13
DLM Forum, 68–69
document imaging, ECM and, 15–17, 22–23, 35–36
DoD 5015.2-STD, *Design Criteria Standard for Electronic Records Management Applications*, 64–65, 88; email archiving and, 147
DoD Manual (DoDM) 8180.01, *Information Technology Planning for Electronic Records Management*, 64
DPC. *See* Digital Preservation Coalition
DPCMM. *See* Digital Preservation Capability Maturity Model
DPC RAM. *See* Digital Preservation Coalition Rapid Assessment Model
Dublin Core: DAM and, 165; digital preservation and, 109; ECM and, 23–24, 28, 47; email archiving and, 141
due diligence: in e-discovery, 239; in GRC, 257–58
duplicate detection. *See* de-duplication

E-ARK. *See* European Archival Records and Knowledge Preservation
EBSCO, 302
ECM. *See* electronic content management
e-discovery, 8, 217–45; AI in, 228, 231; analysis of, 232–33; audits in, 239; business need for, 220–21; centralized repository with, 230; cloud services for, 220, 226, 240–43; collaboration in, 231–32; cost of, 221, 228; data collection in, 225–27; data compression in, 228; de-duplication in, 228–29; EDRM for, 221–23; encryption in, 229, 239; features and capabilities of, 225–37; history of, 219–20; implementation of, 237–43; integration of, 236–37; legal holds in, 237; machine learning in, 219, 228, 230; malware detection in, 229; metadata in, 227, 228, 229, 237; on-premises, 226, 240–43; password protection in, 229; presentation of, 235–36; privacy in, 239; processing of, 227–28; product evaluation for, 238–40; production of, 233–35; review in, 229–32; scalability of, 226; search and retrieval with, 230–31; standards and guidelines for, 221–25
EDMS. *See* electronic document management system
EDRM. *See* Electronic Discovery Reference Model
EIM. *See* enterprise information management
electronically stored information (ESI). *See* e-discovery
electronic content management (ECM), 8; access control with, 33–35; in active phase of information lifecycle, 14–15, 25; AI and, 29–30; audit logs in, 34; audit trails of, 26, 36, 91; authorized users of, 25–28, 30, 36, 49; Boolean operators in, 31, 32; business need for, 17–19; checksums in, 26; cloud services for, 39–40, 44, 51–53; confidentiality with, 33–35; content capture in, 25–27; content locking in, 35; cost of, 48–51; cost overrun with, 54–55; customer base of, 14; DAM and, 159, 166–67, 174, 177, 178; digital preservation and, 97, 108, 114; document imaging and, 15–17, 22–23, 35–36; Dublin Core and, 23–24, 28, 47; electronic signing in, 36; encryption in, 34, 52; features and capabilities of, 24–37; file plans for, 26–30, 45–47; folder taxonomy in, 46, 140; for full-text, 29, 30, 31–32; functionality shortfall with, 54; governance of, 42–45; growth of, 19; history of, 15–17; implementation of, 37–56; infrastructure shortfall

with, 53–54; integration with, 37; legal affairs with, 42; lifecycle management for, 90; machine learning in, 37; metadata in, 23–24, 26–30, 34, 47–48; mobile apps and, 36; OCR and, 28–29; on-premises, 51–53; paper records and, 15–16, 17, 22, 24, 46; PDF and, 36–37; privacy in, 27, 52; product evaluation for, 38–41; production and marketing of, 19, 38–41; project manager for, 42, 44–45; retention policies in, 90; risk analysis for, 53–56; RMA and, 60–62, 71, 86, 89–91; schedule overrun with, 55; search and retrieval with, 30–33; security with, 33–35, 52–53; shared drives and, 17–19, 44, 46; sponsorship shortfall with, 56; standards and guidelines for, 19–24; superiority of, 15; term truncation and, 31; unstructured information and, 13–14, 16, 25; user pushback with, 55; web and social media archiving and, 203; wildcards in, 31; workflows in, 35, 178

Electronic Discovery Reference Model (EDRM), 221–23, 225–37

electronic document management system (EDMS), 17

electronic signing, in ECM, 36

email archiving, 127–58; access control with, 139–40, 142–44; appliance/server, 151–52; audit logs in, 145; audit trails in, 145; automatic classification/categorization in, 142; automaticity in, 128, 134–35, 137; backup copies in, 150; Boolean operators in, 143; business need for, 130–32; cloud services for, 130, 150–51, 153–55; content screening in, 146–47; cost of, 131; data compression in, 139; de-duplication in, 131, 139; direct transfer to email repository in, 134–35; disaster recovery in, 131, 154–55; encryption in, 139–40, 150, 154; features and capabilities of, 133–49; federated searches in, 143; file formats in, 129, 138; folder taxonomy in, 140; full-text in, 147; full-text indexing in, 141–42; history of, 129–30; hybrid installations for, 155–56; implementation of, 149–56; inactive phase of information lifecycle for, 129; indexing in, 141–42; information lifecycle of, 138, 144; legal holds in, 131–32, 145–46, 156; lifecycle management for, 134; local copies in, 147; machine learning in, 148; message storage in, 137–40; metadata in, 129, 140–42, 143, 147; on-premises, 130, 150–51, 154; project manager for, 143; PST files in, 148; real-time, 136, 137, 141; replication in, 137; retention in, 129, 131–32, 144–46; retrieval with, 133–34, 142–44; RMA and, 146, 147–48; scalability of, 137, 152; security in, 133; Sedona Conference on, 133; single-silo, 132; standards and guidelines for, 132–33; stub files in, 135, 138–39; wildcards in, 143; write-once storage for, 138

Email Archiving, 8

embedded metadata: in DAM, 170; in ECM, 28; in RMA, 86

emulation software: for digital preservation, 96, 98; OAIS and, 98

encapsulation, for digital preservation, 96

encryption: in DAM, 175; in database archiving, 282, 288; digital preservation and, 105; in ECM, 34, 52; in e-discovery, 229, 239; in email archiving, 139–40, 150, 154; in ESI, 227; in GRC, 269; in RMA, 85

Enhancing Board Oversight, of COSO, 254

enterprise content management (ECM), 13–57

enterprise information management (EIM), 21, 22, 23, 62

Enterprise Risk Management (ERM), of COSO, 254
ESG, in GRC, 248, 267
European Archival Records and Knowledge Preservation (E-ARK), 280
European Commission, 68
European Union, 68–69
event-based retention, 75–76
eWeek, 301

Federal Electronic Records Modernization Initiative, 66
Federal Rules of Civil Procedure (FRCP), 217–19
federated searches: in DAM, 174; in ECM, 32–33; in email archiving, 143; in RMA, 114
file formats: DAM and, 177; in database archiving, 282, 287; digital preservation and, 106–7, 111; in email archiving, 129, 138; in web and social media archiving, 196, 203
file plans: for DAM, 168–71; for digital preservation, 108–9; for ECM, 26–30, 45–47; for RMA, 83–85
FINRA Rule 2210, 194
fixity: in digital preservation, 106, 110–11, 123; in ESI, 227
folder taxonomy: in DAM, 163; in ECM, 46, 140; in email archiving, 140; in RMA, 140
Forrester, 300
FRCP. *See* Federal Rules of Civil Procedure
freedom of information: email archiving and, 142; RMA and, 65; web and social media archiving and, 195
FTP server, for DAM, 167–68
full-text: in database archiving, 286–87; in ECM, 29, 30, 31–32; in email archiving, 141–42, 147; in web and social media archiving, 206
functionality shortfall, with ECM, 54
fuzzy searches: in DAM, 171; in digital preservation, 114; in ECM, 31

G2, 302
Gale, 302
Gartner, 300
The Gartner Information Technology Glossary, 2
Gartner Peer Insights, 302
General Data Protection Regulations, 213
Generally Accepted Recordkeeping Principles, of ARMA International, 2, 81
Glossary of Records and Information Governance (ARMA International), 2
Google Scholar, 7, 249, 302
Google Trends, 7; on DAM, 162; on database archiving, 277; on DoD 5025.2-STD, 66–67; ECM and, 16; on e-discovery, 219; on email archiving, 130; on GRC, 249–50; on MoReq, 69; on web and social media archiving, 193
governance, risk, and compliance (GRC), 8, 247–73; access control in, 265; AI in, 258; audits in, 248, 261, 263–64; audit trails in, 256, 259, 262, 265; board management and, 264–66; business continuity module in, 266–67; business need for, 250–51; centralized repository with, 259, 261–62, 264–65; cloud services for, 268–69; compliance in, 258–61; confidentiality in, 257; disaster recovery in, 266, 269; encryption in, 269; ESG in, 267; features and capabilities of, 255–67; history of, 248–50; implementation of, 268–72; incident management in, 257; for information technology, 248, 253; malware detection in, 269; on-premises, 268–69; performance management in, 267; policy management in, 261–63; privacy in, 262, 267; risk management in, 255–58; scalability of, 269; software vs. standalone applications, 270–71; standards and guidelines for, 251–55; workflows in, 257, 262

HTML, 13–14, 25, 205
HTTP, 200

ICIF. *See* Internal Control-Integrated Framework
IDA. *See* Interchange of Data Between Administrations
IEC 82045-1:2001, *Document management-Part 1: Principles and methods*, 24
IEC 82045-2:2004, *Document management-Part 2: Metadata elements and information reference model*, 24
IEEE 2418.10-2022, *Standard for Blockchain Based Digital Asset Management*, 166
IEEE 3207-2022, *Standard for Blockchain Based Digital Asset Identification*, 166
IHS Markit, 302
IIPC. *See* International Internet Preservation Consortium
image recognition, in DAM, 172
Improving Organizational Performance and Governance, of COSO, 254
inactive phase of information lifecycle: DAM and, 160; for digital preservation, 94; ECM in, 14; for email archiving, 129; RMA and, 60
incident management, in GRC, 257
indexing: in DAM, 160; in database archiving, 285–87; in email archiving, 141–42; in web and social media archiving, 196, 205
information governance: business need for, 6–7; constituent disciplines of, 4–9; defined, 1–3; professional associations and, 2–3; technology for, 7–9. *See also specific topics*
Information Governance Body of Knowledge, of ARMA International, 2
Information Governance Implementation Model, of ARMA International, 2

information lifecycle: database archiving in, 276, 284; of email archiving, 138, 144; of RMA, 59, 60; RMA and, 59. *See also* active phase of information lifecycle; inactive phase of information lifecycle; lifecycle management
Information Security, 4–5
information technology, 4; DAM and, 183; for ECM, 52; e-discovery and, 224; email archiving and, 152; GRC for, 248, 253
InfoWorld, 301
infrastructure shortfall, with ECM, 53–54
in-place records management, with RMA, 72–73
Institute for Legal Reform, 220
intellectual property: in web and social media archiving, 201. *See also* copyright
Interchange of Data Between Administrations (IDA), 68
Internal Control-Integrated Framework (ICIF), of COSO, 254
International Data Corporation, 300
International Internet Preservation Consortium (IIPC), 191; on web and social media archiving, 196, 203
International Legal Technology Association, 301
International Press Telecommunications Council, 165
International Standardization Organization. *See* ISO
Internet Archive, 192–93
InterPARES 3 Project, 94
Intertek Inform, 302
IPTC Photo Metadata, 165
ISO (International Standardization Organization), 302–3
ISO 877:1993, *Information and documentation-Commands for interactive text searching*, 24
ISO 5127:2017, *Information and documentation-Foundation and vocabulary*, 20, 133

Index

ISO 5477:2023, *Health informatics-Interoperability of public health emergency preparedness and response information systems*, 3

ISO 5963:1985, *Documentation-Methods for examining documents, determining their subjects, and selecting indexing terms*, 24

ISO 12651-1:2012, *Electronic document management-Vocabulary-Part 1: Electronic document imaging*, 13, 20

ISO 12652-1:2014, *Electronic document management-Vocabulary-Part 2*, 20

ISO 12653-1:2000, *Electronic imaging-Test target for the black and white scanning of office documents-Part 1: Characteristics*, 22

ISO 12653-1:2000, *Electronic imaging-Test target for the black and white scanning of office documents-Part 2: Method of use*, 22

ISO 12653-3:2014, *Electronic imaging-Test target for scanning of office documents-Part 3: Test target for use in lower resolution applications*, 22

ISO 13008:2022, *Information and documentation-Digital records conversion and migration process*, 21, 102; database archiving and, 279

ISO 13072:2022, *Health informatics-Clinical information models-Characteristics, structures, and requirements*, 3

ISO 14641:2018, *Electronic document management-Design and operation of an information system for the preservation of electronic documents-Specifications*, 21, 100–101

ISO 14721:2012, *Space data and information transfer systems-Open archival information system (OAIS)-Reference model*, 97–98, 166; database archiving and, 279; for web and social media archiving, 195–96; DPCMM and, 102

ISO 15489-1:2016, *Information and documentation-Records management-Part 1: Concepts and Principles*, 85; for ECM, 23; for RMA, 64, 85

ISO 15836-1:2017, *Information and Documentation-The Dublin Core metadata element set-Part 1: Core elements*, 141; for ECM, 23–24; for RMA, 86

ISO 15836-2:2019, *Information and documentation-the Dublin Core metadata set-Part 2: DCMI properties and classes*, 23–24

ISO 16175-1:2020, *Information and documentation-Processes and functional requirements for software for managing records-Part 1: Functional requirements and associated guidance for any applications that manage digital records*, 20–21, 64

ISO 16175-2:2020, *Information and documentation-Processes and functional requirements for software for managing records-Part 2: Guidance for selecting, designing, implementing and maintaining software for managing records*, 21, 64

ISO 16363:2012, *Space data and information transfer systems-Audit and certification of trustworthy digital repositories*, 98–99, 118; DPCMM and, 102

ISO 16919:2014, *Space data and information transfer systems-Requirements for bodies providing audit and certification of candidate trustworthy digital repositories*, 99

ISO 17068:2017, *Information and documentation-Trusted third-party repository for digital records*, 101

ISO 18128:2024, *Information and documentation-Record risks-Risk assessment for records management*, 253

ISO 18829:2017, *Document management-Assessing ECM/EDRM implementations-Trustworthiness*, 21, 64

ISO 19005-1:2005, *Document management-Electronic document file format for long-term preservation-Part 1: Use of PDF 1.4 (PDF/A-1)*, 101–2

ISO 19165-1:2018, *Geographic information-Preservation of digital data and metadata-Part 1: Fundamentals*, 100

ISO 19263-1:2017, *Photography-Archiving systems-Part 1: Best practices for digital image capture of cultural heritage material*, 22

ISO 19264-1:2021, *Photography-Archiving systems-Imaging systems quality analysis-Part 1: Reflective originals*, 22

ISO 19264-1:2021, *Photography-Archiving Systems-Vocabulary*, 22

ISO 20104, *Space data and information transfer systems-Producer-Archive Interface Specification (PAIS)*, 100

ISO 20652, *Space data and information transfer systems-Producer-archive interface-Methodology abstract standard*, 100

ISO 22287:2024, *Health informatics-Workforce roles and capabilities for terminology and terminology services in healthcare (term workforce)*, 3

ISO 22938:2017, *Document management-Electronic Content/Document Management (CDM) data interchange format*, 21

ISO 23081-1:2017, *Information and documentation-Records management processes-Metadata for records-Part 1: Principles*, 85

ISO 23081-2:2011, *Information and documentation-Metadata for managing records-Part 3: Self-assessment method*, 23

ISO 23081-2:2021, *Information and documentation-Metadata for managing records-Part 2: Conceptual and implementation issues*, 23

ISO 24143:2022, *Information and documentation-Information Governance-Concept and principles*, 2, 252

ISO 25964-1:2011, *Information and documentation-Thesauri and interoperability with other vocabularies-Part 1: Thesauri for information retrieval*, 24

ISO 25964-2:2013, *Information and documentation-Thesauri and interoperability with other vocabularies-Part 2: Interoperability with other vocabularies*, 24

ISO 28500:2017-*Information and documentation-WARC file format*, 196

ISO 30301:2019, *Information and documentation-Management systems for records-Requirements*, 64

ISO 30302:2022, *Information and documentation-Management systems for records-Guidelines for implementation*, 64

ISO 31000:2018, *Risk management-Guidelines*, 253

ISO 31022:2020, *Risk management-Guidelines for the management of legal risk*, 253

ISO 31073:2022, *Risk management-Vocabulary*, 247, 253

ISO 37000:2021, *Governance of organizations-Guidance*, 247, 252, 261

ISO 37004:2023, *Governance of organizations-Governance maturity model-Guidance*, 252

ISO 37301:2021, *Compliance management systems-Requirements with guidance for use*, 247, 253, 258–59

ISO 55000:2024, *Asset management-Vocabulary, overview, and principles*, 159

ISO 55001:2018, *Asset management-Management systems-Guidelines for the application of ISO 55001*, 165

ISO 55001:2024, *Asset management-Management systems-Requirements*, 165

ISO/IEC 2382-32:1999, *Information Technology-Vocabulary-Part 32: Electronic Mail*, 133

ISO/IEC 2382-32:2015, *Information Technology-Vocabulary*, 133

Index

ISO/IEC 15938-5:2003, *Information technology-Multimedia content description interface-Part 5: Multimedia description schemes*, 166

ISO/IEC 17021-1:2015, *Conformity assessment-Requirements for bodies providing audit and certification of management systems-Part 1: Requirements*, 99

ISO/IEC 19770-1:2017, *Information technology-IT asset management- Part 1: IT asset management systems- Requirements*, 159

ISO/IEC 19770-1:2017, *Information technology-IT asset management-Part 1: IT asset management systems- Requirements*, 165

ISO/IEC 19770-3:2016, *Information technology-IT asset management-Part 3*, 165–66

ISO/IEC 19770-4:2017, *Entitlement schema; Information technology-IT asset management-Part 4*, 166

ISO/IEC 19770-11-2020, *Information technology-IT asset management-Part 11: IT asset management systems- Requirements for bodies providing audit and certification of IT asset management systems*, 166

ISO/IEC 20546:2019, *Information Technology-Big Data-Overview and Vocabulary*, 13

ISO/IEC 23681:2019, *Information technology-Self-contained Information Retention Format (SIRF)*, 101

ISO/IEC 27000, 224

ISO/IEC 27000:2018, *Information technology-Security techniques-Information security management systems-Overview and vocabulary*, 253

ISO/IEC 27001:2022, *Information security, cybersecurity and privacy protection-Information security management systems-Requirements*, 253

ISO/IEC 27050-1:2019, *Information technology-Electronic discovery-Part 1: Overview and concepts*, 223–24

ISO/IEC 27050-2:2018, *Information technology-Electronic discovery-Part 2: Guidance for governance and management of electronic discovery*, 224

ISO/IEC 27050-3:2020, *Information technology-Electronic discovery-Part 3: Code of practice for electronic discovery*, 224

ISO/IEC 27050-4:2021, *Information technology-Electronic discovery-Part 4: Technical readiness*, 224

ISO/IEC 30121:2015, *Information technology-Governance of digital forensic risk framework*, 224

ISO/IEC 31010:2019, *Risk management-Risk assessment techniques*, 253

ISO/IEC 38500:2024, *Information technology-Governance of IT for the organization*, 253

ISO/IEC TR 19583-1:2019, *Information technology-Concepts and usage of metadata-Part 1: Metadata concepts*, 23

ISO/IEC TS 22424-1:2020, *Digital publishing-EPUB3 preservation-Part 1: Principles*, 166

ISO/IEC TS 22424-1:2020, *Digital publishing-EPUB3 preservation-Part 1: Principles* and ISO/IEC TS 22424-2:2020, *Digital publishing-EPUB3 preservation-Part 2: Metadata requirements*, 100

ISO/IEC TS 22424-2:2020, *Digital publishing-EPUB3 preservation-Part 2: Metadata requirements*, 166

ISO/TR 12033:2009, *Document management-Electronic imaging-Guidance for the selection of document image compression methods*, 22

ISO/TR 12654:1997, *Electronic imaging-Recommendations for the management of electronic recording systems for the recording of documents that may be required as evidence, on WORM optical disk*, 23

ISO/TR 13028:2010, *Information and documentation-Implementation guidelines for digitization of records*, 22

ISO/TR 14105:2011, *Document management-Change management for successful electronic document management system (EDMS) implementation*, 21
ISO/TR 14873:2013, *Information and documentation-Statistics and quality issues for web archiving*, 196
ISO/TR 15801:2017, *Document management-Electronically stored information-Recommendations for trustworthiness and reliability*, 21, 100–101
ISO/TR 18492:2005, *Long-term preservation of electronic document-based information*, 101
ISO/TR 21548:2010, *Health informatics-Security requirements for archiving of electronic health records-Guidelines*, 100
ISO/TR 22299:2018, *Document management-Digital file format recommendations for long-term storage*, 101
ISO/TR 22957:2018, *Document management-Analysis, selection and implementation of enterprise content management (ECM) systems*, 13, 20
ISO/TS 14441:2013, *Health informatics-Security and privacy requirements of EHR systems for use in conformity assessment*, 3
ISO/TS 31050:2023, *Risk management-Guidelines for managing an emerging risk to enhance resilience*, 253
IS/TS 21547:2010, *Health informatics-Security requirements for archiving of electronic health records-Principles*, 100
ITProToday, 301

Joint Interoperability Test Command (JITC), 65

keywords: in database archiving, 286; in digital preservation, 113; in e-discovery, 227; in RMA, 86; in web and social media archiving, 205, 206

Lawyers for Civil Justice, 220
legal affairs, 5; with DAM, 163; with database archiving, 285; with digital preservation, 103, 111, 118; with ECM, 42; with email archiving, 128, 130–31; with RMA, 42, 70, 71, 76–78, 86. *See also* e-discovery
legal holds: in e-discovery, 237; in email archiving, 131–32, 145–46, 156; in RMA, 77
Levels of Digital Preservation Matrix (LoP), 102
lifecycle management: for ECM, 90; for email archiving, 134
lightbox function, in DAM, 176–77
local copies, in email archiving, 147
LoP. *See* Levels of Digital Preservation Matrix

machine learning: in DAM, 170–71; in ECM, 37; in e-discovery, 219, 228, 230; in email archiving, 148
malware detection: in DAM, 168; in digital preservation, 105; in e-discovery, 229; in GRC, 269
MAM. *See* Media Asset Management
maturity model: for DAM, 165; for digital preservation, 102–3
Media Asset Management (MAM), 162
metadata: in DAM, 165, 166, 168–71, 177; in database archiving, 282–83, 286, 288; in digital preservation, 100, 103, 104, 106, 108–9, 113–14, 120; in ECM, 23–24, 26–33, 34, 47–48; in e-discovery, 227, 228, 229, 237; in email archiving, 129, 140–42, 143, 147; OAIS and, 98; RMA and, 73–74, 80, 85–86; in web and social media archiving, 196, 205
Metadata Object Description Schema (MODS): for DAM, 165; for digital preservation, 109
microfilm, 16, 95, 123
mobile apps: DAM and, 168; ECM and, 26, 36; email archiving and, 130

Model Requirements for the Management of Electronic Records (MoReq), 68–69
MODS. *See* Metadata Object Description Schema
MoReq. *See Model Requirements for the Management of Electronic Records*
MPEG-7 standard, 166

National Archives and Records Administration (NARA), 66–67; Capstone of, 75; TRAC of, 98–99
National Digital Stewardship Alliance, 94, 102
National Institute of Standards and Technology. *See* NIST
National Institutes of Health, 3
National Records and Archives Authority (NRAA), of Sultanate of Oman, 64
National Software Reference Library (NSRL), 228
natural language processing: ECM and, 37; in e-discovery, 230–31
need-to-know: for DAM, 174; for database archiving, 287; for GRC, 261
NIST (National Institute of Standards and Technology), 228; on GRC, 254–55
NIST SP 800-45, *Guidelines on Electronic Mail Security*, 133
NIST SP 800-177, *Trustworthy Email*, 133
NIST SP 1800-6, *Domain Name System-Based Email Security*, 133
NIST Special Publication 800-30, *Guide for Conducting Risk Assessments*, 255
NIST Special Publication 800-37, *Risk Management Framework for Information Systems and Organizations: A System Lifecycle Approach for Security and Privacy*, 254–55
NIST Special Publication 800-39, *Managing Information Security Risk: Organization, Mission, and Information System View*, 254

NIST Special Publication 800-53, *Security and Privacy Controls for Information Systems and Organizations*, 255
Not Only SQL (NoSQL), 275
NRAA. *See* National Records and Archives Authority
NSRL. *See* National Software Reference Library
Nucleus Research, 300

OAIS. *See* Open Archival Information System
OCEG. *See* Open Compliance and Ethics Group
OCLC, 98–99
OCR. *See* optical character recognition
Omdia, 300
on-premises: DAM, 181–85; database archiving, 282, 290–93; digital preservation, 116–17, 120–21; ECM, 51–53; e-discovery, 226, 240–43; email archiving, 130, 150–51, 154; GRC, 268–69; web and social media archiving, 211
Open Archival Information System (OAIS), 94, 97–103, 107; AIP of, 103, 109–12; DAM and, 166; database archiving and, 279; DIP of, 112–13; SIP of, 100, 103, 104, 109–12, 116; web and social media archiving and, 195–96
Open Compliance and Ethics Group (OCEG), 248–49
open-source applications: for digital preservation, 115–16, 120–21; for web and social media archiving, 209–10
optical character recognition (OCR), 28–29
opt-in provision, for web and social media archiving, 213

PAIS. *See* Producer-Archive Interface Specification
paper records: digital preservation and, 97, 105, 123; ECM and, 15–16, 17, 22, 24, 46; RMA and, 63, 80–81

password protection: in DAM, 175; for database archiving, 287; for digital preservation, 105, 113; in e-discovery, 229
PDF: in database archiving, 287; in ECM, 25, 36–37; in e-discovery, 229, 236; in email archiving, 138; in web and social media archiving, 201, 205
PDF/A: in digital preservation, 122; in ISO 19005, 101–2; in RMA, 79
peer-to-peer digital preservation, 111
performance management: in database archiving, 288; in GRC, 267
personally identifiable information: in ECM, 18; in e-discovery, 231; in email archiving, 140, 150
preservation copies, in digital preservation, 107, 114
preservation repository: for digital preservation, 98, 99, 105, 106; for web and social media archiving, 202–4
privacy, 7; with digital preservation, 118; in ECM, 27, 52; in e-discovery, 239; in GRC, 262, 267; in RMA, 86; in web and social media archiving, 213–14
Privacy Act, 65
Producer-Archive Interface Specification (PAIS), 100
professional associations, 300–301
project manager: for digital preservation, 117–18; for ECM, 42, 44–45; for email archiving, 143
PRONOM, 106–7
ProQuest, 302
PROS 19/05, *Create, Capture, and Control Standard*, 67–68
PROS 19/05 S2, *Minimum Metadata Requirements Specification*, 68
PROS 19/05 S3, *Long Term Sustainable Formats Specification*, 68
PROS 99/007, *Standard on the Management of Electronic Records*, 68
PROV. *See* Public Record Office Victoria
proximity searching: in ECM, 32; in e-discovery, 230; in email archiving, 143

PST files, 148
Public Record Office Victoria (PROV), 67
Public Records Act of 1973, of Victoria, Australia, 67

read-only access: in DAM, 175; in email archiving, 143
Real Story Group, 165
real-time email archiving, 136, 137, 141
record declaration, RMA and, 70–73
Records Management, 5
records management application (RMA), 8, 59–92; access control with, 63, 80; alternatives for, 89–90; audit logs in, 80; authorized users of, 70, 80–81, 85–86, 90; Boolean operators in, 79; business need for, 62–63; centralized repository with, 72–73, 80; cost of, 89; DAM and, 159; database archiving and, 276; data compression in, 85; destruction date in, 81, 94; digital preservation and, 97, 108, 114; disposition with, 77–78, 85; ECM and, 60–62, 71, 86, 89–91; EIM and, 62; email archiving and, 146, 147–48; encryption in, 85; features and capabilities of, 70–81; file plans for, 83–85; folder taxonomy in, 140; history of, 61–62; implementation of, 81–90; information lifecycle of, 59, 60; in-place records management with, 72–73; legal affairs with, 42, 70, 71, 76–78, 86; legal holds in, 77; metadata in, 73–74, 80, 85–86; paper records and, 63, 80–81; privacy in, 86; product evaluation for, 87–88; record declaration and, 70–73; retention guidance with, 70–71, 82–83, 92; retention in, 70–71, 82–83, 92, 146; retention period with, 74–76, 81, 85; search and retrieval with, 78–79; security in, 86; security with, 80; shared drives and, 63; standards and guidelines for, 64–69; unique record identifier and, 74, 85–86; web and social media archiving and, 193, 203; wildcards in, 79

Index

replication: in digital preservation, 111–12; in email archiving, 137
request for information (RFI), 54
request for proposal, 88
retention: in database archiving, 278, 280, 281–82, 283, 284–85, 289–90; in digital preservation, 191; in ECM, 90; in email archiving, 129, 131–32, 144–46; in RMA, 70–71, 82–83, 92, 146
retention period: with DAM, 161; with database archiving, 278; with email archiving, 144–45; with RMA, 74–76, 81, 85
retrieval: with DAM, 160, 162, 171–74; with database archiving, 285–87; with digital preservation, 112–15; with ECM, 30–33; with e-discovery, 230–31; with email archiving, 133–34, 142–44; with RMA, 78–79; in web and social media archiving, 204–7
RFI. *See* request for information
rich media assets, 160
rights metadata, DAM for, 169, 170, 186
risk management, 5; for ECM, 53–56; in GRC, 255–58
RLG, 98–99
RMA. *See* records management application

Sarbanes-Oxley Act of 2002, 249
scalability: of digital preservation, 121; of ECM, 27, 46; of e-discovery, 226; of email archiving, 137, 152; of GRC, 269
schedule-based retention, with email archiving, 144–46
schedule overrun, with ECM, 55
search: with DAM, 171–74; with database archiving, 285–87; with ECM, 30–33; with e-discovery, 230–31; with RMA, 78–79. *See also specific types*
security, 7; in DAM, 174–75; in database archiving, 287–88; with

ECM, 33–35, 52–53; in email archiving, 133; in RMA, 80, 86
Sedona Conference, 2–3, 301; *Commentary on Information Governance* of, 218–19; on e-discovery, 218–19, 224–25; on email archiving, 133; on ESI, 218; on technology, 7–8
Self-contained Information Retention Format (SIRF), 101
semantic analysis, in e-discovery, 230–31
sentiment analysis: in DAM, 171; in web and social media archiving, 201
shared drives: DAM and, 167; ECM and, 17–19, 44, 46; e-discovery and, 225; RMA and, 63
SIARD. *See* Software Independent Archival of Relational Databases
SimpleDAM API Protocol, 164
single-instance storage. *See* de-duplication
single-silo email archiving, 132
SIP. *See* Submission Information Package
SIRF. *See* Self-contained Information Retention Format
social media. *See* web and social media archiving
Society of American Archivists, 93–94
Software Independent Archival of Relational Databases (SIARD), 279–80
software review sites, 301–2
SourceForge, 302
sponsorship shortfall, with ECM, 56
structured data, 13. *See also* database archiving
stub files, in email archiving, 135, 138–39
Submission Information Package (SIP), 100, 103, 104, 109–12, 116
Sultanate of Oman, 64
sustainability: in digital preservation, 121–23; in GRC, 254

syntactical analysis, in e-discovery, 230–31
system administrator: for database archiving, 284, 287; for digital preservation, 113; for ECM, 33; for RMA, 73–74

TAR. *See* technology-assisted review
technical metadata, 26–27
technology-assisted review (TAR), 231
technology news websites, 301
Techstreet, 302
term truncation: ECM and, 31; RMA and, 79
time-based retention, 75
timestamps: in DAM, 160, 178; in web and social media archiving, 204
TRAC. *See* Trustworthy Repositories Audit and Certification
transfer the records to a designed repository, with RMA, 77
TrustRadius, 302
Trustworthy Repositories Audit and Certification (TRAC), 98–99

UERM. *See* Universal Electronic Records Management
UNESCO General Conference, 191
uniform retention: with email archiving, 145–46; with RMA, 75
unique record identifier, RMA and, 74, 85–86
Universal Electronic Records Management (UERM), 66–67
unstructured information: DAM and, 167; ECM and, 13–14, 16, 25, 167
user pushback, with ECM, 55

vendor information, 299–303
VEO. *See* VERS Encapsulated Object
VERS. *See* Victorian Electronic Records Strategy
VERS Encapsulated Object (VEO), 68
Victoria, Australia, 67–68
Victorian Electronic Records Strategy (VERS), 67–68
Visual Resources Association, 165
voice recognition, in DAM, 171
VRA Core, 165

WACZ. *See* Web Archive Collection Zipped
WARC, 196, 203
Wayback Machine, 192, 205
web and social media archiving, 8, 189–216; access control in, 204–7; AI in, 206–7; authorized users for, 206; business need for, 193–95; checksums in, 204; cloud services for, 206, 211; content capture in, 197–202; content selection for, 208–9; copyright and, 211–13; data compression in, 196; de-duplication in, 203–4; digital preservation in, 190–91, 202–4; ECM and, 203; features and capabilities of, 196–208; file formats in, 196, 203; history of, 191–93; implementation of, 208–14; metadata in, 196, 205; on-premises, 211; open-source applications for, 209–10; opt-in provision for, 213; preservation repository for, 202–4; privacy in, 213–14; retrieval in, 204–7; RMA and, 193, 203; standards and guidelines for, 195–96; timestamps in, 204
Web Archive Collection Zipped (WACZ), 196
Webrecorder, 196
wildcards: in DAM, 171; in database archiving, 286; in digital preservation, 113–14; in ECM, 31; in e-discovery, 230; in email archiving, 143; in RMA, 79
workflows: in DAM, 177–78; in ECM, 35, 178; in GRC, 257, 262
WorldCat, 302
write-once storage, for email archiving, 138

XML: in database archiving, 287; in ECM, 25

ZDNet, 301
ZIP compression, 196
Zubulake v. UBS Warburg LLC, 219

About the Author

William Saffady is an independent records management and information governance consultant and researcher based in New York City. He is the author of over three dozen books and many articles on records management, record retention, document storage and retrieval technologies, and other information management topics. His latest books are *Information Compliance: Fundamental Concepts and Best Practices*, which was published by Rowman & Littlefield in 2023, *Managing Information Risks: Threats, Vulnerabilities, and Responses*, which was published by Rowman & Littlefield in 2020, and *Records and Information Management: Fundamentals of Professional Practice, Fourth Edition*, which was published by Rowman & Littlefield in 2021. He received his BA degree from Central Michigan University and his MS, PhD, and MSLS degrees from Wayne State University. Before establishing his full-time consulting practice, he was a professor of library and information science at the State University of New York at Albany, Long Island University, Pratt Institute, and Vanderbilt University. He is a fellow of ARMA International and is profiled in the *Encyclopedia of Archival Writers, 1515–2015*, a reference work published by Rowman & Littlefield in 2019.